# ESKIMO-ENGLISH ENGLISH-ESKIMO DICTIONARY

## INUKTITUT-ENGLISH ENGLISH-INUKTITUT DICTIONARY

# ESKIMO-ENGLISH ENGLISH-ESKIMO DICTIONARY

INUKTITUT-ENGLISH
ENGLISH-INUKTITUT
DICTIONARY

**ARTHUR THIBERT, O.M.I.**

**REVISED EDITION**

GYAN

*Published by*

GYAN

Gyan Publishing House
5, Ansari Road
Daryaganj, New Delhi-110002
Phone: 011-47034999, 9811692060
E-mail: books@gyanbooks.com

*Distribution Network*
gyanbooks.com
India, USA, Canada, UK, Australia, France



ISBN : 978-81-212-4369-8 (PB)
First Published, Ottawa, 1954

2nd Impression 2020

*Printed at:* Gyan Press, Delhi.



The book at your disposal is the edition of an old book originally published long back. The Text quality of this book may not be at par as compared to our other books but many readers approached us to reprint this important book so that it could satiate their hunger. We request all the readers of this book to help us to improve its quality by providing the necessary text of those pages which are not properly visible. Your valuable support in this case will be highly appreciated and acknowledged and our future readers will be benefitted immensely.

ARTHUR THIBERT, O.M.I.

# ENGLISH-ESKIMO

# DICTIONARY

# ESKIMO-ENGLISH

*Revised Edition*

Centre Canadien de Recherches en Anthropologie
Canadian Research Centre for Anthropology
Université Saint Paul University
Ottawa Canada

1970

To the memory of

Rev. J.E. Champagne, O.M.I.,

the Founder and first Director

of the

Canadian Research Centre

for Anthropology

1905 - 1969

*1954: First Edition*
*1958: Revised Edition 1st Printing*
*1970: Revised Edition 2d Printing*
*1976: Revised Edition 3rd Printing*

# *FOREWORD*

*This dictionary is the result of twenty-seven years of missionary work among the Eskimos. Chesterfield, Eskimo Point, Southampton Island, Baker Lake and Churchill were the chief headquarters from which I traveled across the Arctic, meeting the Eskimos and studying their language, ways and manners.*

*Besides my personal knowledge, the Eskimo dictionary embodies pioneer works and manuscript essays of such eminent linguists as Bourquin and Erdmann, of Bishop Turquetil, O.M.I. and Fathers Ducharme and Fafard, O.M.I. These works or notes have been most helpful, and I am glad to seize this opportunity to express my gratefulness to their authors.*

*In compiling this dictionary, I have had no other aim than to provide the Missionaries and all those who work in the Arctic or care for the social welfare of the Eskimos with a suitable tool for their task. I do hope that this work will prove beneficial to the mutual understanding of two widely different cultures of our Country.*

*Arthur Thibert, o.m.i.*

# INTRODUCTION

1) This dictionary covers practically all the words generally used by the Canadian Eskimos. A certain number of words used only by local bands of Eskimos have been added on account of their particular interest and usefulness. In this case we have always taken care to note their local origin, as : Padl. for Padlermiuts, Eskimos of Eskimo Point, Padlei district.

2) As there is no infinitive mode in Eskimo, all the verbs are given in the indicative mode, in the third person singular. As a rule when the subject of a verb is a personal pronoun, it is not expressed but included in the verb. For instance : pissuktok, means he, she or it walks. So we have given the verbs in the third person without expressing the subject.

3) Besides the words that we have compiled in this dictionary, new words may be created by the use of infixes. So we have given a list of infixes in Appendix I.

4) **PRONOUNCIATION.** Eskimo pronounciation does not present as much difficulty as some of the other Amerindian languages. The different letters are pronounced mostly as in Latin. Here are a few letters or sounds that present certain difficulty :

**K** — The k has two distinctly different pronounciations. The first one is that of the **k** in king, vg. ikkitit, matches; the second one is pronounced deep in the throat. It is very similar to a **Kr** and we have written it thus. But this **r** is choked in the throat, it is never distinctly pronounced or rolled.

**J** and **Y** — The j and the y are interchangeable and should be pronounced as **y** in you.

**S** — The **s** is generally pronounced as **sh**, vg. amisut (amishut). Some bands in the Eskimo Point region pronounce it as an **h**, vg. asso (aHo).

**I** — The **i** is pronounced as ee, vg. inuk (eenuk).

**U** — The **u** is pronounced **oo** as in shoot, or better as in the latin "una".

**NG** — The **ng** is pronounced with a single sound, as in singing and never as in "ungodly".

**DLERK** — at the end of a word is pronounced like **TSLERK.** It is in fact the only really difficult pronounciation, along perhaps with the **KR.**

5) The use of **SYLLABIC** in Eskimo. — It is well over 120 years since the syllabic system of writing was introduced in the Amerindian languages of Western Canada. Syllabic writing, however, was unknown to the Eskimos as late as 1885, when it was adapted to their language with a few additional signs to express the syllables: wai, wi, wo, wa (ᐍ ᐏ ᐓ ᐗ).

The syllabic system is a very simple way of writing syllables (not letters) with signs. Although it is very practical in many ways, it is not a precise manner of writing. Indeed, it is often ambiguous. For instance, ᑲᓂ may mean, **karnerk,** hunger; **kranerk,** mouth; **kannerk,** snow; **krarnerk,** burst; **kramnerk,** water flowing under the snow; etc. One must rely entirely on the context for the precise meaning of a word.

Here is the syllabary used by the Eskimos:

| | | | | | | | |
|---|---|---|---|---|---|---|---|
| ᐁ | ai | ᐃ | i | ᐅ | o | ᐊ | a |
| ᐯ | pai | ᐱ | pi | ᐳ | po | ᐸ | pa |
| ᑌ | tai | ᑎ | ti | ᑐ | to | ᑕ | ta |
| ᑫ | kai | ᑭ | ki | ᑯ | ko | ᑲ | ka |
| ᒉ | gai | ᒋ | gi | ᒍ | go | ᒐ | ga |
| ᒣ | mai | ᒥ | mi | ᒧ | mo | ᒪ | ma |
| ᓀ | nai | ᓂ | ni | ᓄ | no | ᓇ | na |
| ᓭ | sai | ᓯ | si | ᓱ | so | ᓴ | sa |
| ᓓ | lai | ᓕ | li | ᓗ | lo | ᓚ | la |
| ᔦ | yai | ᔨ | yi | ᔪ | yo | ᔭ | ya |
| ᐍ | wai | ᐏ | wi | ᐓ | wo | ᐗ | wa |

## ABBREVIATIONS USED

### IN THIS DICTIONARY

**Aiv.** — Aivilingmiuts, Eskimos of Chesterfield, Repulse, etc.

**anat.** — anatomy.

**bot.** — botany.

**cf.** — see.

**Eng. cor.** — corruption of an English word.

**ex.** — example.

**exclam.** — exclamation.

**imp.** — imperative.

**instrum.** — instrumental.

**K.** — Krernermiuts, Eskimos of the Baker Lake region.

**Kidl.** — Kidlinermiuts, Eskimos of the MacKenzie region.

**lit.** — literally.

**n.** — noun.

**Net.** — Netsilingmiuts, Eskimos of the Pelly Bay region.

**Okk.** — Okkomiuts, Eskimos of Baffin Land and Ungava regions.

**ornith.** — ornithology.

**Padl.** — Padlermiuts, Eskimos of the Eskimo Point region.

**plur.** — plural.

**poss.** — possessive.

**sing.** — singular.

**s.o.** — some one.

**s.t.** — something.

**subst.** — substantive.

**v.** — verb.

**vg.** — (verbi gratia) for example.

**- . . . -*** means that this particle is an infix.

## A SHORT BIBLIOGRAPHY OF THE ESKIMO LANGUAGE


BALMES, O.M.I., R.P. Joseph, Traduction française manuscrite de la Grammaire Bourquin, Chesterfield Inlet, N.W.T., 1934.

BOURQUIN, Theodor, Grammatik der Eskimo-Sprache, London, England, 1891.

BUGGE, Aage, Grönlandsk Rejseparlor, Kjöbenhavn, 1952.

ERDMANN, Friedriich, Eskimoisches Worterbuch, Budissin, Volume I, 1864; Volume II, 1866.

KJER, J. and RASMUSSEN, Chr., Dansk-grönlandsk Ordbog, Kjöbenhavn, 1893.

KLEINSCHMIDT, Von S., Grammatik der grönlandischen sprache, Berlin, 1851.

KLEINSCHMIDT, Von S. P., Den grönlandske Ordbog, Kjöbenhavn, 1871 [a dictionary].

PECK, Rev. E. J., A Dictionary of the Eskimo Language, Hamilton, Ont., 1925.

PECK, Rev. E. J., Eskimo Grammar, Ottawa, Ont., 1919.

PETITOT, O.M.I., R.P. Emile, Vocabulaire Français-Esquimau, Paris, E. Leroux, 1876.

PILLING, James Constantine, Bibliography of the Eskimo Language, Washington, D.C., 1887.

RASMUSSEN, Chr., Grönlandsk Sproglaere, Kjöbenhavn, T888 [a grammar].

RYBERG, C., Dansk-Grönlandsk Tolk, Kjöbenhavn, 1891 [Exercises in language].

SCHULTZ-LORENTZEN, A Grammar of the West Greenland Eskimo Language, Copenhagen, 1945.

SCHULTZ-LORENTZEN, Dictionary of the West Greenland Eskimo Language, Copenhagen, 1927. cf. Vol. LXIX of MEDDELELSER om Grönland.

SCHULTZ-LORENTZEN, Undervisning I Grönland, AF, Kjöbenhavn, 1939, [Exercises in language].

THALBITZER, William, A Phonetical Study of the Eskimo Language, Copenhagen, 1904.

VIBAEK, P., 100 Timer i Grönlandsk, Kjöbenhavn, 1952.

WASHINGTON, Capt. John, Eskimo and English Vocabulary, London, England, 1850.

## CONTENTS

## PART I

# ENGLISH-ESKIMO

# PART I

# ENGLISH-ESKIMO

## — A —

**Abandons** v. — Iperainnarpok, kremaiwok.

**abdomen** — naak.

**abdomen (obese)** — naartok.

**abdomen (aches)** v. — naarluktok, nadjeriyok.

**abed** (is) — iglertok.

**abides with** — najortok, nayortok.

**ablactates** v. — amâmaruerpok.

**ableness** — -yungnar-*.

**aborts** v. — avuyok, aliptortok.

**abounds** — pitaliâluk.

**about (is about to)** — -lertok-*, -langayok-*.

**above (passes)** — kollângorpok.

**abreast** — nellâni.

**abroad** — âwani.

**abrupt** — imnark.

**abscess** — âjuwak.

**abscess** (has an a.) — âjuwalik.

**absent (is)** — pitakangitok, makreitok.

**absent** (is long absent) — nipamayok.

**absorbent cotton** — nerromiktouyartok, ukaleuyak.

**abstains from** — pitailiwok.

**abstinence** (from meat) — nerkritortailibviksak.

**absurd** (is) — tukikangitok.

**accepts** — angerpok, pibviriyauyok.

**accompanies (at departure)** — kaniorpok.

**accumulates** v. — ivuyiyok, (pushes one against the other).

**accumulation** — ivunerk (pushed one against the other).

**accuses** — passiyok, passitiksakartok.

**acquires** — pissiariwok, pitârpok, -târ-*.

**across (goes)** v. — ikârpok.

**action** — illiornerk, suliyak, piliyak, -nerk-*, -ar-*.

**action in the future** — piniarsartanga (possessive).

**action in the past** — pilereavinerk.

**active (is)** — nutkarsuitok, pilerikattartok.

**acts** v. — pilerpok.

**acts well** — pitsiarpok, idluarpok, nakoarpok, nakoarsarpok.

**acts without being seen** — tireksorpok.

**actually** — mânna, tagva-tagva.

**adage (is an a.)** — okrauseôyok.

**added (to be added)** — illaksak.

**addresses s.o.** — illaksiorpok, illaksiorpâ.

**adds to** — idleriwok.

**adequate (is)** — nâmakosartok, nâmaktok.

**adheres** v. — nippittok, nippingayok.

**adherence (protector against)** — nippidjaekut.

**admiration** (exclam.) — mai ! maitsiak !

**admires** v. — ôpipok, ôpigosukpok.

**admonishes** v. — inerterpok, (innerterpok).

**adopted** — tiguak.

**adopting** — tiguarsiye.

**adores** v. — nertormarikpok, nertorpok.

**adrift** (is) — sâvidyauyok.

**adult** — innark, aktok.

**adultery (commits)** — aipaksauyok.

**advances** v. — sivumuarpok.

**advantageous** — ikayornartok.

**advice (gives advice)** — issumaliorpok, tilliorpok.

**affection (has a.)** — ungayok, nagliktok, pinnariyok.

**affirms** v. — angerpok.

**afflicted** (is) — nikadlortok.

**afraid** (is) — kappiasuktok, erksiyok.

**after** — kingudlermik.

**again** — sulli, -kanner-*.

**age** — ukkiulik, alragolik.

**aged** — ôtokrak; aged woman: arnakoaksak.

**aggravates** v. — piwallialerpok, piluarpallialerpok.

**agitated** (is) —ôminisartok.

**ago** — taimangat.

**agreement** — issumakattigengnerk.

**agrees** — issumakattauyok, angertok.

**ahead of time** — sivusiktok, sivuvasiktok.

**aid** — ikayorte.

**aims at** v. — tôrarpok.

**air** — sila.

**airless** (no air) — silakangitok.

**airplane** — tingmisût, kangatayût.

**alcohol** — angayarnartok, immerluk.

**alike** (is) — adjiriwâ.

**alive** (is) — ômayok.

**all at once** — tagvadlaksinnar, erneinnar.

**all of it** — tamaluktar, tamatkertok.

**all of them** — tamaita, illunatik (Okk.).

**all of us** — tamapta, illunata (Okk.).

**all of you** — tamapsi, illunasi (Okk.).

**allows** v. — perkoyiyok.

**almighty** — ajugakangitok.

**almond** — sauniub inua.

**almost**—eiei, -kasak-*, -gayar-*

**alone** — (he) : kissimi; (I) : kissima; (you) : kissipsi.

**alone by himself** — ingmikortok.

**alone to do it** — piyotuar.

**alone not to do it** — pingitotuar.

**alongside** — senniagut.

**aloof (is)** — sâviktok.

**aloud** — nippikortuyomik piyok.

**alphabet** — illisautit (anything to help learning).

**also** — -lu-*, -tauk-*.

**altar-boy** — ikayorte.

**altered** (is) — assiangoyok.

**alternates** — nikitarpok.

**always** — atayomik, krangaluktar (past), krakugoluktar (future).

**ambitious** (is) — piyomadluartok, piyomittartok.

**amends himself** — piosiyok.

**amiable** — naglingnartok, ikpanartok.

**ammunition** — kardjuk, (pl: kardjuit).

**among** — akkuningani.

**ample** (is) — nerrotuyók.

**amulet** — pittokutit, anruark.

**amusing** (is) — tipsinartok, iglarnartok.

**ancestors** — sivudlit.

**anchor** — kîsaut.

**anchors** v. — kîsarpok.

**anchorage** — kîsarviksak.

**ancient (formerly of)** — -vinerk-*, -tokrak-*.

**and** — -lu-*, -tauk-*.

**anew** — attilu, sulli, -kannerk-*.

**angel** — anernerk.

**angle** — tiretkroak.

**angry** (is) — ningartok, ningaktok.

**anger** — ningarnerk.

**animal (land animal)** — nergdjut, pissukte.

**animal (sea animal)** — puiye, (pl: puiyit).

**ankle** — signernerk.

**annoying** (is) — anarsitauyok.

**another** — assi (poss.assia), pikattar, aipa etc.

**answers** v. — kiowok, akkiwok, akpiusarpok.

**antler** — nagdjuk.

**anus** (anat,) — itterk, ittierk.

**anvil** — kautauyarvik.

**anxious** (is) — niviorpok, akkunigosukpok.

**anyone** — kinatuinnar, (person), -tuinnar-*.

**anything at all** — sutuinnar, sunatuinnar.

**appears** v. — takuksauyok, satkomertok.

**appears from behind**—uyaktok.

**appendix** (anat.) — krepingut.

**appetizer** — kâlersaut.

**applauds** v. — patiktarpok.

**apple** (fruit) — paunrak aupaluktok.

**apple (Adam's apple)** — tupingoark.

**apple of the eye** — takubvik, iyaroak.

**approachable** (is) — illeranaitok (morally). tikitarealik (physically).

**approves with one's head** — okkungiarpok, angerpok.

**apron** — mamautalitak.

**apt** (is) — piyungnartok, ayungitok, nâmaktok.

**areola** — awaliarutak.

**arises** v. — makkitpok, makkilerpok.

**arm** — tallerk.

**arm** (right arm) — tallerpidlerk.

**arm** (left a.) — saumidlerk.

**arm** (outside upper arm) — aksakrok.

**arm** (strong a.) — talleriktok.

**arm** (at arms length) — issâusimayok.

**armpit** — unerk (or: ônerk).

**around** — awatani.

**around us** — awatiptingni.

**arranges** v. — ikpariksarpok, atkrikpok, senneyok etc.

**arrested** (is) — atungersimayok, pangnaersimayok.

**arrives** — tikitpok.

**arrives from far** — tikitpok.

**arrow (for bow)** — kardjuk.

**artery** (anat.) — tiglertak.

**artery** (main a.) — torkluk.

**articulates well** (words) — katsukpok, okratsiarpok.

**artificial** — -ngoar-*.

**Ascension Day** — Jesusib Majorarvia.

**ashamed** (is) — kangusuktok.

**ashamed (makes one a.)** — kangunartok.

**ash** (ashes) — arjalinerk.

**ashes (cooked under a.)** — adgerk.

**ashore (goes a.)** v. — nunalikpok, sammurpok.

**aside** (left) — issumariyaungitok (no one thinks of him).

**as if** — sorlo, -uyar-*, -tut-*.

**asks** (begs for, v.) — tuksiarpok, tukserarpok.

**asks questoins** v. — apersorpok.

**asleep** (is) — sinniktok.

**assembly** — inugiarâluit, kadgemioyut.

**assistant** — ikayorte.

**associated** (is a. with) — illamar, illagektok, kattutiyok.

**astern** — kingumut.

**astonishment** (exclam.) — sunaubva ! (I thought it was otherwise, but . . .).

**astride** — ablangayok.

**at** — -mi-* or -mut * etc.

**attempts** v. — pinasukpok.

**attentive (is)** — udjertorpok, illimasukpok, ulureasukpok.

**attention (pays a.)** — nautsertorpok, aulaiyiyok.

**attention not to fall** — pinaimiyok.

**attracks (with fish hook)** — kikparpok, aulasarpok.

**audible** — tussarsauyok.

**aunt** (father's sister) — attak, atsak, attak.

**aunt** (mother's sister) — arnabvik, arnadjak, ayak.

**aurora borealis** — aksarnerk.

**automobile** — nunakorutiâlak.

**avaricious** (is) — uivituyok, tutkuitok, nerdlingoyok, erligosuktok.

**avenges** — akkisartorpok.

**avoids** v. — uivarpok, nigorpok.

**awake** (is) — tupaksimayok, erkromayok.

**awake all night** — sinningitainnartok.

**awake all night** (voluntarily) — pigârtok.

**awakes s.o.** v. — tupatitsiyok, ittersarpok.

**aware** (is) — illimasuktok, ulureasuktok.

**awful** (is) — kappianartok.

**axe** — ulimaut.

**axe (uses an a.)** — ulimarpok.

## — B —

**baby** — nutaralak.

**bachelor** (not married) — nulliakangitok.

**back** — tunr.u.

**back (lying on the b.)** — nivralayok.

**back (comes b.)** v. — utterpok.

**back (comes b. without success)** — sunamerpok, angiinarpok.

**back (gives b. to owner)** — satorpok.

**backwards** (leans b.) — niverpok.

**bad person** — idluitok, piktaungitok, înuguserk. suinnak, piungitok, pitsiangitok, idluangitok.

**bad thing** (excl.) — maiksuk !

**bag** — pokattar, ikpiardjuk, pôk, pôksak.

**bag for meat** — puguserk, pubverark.

**baggage** (carries b. ahead) — kanigiyok.

**bait** (for traps etc.)—nareaksak.

**bait** (smells the b.) — narearpok.

**bait (for fish)** — manak.

**Baker Lake, NWT** — Kramaniktuark.

**baking powder** — illaksaut, publurterut, publursaut.

**baleen** — sokrark.

**ball (foot-b.)** — aksark.

**ball** (base-b. etc.) — anauligak, aitaliyak.

**ballast** — okkomaidjutiksak.

**balloon** — pubviark.

**bandage for wounds** — matutiksak, immutiksak.

**bank** (institution) — kinauyaleribvik.

**bannock** — alaksauyartok, adgiksak.

**banquet** — nerrevigdjuark.

**baptizes** v. — kobverinayok, kobveriyok.

**baptized (is)** — kobverinilik, kobverisimayok.

**baptized** (is to be b.) — kobveriniliksak.

**baptism** — kobverinerk.

**barber**—nuyaiyarte, umgiyarte.

**bare** (naked) — ussertok, ussingayok.

**bare-footed** — kamidlartok.

**barks** v. (dog b.) — krelukpok.

**bark** (of trees) — amerark, amânga.

**barrage** — sapputit.

**barrel** — kattauyak.

**barren land** — nuna sutakasuitok.

**barren woman** — arnak ernesuitok.

**base** (stool)—ikuvrark, tungavik.

**bashful** (is) — illerasukpok, kangusukpok.

**basking seal** — ôtok.

**bass voice** (has) — kattituyok.

**battery** (electric)—aumagertaut.

**battle** — unatarvik.

**bay** — kangerdluk, kangersuk, (Okk.).

**beacon** — inuksuk.

**beads** (decorative)—sungauyait, sappagnait, (Okk.), uyamit.

**beak,** bill — sigguk.

**beans** — nilernait.

**bear** (polar) — nanuk.

**bear** (brown) — aklark.

**bear cub** — nanertak, âtertak.

**bear skin** — nanurark.

**beard** — umerk, umik.

**bearded one** — umilik.

**beater (snow b.)** — tiluktût, anautark.

**beats (snow from clothes)** — tiluktorpok.

**beautiful !** — pitsiark ! maitsiak ! ânana !

**beautiful,** fair (is) — inekonartok.

**beaver** — kiggiark.

**because** — ilar, (or the verbal form -mat etc.).

**becomes** v. — -ler-*-ngor-*.

**bed** — iglerk.

**bed** (is in b.)—igliktok, innartok.

**bed** (is making a b.) — igliliorpok.

**bed pan** — kôrvik.

**bee** — iguptark, igupsak, iguppak.

**begins** v. — pilisarpok, pigiorpok, pigiarpok.

**begs insistantly** — krenutuyok.

**behaviour** — illiornerk.

**behind time** (is) — kingurarpok.

**belches** v. — niksarpok.

**believes** v. — okperpok.

**believers** — okperkutit, okpertokutit.

**bell** — sivanerteraut, sâviarpalût, (Padl.).

**bell-ringing** — sivanerteriyok, sâviarpaluktok.

**belly** — naark.

**belly** (obese) — naartok.

**belly** (empty b.)—naklisimayok.

**belly ache** (has a b.) — nadjeriyok, naarluktok.

**belongings** — perkutit.

**belongs to him** — perkutiriwâ, pigiwâ (sing).

**belt** — tapsi, kritikisautit.

**beluga** (white whale) — kenalogak, (kelalogak).

**beneath** — atâni, atâgut, etc.

**bent** (is) — niungayok.

**bent** (is becoming) — niortitok.

**berries** — paunrait.

**berry** (black b.) — kablak, (plur: kablait).

**berry** (yellow b.) — akpik.

**berry shrub** — paunrakutit, akpikutit, kablakutit.

**beseeches** v. — tukserarpok.

**besides** — amma.

**best** — piolak.

**between** — miksa, miksani.

**between us** — akkunaptingni.

**between you** — akkunapsingni.

**beverage** — immiyaeksak.

**beyond** — ikkani, akkiani.

**biceps** — katsoark.

**big** (is) — angiyok, takiyok.

**big** — -âluk-*, -djuark-*, -kortuyok-*.

**big** (as b. as) — aktiriyok.

**big thing** — apikdjuark !

**biggest** — angilak.

**big (more or less b.)** — -ralla-*.

**bile** — sungark.

**bile** (gives b. v.) — sungonartok.

**bill (bird's b.)** — sigguk.

**billiard ball** — tûgagak.

**billiard cue** — tûgaut.

**billiards (plays b.)** v.—tûgarpok.

**billiard-table** — tûgarvik.

**bird** — tingmiark (plur: tingmidjet).

**bird** (male) — angutiviark.

**bird** (female) — arnaviark.

**bird nest** — upluk.

**bird (snow bird)** — kopanoar, amauligak.

**bird (young b.)** — pialak, aitortungiark.

**birth** — anibvik.

**birth (about to give b.)** — ernesukpok.

**birthday** — anibviksak, anibvik.

**birth (gives b.)** — erniwok.

**biscuit** — sigalak, nerdleogak.

**bit** (a piece) — mikiyomik, illanga, serdlerk.

**bit** (tool) — niortût.

**bitch** — ârnaluk.

**bites** v. — kiisiwok, mikkikpok.

**bites** (takes b.) — tamuarpok, tamuawok.

**bitter** (is) — sernartok.

**black** (is) — krernertok.

**Black Lead Island** — Omanerdjuark.

**bladder** (anat.) — nakkasuk.

**blames** v. — sukkorpok.

**blanket** — krepik, ôlik.

**bleeding** (is) — aokpok, aonarpok.

**blessing** — saimartidjut.

**blind** (is) — tautujuitok, takuyuitok.

**blind-man's buff** (they play v.) — taptauyartut.

**blistered** (is) krarsortok.

**blood** — aok.

**bloomers** — awadluk.

**blooms** (flower etc.) — erkpakpok.

**blows** (wind) — subluarpok.

**blows a little** — subluksungnartok.

**blows with one's mouth** — suppiwok.

**blubber** — orkso.

**blue (is)** — tungortok.

**blushes v.** — kangusukpok, aupadlakpok.

**board** (plank) — kreyuksak, igluksak.

**boat** — umiark.

**boat** (Peterhead) — naparotatualik, umiardjuk, ikkumaligdjuark.

**boat (schooner)**—umiardjuatnar.

**boat** (steamer) — umiardjuarâluk.

**boat (is travelling by b.)** — umiartortok.

**boat wreck** (has a) — umiiyarpok.

**bob-tail** — papikattok.

**bogey** — kadlupidluk, paiyâ, payâ.

**body** — timik.

**boil** (blister) — ajuwak.

**boils** v. — kalârpok.

**bone**, frame — saunerk.

**bone (for dog food)** — kipkark.

**book** — makpertak, titirkret ibjoyut.

**boot** — kamik.

**boot (waterproof)** — iperauserk (seal skin), attirak (deer skin).

**bores** — ikkûrpok.

**born** (is newly b.) — anilisartok, inolisartok.

**borrowed** (is) — atortugak, atortuinnartok.

**boss** (chief) — angayokrark, issumatak, atanerk.

**both hands or feet** — igluktût, iglugeik.

**both (uses both hands or feet)** — iglutorpok.

**bothers** — pagvisarpok.

**bottle** — allegor, publauyak.

**bottom of the sea** — allua.

**boulder** — uyarasukdjuk.
**bounces** v. — piglertarpok.
**bouncing ball** — piglertak.
**bow** (for arrows) — pitiksik.
**bow** (for Eskimo bit)—pitikserak.
**bow** (shoots with b.) — pitiktarpok.
**bowel** (anat.) — inaluak.
**bowels** (one's b. move) — anârpok.
**bowl** — makkauyak.
**bows** v. — ukkungawok.
**box**—kreyukut, iklervik, illiviak.
**box (with cover)** — matulik.
**boy** — nukapiak, inosuktok, sorûserk (Okk.).
**brace** (tool) — ikkûtak, illiorut.
**braids** v. — aglakpok.
**braidings** — aglait.
**brain** (anat.) — karetak, karesak (Okk.).
**brakes** v. — tukertarpok.
**brakes** (n.) — tukertarutit.
**branch** — issarutak, akkerok.
**brave** (is) — kappiasuksuitok, kappiataitok.
**bread** — akrelkoyak, adgiksak, niakrouyak.
**breakfast** — tuparomitarvik.
**breakfasts** v. — tuparomitarpok.
**breaks** v. — sirkropterpok, sirkromikpok.
**breaks** (wood etc.) — sigittok, nakattok, illingartok.
**breakup (of sea ice)** — tuwaertok.
**breast** (mamma) — iviangek.
**breast** (extremity of b.)—milluk.
**breathes** v. — ânerteriwok.
**breath** (holding back one's b.) — ânernasarpok.
**breathes** (sighing)—ânersarpok.
**breathes no more** (is dead) — ânernangertok.
**breathes (holding on'e nose)** — sertuwok.
**breathing hole** (for seals) — aglu.
**breeches** — karlik, kadleroat.
**breeze** (windy) — anoretuyok.
**bridge** (over water) — ikârviksak.
**bright** (luminous) — kraumayok, kiblariktok.
**bright** (intelligent) — silatuyok, pokrittok.
**brings** v. — adgiarpok, nerksarpok.
**broad, wide** (is) — siliktok.
**broadness** — silingnerk.
**broken** (is) — sorartok, illingartok, sirkomittok.
**broken wood** — napiyok.
**broken line,** string—kiktorartok.
**broods** (sits on eggs) — ivayok.
**broom** — sanniutit, sannerut.
**brother (of a man)** — elder: angayok; younger: nuka.
**brother (of a woman)** — anik.
**brother-in-law** — ai, sakkiak.
**brown** (is) — aupayartok.
**brush** (for clothes) — siangiyaut.
**buck** — pagnerk.
**builds** v. (a house)—igluliorpok.
**bullets** (small) — kardjurauyait.
**bullet hole in game** — tudlak.
**bumps** v. — tullurpok.
**bundle** — kidlartak.
**bundle (makes a b.)** v. — immuserpok, kidlartaliorpok.

**burns** (it b.) — ôtarpok, ikkuadlakpok.

**bush,** forest — napârtolik.

**bursts** v. — krarpok.

**busy** (is) — pileriyok, piyareakartok, suliwok, nuutok.

**but** — -li-*.

**but** (I thought, but . . .) — sunaubva, ussiomali.

**butt** (of rifle) — kangia.

**butter** — immuyak.

**butterfly** — tarralikitak.

**buttock** (anat.) — mimerk; (both: ôpatik).

**button** — siarut, unguark (Padl.).

**buys,** trades — nioverpok.

**buzzing in ears** — avioyok.

— C —

**cache** — perôyak, krematût.

**calendar** — ublursiutit, naisautit.

**calf** (fawn) — norrak, (aupilaktok).

**calls** v. — krainkoyiyok.

**calls dogs** — kammarpok.

**calm** (is morally c.) — uimaitok.

**calm water** — orksuartok.

**calm weather** — ikubliartok.

**calumniates** v. — pipkartitsiwok.

**camera** — adjiliorut.

**camps** v. — tangmârpok.

**can** (tin can) — ipuitok.

**can do it** v. — piyungnartok.

**candle** — nâpartak, ikkumayak.

**candlestick** — nâpartarvik.

**candy** — nunguserak, okkomiakattar.

**cannot do it** — pidjangitok, pilangitok.

**canoe** (Eskimo c.) — kayak.

**canoe from stores** — kayareak.

**canvas for tent** — tupiksak.

**canvas (under load)** — ignorêk.

**cap** (headgear) — nassak.

**carcass (of bird)** — kattik, (krattik).

**carcass (of any animal)** — sauningit.

**cards** (playing cards) — kritkutit, pattait, sipiatsit (Okk.).

**careful** (is) — udjertortok.

**caribou** — tuktu.

**cargo** — ussik (poss: ussiyanga).

**carp** (fish) — atniyark.

**carries** v. — adgiarpok, nerksarpok.

**carries on shoulder** — erksukpok.

**carries on one's self** — taglerpok.

**carries under cover** — komiukpok.

**carries with frontal band** ikkajût attorlugo.

**carrion** — silu.

**cart** — aksalualik.

**cartridge** (ammunition) — kardjuk.

**casting** (is c. stones etc.) — egitsiwok, milorpok.

**cascades** — kôrluktok, kipputit, kurluktok.

**cat** — pussi.

**catches** v. — tigusiwok.

**catches a flying ball** — akkorpok.

**catechism** — ajokertuserk.

**caterpillar** (insect) — nanuyak.

**catholics** — okperkattigêtsiartut, (seningayolingmiutait).

**caught** (is) — piyauyok, tiguyauyok.
**cause of** — -lutau-*.
**cautious** (is) — illimasukpok.
**ceases** v. — areowok, pianikpok.
**ceiling** — krilak.
**celebrates the day** — ublursiorpok.
**cement** — kreku, krekô.
**center** — kerkra.
**certain, sure (is)** — kollarnangitok.
**cerumen** (anat) — tikte.
**chain** — ipiutak.
**chair** — iksiwautak.
**changed into** — -ngor-*.
**changes** v. — sanguwok, sokosiwok.
**changes often** — sangusareitok.
**changes place** — nukterpok.
**chapel**, church — tuksiarvik.
**charitable** (is) — nagliktartok, nagliktok.
**cheats** v. — sagluwok, tiglikpok.
**cheek** (anat.) — ulluak.
**cheek** (lower ch.) (anat.) — tutak.
**cheerful** — kuviasukattartok, kakrayok.
**cheese** — immuyartok.
**chequers** — ayakattar.
**chest** (anat.) — sagvik, sakkrark.
**Chesterfield Inlet, N.W.T.** — Igluligardjuk.
**chewing gum** — tamuatuar.
**chews** v. — tamuawok.
**chicken** — akrigeuyak.
**chief** — issumatar, âtanerk, angayokrak.
**child** — nutara, soruserk; krittongak, piarak.
**child of same age** — nutarangokattigeit.
**chilly** (is) — pattangayok.
**chimney** — igalerk.
**chin** (anat.) — tablu.
**chin (under c.)** — kakerdluk.
**chin (tatooing)** — tablurutit.
**chip** (of wood, iron etc.) — uluarnikut, sâvinikut.
**chisel** for ice — tôrk.
**chisel (uses c. for ice v.)** — tôrkpok.
**chisel (cold c.)** — ulurksit.
**chisel (wood c.)** — pokuliut.
**chocolate** — koko (Engl. corr.).
**chokes** v. — tupittok, ibjangoyok, saunittok.
**choke** (makes one c.) — tupinartok.
**chooses** v. — anneriwok.
**chooses the best** — narroadlerpok.
**Christmas** — Jesusib Anibvia.
**church** — tuksiarvik.
**Churchill**, Man. — Kûrdjuark, Kordyuark.
**chyle** (anat.) — sirkreark.
**cigarette paper** — immutiksak.
**cinders** — arialinerk.
**cinema show** — tarraiyartut.
**circle for barrel** etc. — erkridjut.
**circles** v. — kaibjayok.
**circumstance** — illayokartok.
**city**, town — iglurdjuartalik.
**clam** — uviluk, orvilruk.
**clay** — marrak.
**claw**, finger nail — kukik.
**clean** (is) v. — salumayok.

**clear sky** — adlartok.
**clear water** — kakiaktok, sikittok.
**clever** (is) — silatuyok, pokrittok.
**climbs** v. — majorarpok.
**clipper** (for hair) — nuyaiyaut.
**cloak** — koliktar.
**clock** (watch etc.) — krauyisaut, sikkrineuyak.
**close** (is) — kanittok.
**close (gets)** — kaglivok.
**close to one another** — kanigektut, akkulaitut.
**cloth (for table** etc.) — mangíptark.
**clothes** — okkorutit, annoradjet, okkoksait.
**clothes from store** — kablunartak.
**clothes** (puts on clothes) — annorarpok.
**cloud** — nuvuyak.
**cloudy** (is) — nuvuyayok.
**clubs** (playing cards) — keslalapar.
**coagulated blood** — augiark.
**coagulates** v. — kekrewok.
**coal** — ariaksak.
**coast** — sinâ.
**coat** — koliktar.
**coat (take off your c.)** — târit.
**coat (taken off)** — tâdgomayok.
**coat of arms** — kilikpak, attikiktok.
**cóccyx** (anat.) — pameodluk.
**cod fish** — ôgark.
**coffee** — kâpik, tîrdlak.
**coffin** — kreyukut, iklervik.
**cog-wheel** — maniilak.
**coin (money)** — kinauyak.

**cold** (is) — nigliktok.
**cold** (feels c.) — ikkiertok.
**cold** (it is) — ikkii, ikkianartok. ikkianartok.
**cold (has a** cold) — nôvaktok.
**collapses** (vg snow house) — immikpok.
**collar bone** — kôtok.
**collects** v. — kattersiwok.
**collide** (v. pl.) — tullurtoraurput.
**colour** — kânga.
**black** — krernertok.
**blue** — tungortok.
**green** — tungoyortok.
**pink** — aupayartok.
**red** — aupaluktok.
**violet** — krenerkasaktok.
**white** — kakortok.
**yellow** — koksortok, kayok.
**comb** — idlaerutit, pilrautit.
**combs** v. — idlaerpok.
**combination-suit** — âtayolik.
**coming crowd** — adgertut.
**coming** (is) — krainyok.
**coming here** (is) — maungarpok.
**coming back without anything** — sunamerpok, angiinarpok.
**commands** (v.) — perkoyiyok.
**commands dogs** — sukasarpok, sakresarpok.
**commission (gives)** v. — akoertorpok, nerksiutiyok.
**commission receives** (v.) — nerksiusarpok, akoertugauyok.
**commissure of lips** — erkri.
**communion** (sacrament) — tamuasungnerk.
**companion** — pikatti, aipa, ingnerattar (Padl.).

**compass** (marine c.) — tammareikut.

**complains** — ipkolukpok, ômilarpok.

**completely** — tamarmik, tamaluktarmik. -luktar-*, -limar-*.

**completely lost** — -ijar-* or -iyar-*.

**completely takes (entirely all)** — tamatkerpok.

**complies** v. — nâleksinnarpok.

**compulsory** (is) — perkoyaumariktok.

**concave** — parangayok, illutortok.

**conceals** v. — iyerartorpok.

**conceives (child)** — singaiyok.

**confession** (sacrement) — piungineiyarnerk.

**confidence** (has) — okpigosuktok, tatiriyok.

**confined in prison** — atungersimayok, pangnaersimayok.

**congratulates** v. — nakoriwok.

**congregation** — kattimayut, tuksiarkattauyut.

**conjectures** v. — passagosukpok.

**conjuring ghosts** v. (is) — tonriyok, sakkayok.

**conjuror** (medecine man) — angatkro.

**connects** v. — kattitsiwok.

**conscious** (is) — krauyimayok, aulayiyok.

**consents** v. — angerpok.

**conserves** v. — papatsiwok.

**consoles** v. — saimarpok, saimaksarpok.

**consolation** (grace etc.) — saimarnerk.

**consolation** (given) — ·saimaksaut, saimaksautit.

**constant** (is) — sangusuitok.

**constrains** v. — pititsiyok.

**container (for liquid)** — immerkraut.

**container (for solids)** — pôksak.

**container (large c).** — illutuyok.

**container (small c.)** — illukiktok, immakiktok.

**contemptable** (is) — issumariyaeksaungitok.

**contended** (is) — nâmariwâ.

**continue ! keep on !** — attilu sulli, kajusilutit !

**contradicts** v. — anârtorpok.

**contrary** (on the c.) — iglunganunga.

**contributes** v. — pikattauyok, illauyok.

**convalescing** (is) — piosiwallialertok.

**convenient**, useful (is) — atuyuyok, atukattartok.

**converges** v. — tôrarpok.

**conversation** (is object of c.) — okrauseôyok.

**converts** v. — sanguniarpok.

**cook** (male or fem.) — îgaye.

**cooked** (is) — ôyok, îgasimayok.

**cooking place** (kitchen) — îgabvik.

**cooking pot** — ukkusik, utkosik.

**cooks** v. — îgayok, îgawok.

**cools**, refreshes v. — niglitserpok, niglikpok.

**copies** v. — adjiliorpok.

**copulates** v. — koayok, nulliakpok.

**cork** — simmik.

**cork-screw** — simmerksit.

**corner** — tiretkrok.
**corrects,** scolds v. inerterpok.
**costless** (is) — akkikangitok.
**costs much** (expensive) — akkituyok.
**costs little** — akkikiktok.
**coughs** v. — koertorpok, kadlaktorpok.
**counts** v. — kissitsiwok.
**countless** — naisagaeksaungitut.
**counter** (cribbage board) — naggavik.
**country** — nuna, perorsêvik.
**countrymen** — nunakattigeit.
**couple** (married c.) — nulliareik, uigeik.
**cousin** — arnakatti.
**Covenant Arch** — najorterut.
**covered completely** (by snow etc.) — sausimayok.
**covets** v. — ikligosukpok, tussuwok.
**cow** — tuktuwak immulik.
**cowardly** (is) — kussuyok.
**crack (in ice)** — nuktak.
**cracks (with noise)** — nuktikpok.
**cramps** (has) — kreluliyok.
**crane** (mechanic) — amuakattaut, amulrut.
**crane** (ornith.) — tatidgak.
**crawls** v. — aorpok.
**creates** v. — pingortitsiwok.
**Creator** — pingortitsiye.
**Creator of the earth** — Nunaliorte.
**credit** — akkiliut.
**crew** — umiartortit.
**crib** (manger) — nerrebvik.
**cries,** yells v. — ereadlakpok, erealârpok, kreayok.
**crooked** (is) — niungayok, krepingayok.
**crooked legs** (has) — iblungayok.
**crop to be reaped** — kattersiutiksak.
**crop of a bird** — illupkut, pubviak.
**cross** — senningayok.
**cross-bar of sled** — nappu.
**cross-eyed** (is) — nakungayok.
**cross** (sign of the c.) — senningayuliornerk.
**cross (makes the sign** of the c.) — senningayuliorpok.
**crosses over** v. — ikârpok.
**crow** (bird) — tullugak.
**crow-bar** — ibyutak.
**crowd** — inugiaraluit.
**crowded** (are) — pangmiortut, nimniortut.
**crown** — niakrorut.
**crown of the head** — kabjerk.
**crucifix** — senningayolik.
**crushes** v. — sêmikpok.
**crutches** — ajaupidjet (sing : ajaupiark).
**cub** (bear cub) — nanertak.
**cultivates** (farming) — perorsaiyok.
**cup** — ermoseuyak, ermoserk.
**cured** (is) — piyungnaertok.
**curled hair** — erkresulingayok.
**curled tail** (dog) — pamiiyok.
**curls up** (as a dog) v. — immorikpok.
**curls up** — erkriwok.
**curtails** v. — nailiwok.
**curved part of sled** — iktak.
**custom** (uses, habits) — illitkoserk.

**cute, intelligent (is)** — silatuyok.
**cuts** v. — kipiwok.
**cuts at cards** — kaurpok.
**cuts blocks of snow** — awiksarpok.
**cuts hair** — nuyaiyarpok.
**cuts into pieces** v. — abgorpok.
**cuts lengthways** — sîgpok.
**cuts sideways** — kipiwok.
**cuts meat** — pilaktorpok.
**cuts tobacco** — kreorpok.

## — D —

**daisy** — kanguyak.
**dam** (to catch fish) — sapputit.
**damaged** (is) — sorortok, illingartok.
**damaged** (is never d.) — soroyuitok.
**damp** (is) — krausertok, sarattok.
**dances** v. **(Eskimo dance)** — momerpok.
**dances** v. **(White men's dance)** — mominguarpok.
**danger** (is in d.) — nanrarpok, nangiarpok.
**danger ahead !** — irk !
**dangerous** (is d.) — erksinartok, kappianartok.
**dark** (is) (without light) — târtok.
**dark** (pitch dark) — tâggarik.
**darkness** — târk.
**dart** — kardjuk.
**daughter** — panik.
**daughter (adopted** d.) — paniksak, tiguak.
**daughter-in-law** — ukkuark.
**dawn** — ublarpaluk.
**day** — ublur.
**day after tomorrow** — ungwatago.
**day (all day long)** — ubluluktar.
**day (in only one day)** — ubluinnar.
**day (every day)** — krau-tamat, ublurât.
**day (longest day)** — ublukortulak.
**day (shortest day)** — ublukilak.
**day (to-day)** — ublumi.
**daylight** — kraumayok.
**dead** (is) — tokoyok.
**dead animal (found)** — kridlok, silu.
**death blow** (gives a d. b.) — puipsarpok.
**deadly poison** — tokonartok.
**deaf** — tussasuitok, tussayuitok.
**dear ones** (relatives) — illamareit, illageit.
**death** — toko.
**death** (as if almost d.) — tokotsertok.
**debt** — akkiitok, akkiksak.
**debt** (something to pay a d.) — akkiliksak.
**debt (pays his d.)** — akkililerpok.
**debts (makes d.)** — akkitoliyarpok.
**deceives** v. — tammarsaiyok.
**deception** (excl.) iak ! aikuluk !
**decoys** — -ngoark-*.
**decreasing** (as moon) — nunguksaiyok.
**deed** — illiornerk.
**deep** — itiyok.
**deer** — tuktu.
**deer (hunts** deer) v. — tuktusiorpok, tuktuliarpok.
**deer calf** — norrak.

**deer skin clothes** — tuktukutit.
**deer buck** — pagnerk.
**deer cow without fawn** — norraitok, kulavak.
**deer horn** — nagdjuk.
**deer migration** — adgerput, aggerput.
**deer skin** — tuktub aminga.
**delayed** (is) — kingusiktok.
**deliriums** (has) — assinik okrarpok.
**delivers child** (birth) — nutakreyok.
**deluge** (flood) — ulingonerdjuark.
**den** (fox d.) — sidjiark.
**den** (for dogs) — sittigak.
**denies** v. — missiarpok.
**denies by sign of nose** — naksitarpok.
**departs** (leaves) v. — audlarpok.
**depreciation** — -kunuk-*, -neluk-*, -ruluk-*.
**descendants** — kinguvangit, kinguvareit.
**desert** (is a d.) — sunakasuitok.
**deserted** (is) — inuilak, inukasuitok.
**desires** v. — tussuyok, pissuartok, ikligosuktok.
**desirable** — tussunartok, iklinartok, pijominartok.
**despicable** — suglunartok.
**despises** v. — suiksarpok, suiriwok.
**despises something** — nakroyarpok, nakrowok.
**despised** — narronikut.
**destitute** (is) — ayuksartok.
**destroys** v. — asserorpok.
**destroyed** (is completely d.) — suteititauyok.
**detonates** v. — sirkropadlakpok.
**develops** — agliwallialerpok.
**devil** — tonrar.
**devours** v. — apkalawok.
**dew** — missuk.
**diamond** (at cards) — kaksungaut.
**diarrhoea (has)** — akritomik anârpok. ittiktartok, anârkrartok.
**dies** v. — tokowok.
**different** (is) — assia, at'la (Padl.). adjigengitok.
**difficult** (is) — ajornartok.
**difficulty (has)** — ajortok.
**digest** (hard to d.) — sidlingonartok, sungonartok.
**digs** v. — adgasarpok.
**dines** v. — ubluromitarpok.
**direction** — -tor-*.
**dirt** — iperk, pilu.
**dirty** (is) — ipaktok, salumaitok.
**dirty clothes** (has) — salumaitok, pujartok.
**disagrees** — issumakattigengitok.
**discouraged** (is) — kevittok, mungovok, sujumiyok.
**disentangles** v. — idlaerpok.
**disguised** (is) — adjortok.
**dish** — pugutak, awapsilak.
**dislikes** v. — mamiasukpok, mamiatsakpok.
**disobedient** (is) — nâlengitok, opalungitok, tussangitok, kamataitok, tussangisartok.
**displeased** (is) — kuviasungitok.
**displeases** v. — kuvianailiorpok.
**disposed (is badly)** — sorangayok.

**disregards** s.o. v. — issumaringitâ.
**dissolves** (vg sugar in tea) — ingularpok.
**distance (long** d.) — sivituyok.
**distance (short** d.) — sivikiktok.
**distasteful** (is) — mamaitok.
**distributes** v. — tuniorkraiyok, ningerpok.
**distribution** — -yorkrai-*.
**distributor (of flame)** — palagêkkut.
**disturbs everybody** — pakadlakpok.
**divides,** separates — awikpok.
**divides into pieces** — abgorpok.
**diving (as a bird)** — auksarpok, auksararpok.
**diving into water** — aglorpok.
**division** — awingnerk.
**divorces** v. — awikpok.
**dizzy** (is) — uibjartok.
**do this** — imanna-pit; pilerit.
**do this for me** — pi'nga (Padl.).
**dock** — kisarvik, iksarvik.
**doctor** (medical) — idluarsaiye.
**does as if** v. — -sertor-*.
**dog** — kringmerk.
**dog (plays)** v. — unayok.
**dog team (on the move)** — kremuksertut.
**dog (leader dog)** — issorartuyok.
**doll** — nutarangoark, inungoark.
**domesticated** (is) — nuutsuitok.
**domicile** — aisimabvik.
**domination** — nalegaunerk.
**done** (is) — pianiktok, pissimayok.
**don't !** — pinnak ! pitaili !
**door,** cover etc. — matu, ukkuark.
**door** (opens the d.) — ukkuerpok.
**door** (closes the d.) — ukkuarpok.
**door frame** — katark or katak.
**Doršet** (Baffin Land) — Kingait.
**doubtful** (is) — kollarnartok.
**down** (hair) — keviork.
**down there** — taunani, taununga etc.
**down the river (goes)** v. — situvok.
**down (goes d.)** — atkarpok.
**downwards** — taununga.
**downward (vertically)** — ammut.
**downward (head d.)** — kudjangayok, napayararpok.
**drags** (by force) v. — nutsukpok.
**drags sled (dogways)** — uniarpok.
**drawers of table** — amuyakattark.
**dreams** v. — sinnektomawok.
**dream** n. — sinnektomanerk.
**dress** (woman's) — arnangodjutit, atailitak.
**dress** (front part of woman's dress) — kînerk.
**dressed** (ready to work) — pigingayok, pigittok.
**dresses wounds** v. — matuserpok.
**dries** v. — pannerserpok.
**dried meat** — mipko.
**dried fish** — pipsi.
**dried oil** on clothes etc. — puyak.
**dried** (is) — pannertok.

**drier for skins** — kaupkoark.
**drifts** (snow d.) — perktok, perksertok.
**drifts a little** — perktudjuktok.
**drifting** (travels when d.) — perktorsiorpok.
**drift wood** — tibjak.
**drifted ashore** — tipiyok.
**drinks** v. — immerpok.
**drunk** (is) — angayartok.
**drips** v. — kussertok, ernrartok.
**drip-flat** — manuilitak.
**driver (of dogs)** — sakrisartok, sukkasartok.
**drop of liquid** — kusserk.
**drops,** falls v. — katakpok.
**drops something** — kataiyok.
**dropsical** (is) — immerolik.
**drowned** (is d. from a canoe) — kayauyok.
**drugs** (medecine) — idluarsautit.
**drum** — krilaut.
**drum (plays,** beats the d.) — kattukpok.
**drunken man** — angayartok.
**dry meat** — mipko.
**dry fish** — pipsi or pepsi.
**drying rack** — pauguserk, innitak etc.
**duck** — mîterk.
**duck (eider** d.) — kringâlik, amaulik.
**duck (squaw duck)** — a'agnerk, agiariardjuk.
**ducklings** — mîterait.
**dug of dog,** cow etc. — mamaut.
**dumb, dummy** — okrajuitok.
**during** — pitillugo, -tillu-*.
**dust** — sannerk or sanerk.
**dust (sweeps d.)** — sannerpok or sanerpok.
**dust** or snow under shoes — alorluk.
**duty** — piyuksak, piyaeksak.
**dwarf** — inugaruvligak, inugaruvligardjuk. plur : inugaruvligardjuit.

## — E —

**each** — atunit; -kraur-*.
**each time** — -lerangat-*.
**eagle** (bird) — nektoralik.
**ear** (anat.) — siut; plur : siutit.
**ear-drum** — igalauyak.
**ear-pendant** — siuterut.
**ear wax** (cerumen) — tikte.
**ears** (has sore ears) — siuseriyok.
**ears falling** (as dog) — padlungayunik siutilik.
**ears (are long)** — siutikortuyok.
**early** — -sar-*.
**early riser** — ublarortok.
**earns** (money) v. — kinauyatârtok.
**earth** — nuna.
**earth map** — nunangoark.
**east** — unani.
**Easter** — Jesusib Makkibvia.
**easy** (is) — ajornangitok, piyareakiktok.
**easy** (the idea of ease is rendered by several infixes) — -qlayok-*, sarei-*, -gayuk-*.
**eats** v. — nerreyok, nerrewok.
**eats (making noise)** — kargolartok.
**eats remains of others** — sunasorpok.
**echoes** (it e.) v. — akkiortok.

**economizes** v. — illipayok.
**eddy of water** — niorluk.
**edge** – kiglerk, siniksak.
**edge of ice** — sina.
**edge of garments** — sinniksak, sinniksaut.
**educated** (is well e.) — pamitsiartok.
**effort, makes an e.** (physical) — aksororpok.
**effort, makes an e.** (moral) — illungertorpok.
**effort,** do make an effort — aksut ! aksororit !
**egg** — mannik.
**egg (found)** — pikjuk.
**eggs (lays e.)** — manniliorpok.
**eggs (month of e., June)** — mannit.
**egg** (fish e.) — suwak, plur. suwait.
**egg out of its nest (laid in a hurry)** — angornikut.
**egg shell** — saunark.
**egg white** — kauk.
**egg yoke** — itserk.
**egoistic** (is) — unwangamiutak.
**eider duck** — kringâlik, amaulik.
**eight** — pingasunik-arvinilli.
**eight** at cards or 8 o'clock — taiyalak.
**either . . . or . . .** — -luba-*, -luba-*. -lonit-*, -lonit-*.
**ejector of a rifle** — piksitaut.
**elastic** (is) — tassiyartok.
**elbow** (anat.) — ikkuserk.
**elbow (pushes with e.)** — ikkusiarpok.
**elbows (leans on one's e.)** — ikkusimigarpok.
**eldest** — angayodlerk.
**elected** (is) — anneriyauyok.
**embarked** (is) — ikkimayok.
**embarks** v. — ikkiwok.
**embraces** v. — erkrikpok.
**embryo** — iplaut, nutaraksak, singaiyak.
**emerges from the water** v. — puiyarpok.
**emetic** — merearnartok.
**emotion** (almost choked by e.) — tupkoyakiktok.
**emotion** (shivers from e.) — kalertanartok.
**empties** v. — immerutiwok, eruipok.
**empties (any liquid)** — kuvisiwok.
**empties (any solid)** — navikpok.
**empty** (is) — immakangitok, inukangitok : (empty house). immaertok, immerutiyok.
**end** — issuk.
**enemy** — akkerark, unalerk.
**engaged couple** (to be married) — nulliaksareik.
**engine** — ikkuma, ikkumalik.
**enlarges** v. — agliwayok.
**enough of that** ! stop ! — asso ! tagva ! assogor !
**enough** (has e.) — areoyok; (fed up : kawaktok).
**entangled** (is) — idlalik, nigaptertok.
**enters** v. — iterpok, illuanuarpok.
**envelope** n. — immût.
**envelops** v. — matuserpok, immuyiyok.
**envious** — idluigosuktok.
**epileptic** — krersortok, âsortok.

**equal** — aktikosartok.
**equalizes** v. — maniksarpok.
**eraser** — pîyaut, nunguterut.
**erect** (is) — napaiyok, napayok.
**ermine** — tireak.
**error** — tammarnerk.
**error** (induces into error) v. — tammarsaiyok.
**escapes** — annakpok.
**Eskimo** — inuk, inumarik, inudlarik, inupiak.
**Eskimo (first ancestors)** — inunrautik.
**Eskimo language** — inuktut, inuktitut.
**Eskimo nun** — inuk-nayangortok.
**Eskimo uses** — illitkosetokrait.
**Eskimos (we, the Eskimos)** — inuktigut.
**Eskimo Point**, NWT — Arviark.
**eternal** (is) — issukangitok, nungusuitok.
**even** (renders surface e.) v. — maniksarpok.
**even** (is) — maniktok.
**even so** — aglat, -lônit-*.
**evening** — unnuk.
**evening prayers** — unnuksiutit.
**every one** — tamarmik, nelliallonit, illunatik.
**every thing** — sunaluktar, sutuinnark.
**evident** (is) — nalunangitok.
**evil** (is) — piktaungitok.
**exceeds** v. — piluartok.
**excessive** — ungatârtok, pidluartok.
**exchange** (root word for e.) — akki.
**excited** (is) —uimaktok, uimayartok.
**excrement** — anâk.
**excrement (evacuates)** — anârpok.
**excrement (smells e.)** — anârnittok, anârsunniktok.
**excuse** (seeks an excuse) — passiyauyungnaerutiksariorpok.
**exempted** (is) — perkoyaukattaungingmat.
**exercises** (does e.) — illisaiyok, piniarsartok.
**exhausted**, tired — erevittok.
**exit** — anigorviksak.
**expands** v. — issiviktok.
**expects** — nerriukpok.
**expects a gift** — arliarpok.
**expects some one** — itsuarkattarpok (goes out often to see if s. o. coming).
**expensive** (is) — akkituyok.
**expires** v. — tokowok, anernangerpok.
**explodes** v. — sirkrortok.
**extension (added)** — uigoriyauyok.
**exterior garments** — silapait, sing. silapak.
**exterminated** — pitakarungnaertok.
**external** — kangagut, silatagut.
**extinguished fire** — kamittok, kamingartok.
**extinguishes fire** — kamitpok.
**extreme** — issudlerk.
**extremity**, end — issuk.
**eye** (anat.) — iye; (plur. : iyit).
**eye (apple of the e.)** — iyaroak
**eyebrow** — kabluk.
**eye (cross-eyed)** — nakungayok.
**eyelash** — kremereak.
**eyelid** — sitkut.

**eye (lost)** — iyarortok.
**eye (orbit of the e.)**—iyauservik.
**eye (pupil of the e.)** — takuvitnar, iyaroak.
**eye (is sore)** — iyeleriyok; (snow-blind: idluktok).

## — F —

**fable,** story — unipkartuar.
**face** (anat.) — kinark, tautu.
**facing** — nellani, akkiani.
**fading** (is) — kokartok.
**fails** (misses one's shot) v. — uniorpok.
**faints v.** — awârpok, âwok.
**fair complexion** (has a) — inekonartok.
**faith** — okpernerk.
**faith (has)** — okperpok.
**fall** (season) — ukkiaksak, ukkiak.
**falls** n. — kurluktok, kôrluktok.
**falls** v. — katakpok.
**falls backwards** — kingupiusarpok.
**falls from high** — iyukarpok, eyukarpok.
**falls head first** — ukpikarpok.
**falls in,** v. — immiktok.
**falls into water** — immarpok.
**falls inside** (vg. igloo) — illusikpok.
**falls (lets fall)** — kataiyok.
**falls sideways** — olrowok.
**falls while walking** (stumbles) — padlakpok.
**falsehood** — saglunerk.
**family** — -kut-*, -miut-*.
**family (complete)** — nutarareit (parents & children).
**famous** Eskimo ancestors — tunit.
**far away** (is) — unvasiktok, awanitok.
**far from one another** — akkulaitok.
**farewell to s.o. going away** — tâwawutit.
**farewell to s.o. staying home** — tagvawutit.
**farm** — perorsêvik.
**farmer** — perorsêvileriye.
**fast** (travels f.) — nakkertok, nakkersartok.
**fast day** (fasting d.) — nerretailibvik.
**fasts** v. (is not eating) — nerretailiwok.
**fat** — tunnu.
**fat** (is) — koiniyok, tunnulik.
**fat of the intestines of deer** — kiksaut.
**fat of the loins of deer** — tunnu.
**fat (part of the hind leg)** — nakkasungnark (the fat of the leg).
**father** — atâtak; (Kidl.: apâk).
**father (adopting f.)** — atâtaksak; angutiksak.
**father-in-law** — sakki or saki.
**fathom** (measure) — issark.
**fault** — tammarnerk.
**fault (it is my f.)** — pidjutauyunga.
**fawn** (calf) — norrak.
**fearful** (is) — kappianartok.
**fearful** (how f.!) — kappiannamik!
**feather** — suluk, eretak.
**feathers** (plucks off f.) v. — eretarpok.

**feeds v.** — nerretitsiwok.

**feeds dogs** — takulukpok, kringmeriwok.

**feels** v. — ikpiriwok.

**feeling (no more f.** in limbs) — —kakilarsarsiyok.

**female,** woman etc. —arnak.

**fence** — sablutak.

**festivity** — pibvikdjuark.

**fetches** v. — aiklerpok.

**fever** (has) — ôternartok, ônartok.

**few** (very f.) — ikkitokoluit, amisungitut.

**fiddle** — agiarialik.

**field** — manerark.

**field** (cultivated f.), garden — perorsêvik.

**fight** (dog fight) — ugiarput, ogiarput.

**fights v.** — unatarpok.

**fights** (as dogs etc.) v. — ugiarpok.

**file** (instrum) — agiark.

**files** v. — agiarpok.

**filings** — agidjakuit.

**fillip** — mitigleraut.

**fills** v. — illudlerpok, tatatpok.

**filter** (for liquid) — kakiaksaut.

**finally** — kingudlerpâmik, -tungar-*.

**finds** (after searching) v. — nennisiwok.

**finds (perchance)** — nagvarpok.

**finds (meets)** — -si-*.

**finger-nail** — kukik.

**finger-tip** — pudjuk.

**fingers** — adgait, inugait, angutinguit.

" **annular** — mikilerark.

" **index; forefinger** — tîkerk.

" **little finger** — ikritkrok.

" **middle finger** — kriterdlerk.

" **thumb** — koblu, (kublu).

**finished** (is) no more of it — nunguktok.

**finishes v.** — pianikpok, nâwok, -anik-*, innerpok, innerpâ.

**fire** — ikkuma.

" **big f., hell** — ikkumaâluk.

" **burning** — ikkiyok, ikkuadlaktok.

" **burns, is on fire** — ikkumayok.

" **camp fire** — kigluk.

" **(puts out f.)** — kamittok.

" **(remains of camp f.)** — ikkumalinerk.

" **starting** — aumaliktok, ikkaksartok.

**firm,** hard — sitiyok.

**first** — sivudlerk.

**first (arrives first)** — tikikrautauwok.

**first (at first)** — sivudlermik.

**first (for the first time)** — -gior-*, -lisar-*.

**first (goes first)** — sivudlerpok.

**fish** — irkaluk.

" **bate** — manak.

" **(cod fish)** — ôgark.

" **eggs** — sûwait.

" **line** — aulasaut.

" **(red trout)** — ivitaruk.

" **scaled f.** — kavisilik.

" **white fish** — anâdlerk, kakiviartok.

**fishing** (goes f.) — irkadliarpok.

**fishing hole in ice** — agluwak.

**fishing with line** — aulasarpok.

**fits well** — nâmatsiartok.

**five** — tadlimat.

**five (every fifth one)** — tadlimerangat.

**five (fifth)** — tadlimât, tadlimangat.

**five (times in a row, 5 days in a row)** — tadlimangorsaiyok.

**fixed** (after being broken) — atkriktok.

**flag** — audlakrut, aulakrut, audlakosiak.

**flame distributor** — palagekkut.

**flashlight**, lamp — ikkittartok.

**flatters** v. — uivilraiyok, âkkakpok.

**flavour** — tipi.

**flees away** v. — kremayarpok, mangatpok, kremayok.

**flesh** — uvinerk, nerkri.

**flexible** (is) — napsiktok.

**flick of the finger** — mitiglerauf.

**flint** — kukiksaut, kukiksak.

**flipper** — tallerok.

**flirts** v. — sivulingayok.

**float** (for nets) — poktakut; poktakutâ (poss.).

**floats** v. — poktalarpok.

**flood** (deluge) — ôlingonerdjuark, ulingonerdjuark.

**floor** — natterk.

**flour** — akrekoyaksak, adgiksak.

**flower** — nunangoark, perusiatsiark.

**flows** v. — kûrktok.

**fluid**, liquid — kuvisuktok.

**fly** (insect) — anângierk, niviugak, milugiak.

**flying** (is) — tingiyok, tingmiyok.

**foam** — krappuk.

**foetus** — iplaut or iblaut, nutaraksak.

**fog** — nipterk, tarkserk.

**foggy** (is) — niptaitok, tarksertok, isserartok.

**folds (lengthways)** v. — koglurpok.

**folds sideways** v. — peritpok.

**folks**, relatives — illageit, illigeit.

**follows** v. — mallikpok.

**followed** (is) — malliktauyok.

**food** — nerkriksak.

**food for dogs** — takulutiksak, kringmisitiksak.

**food for family left home** — pagetaeksak, ikkupiksak (Net.).

**food marks in face** etc. — tiblit.

**fool** — pokreitok, issumakangitok, tukikangitok.

**foot** (anat.) — ittigak; Okk: issigak.

**for** — -uti-*.

**forbids** v. — pitailiwok, perkoyingitok.

**force** (compels by strength) — -ti-*, -titsi-*.

**forceps** — kîyautit.

**ford** — ikârvik.

**forefathers** — sivudlit, sivudlivinit.

**forefinger**, index — tîkerk.

**forehead** (anat.) — krau.

**forehead band** (decorative) — kraurut.

**forehead band** (to help carrier) — ikayût.

**forehead of deer skin** — kringôk.

**forenoon** — ubluromitarvik pingitillugo sulli.

**foresight** (of rifle) — nakatak, ulurnerk.

**forest** — napârtolik.
**forgets** v. — puigorpok.
**forgets easily** — puigudguyok (Padl.).
**forgives** v. — issumariyungnaerpok.
**fork** (table f.) — kakiak.
**formerly of** — -vinerk-*.
**forsakes** v. — iperainnarpok.
**fortunately !** — anerta !
**forty** adj. — awatit-malrok, sitamat-adgait.
**forward** — sivumut.
**foundation,** base — tungavik, ikkuvrark.
**four** adj. — sitamat; (Okk: tisamat).
**four times** (used only with a verb. vg. he does it f.t.) — sitamaertarluni.
**four** (obtains, gets f.) — sitamararpok.
**fourth** — sitamât, sitamangat.
**fourth, (every fourth one)** — sitamerangat.
**fox** — tireganierk; (Okk: nappatak).
**fox (blue fox)** — krearnartok.
**fox trap** — tireganiersiut, kiiyakattar, mikkigiak.
**frame** (of picture etc.) — awadluk.
**frank** (is) — saglusuitok.
**free** (not caught) — annakpok.
**freezes** — kekrewok, koangowok.
**freezes to death** — kekrarpok.
**frequency** (easiness) — -gayuk-*.
**friend** — illamar, pinnariyauyok.
**fries in pan** v. — tertittok.
**frightened** (is) — kappiasuktok, aliasuktok.
**frightened (suddenly)** — tatabjiyok.
**fringe of garment** etc. — nidgiak; plur: nidgiet or nidgiait.
**from** — -mit-*; nakit.
**from (where do you come f.) ?** — nakingiarpit ?
**front** (goes in front of him) — sâgiarpa.
**front** (in front of.) — sangani.
**front part of** — sivu, poss: sivua or sivunga.
**frost** — patu, (light frost : minu).
**frost (in window)** — illuyok.
**frost (new frost on sea ice)** — krenu.
**frost (scrape f.)** — illuiyarpok.
**frozen** (is) — kekreyok, koangoyok.
**frozen meat** — koak.
**frozen to death** — kekrarmago.
**fruits** — paunrait.
**frying pan** — ipualik.
**fuel** — orkso.
**fulfils** v. — nedliutikpok.
**full** (is) — tatattok, imagtok.
**Fullerton** NWT — Kattiktalik.
**functions no more** (broken) — illingartok.
**funnel** — kubvivik, kuvitît, ikkiyarsît, uksavik.
**funny** (is) — tipsinartok, iglarnartok.
**fur** — amerk mitkrolik.
**furnace** — ikkualausibvik.
**further in the igloo** (goes) v. — kilusikpok.

**furthest (to the end)** — issudlerpak.

**furuncle** — ajuwak.

**future** (gramm.) — -niar-*, -omar-*, -lar-*.

## — G —

**gale** (their is a g.) — anoretuyok.

**gallops** v. — pangalikpok.

**game** (at hunt) — anguyaeksak.

**game** (a play) — pinguaruserk.

**gargle** (mouth wash) — erortût.

**gasolene** — ikkisareitok, orkso.

**gathering** (takes part in g.) — kadgemiôyok.

**gathering house** — kadgek.

**gathering place** — kattimavigdjuark.

**generates** — nutaraliorpok.

**gear** — maniilait.

**generous** (is) — tukkuttok.

**genuine** — -luavik-*.

**get out of my way !** — akkâ ! perit !

**gets up** — makkitpok.

**ghost,** spirit — tonrar.

**giant (man)** — inukpak, inukpassuk.

**gill** (of fish) — massik.

**girdle** — tapsi, kritikisautit.

**girl** (young g.) — niviasar.

**gives** v. — tunisiyok, kraintsiyok.

**gives back** — tunimiyok, utterpok, satorpok.

**gives his word** — tunersiyok.

**gives food** (to whole family at home) — payukpok.

**gift** — aitût, aituserk, tunerk.

**gift** (received at festival) — kuviasuguserk.

**glass** — alegor, nilauyark.

**glass window** — igalak.

**glass (spectacles)** — îgak.

**globe** (map) — nunangoark.

**glorious** — nertornartok.

**glossy** — kiblariktok, piaktok.

**gloves** — adgauyait, poalu.

**glue** — nipiterut.

**gnashing of teeth** (has) — aglerolarpok.

**gluttony** — nerretunerk.

**go on !** — atti, aksut, attai.

**God** — Anernealuk, Nunalîorte.

**goes for** — -jartor-*, -rear-*.

**goes home** — aiwok.

**goes in** — iterpok.

**goes out** — aniyok.

**goes** (people are gone) — inuerutiyok.

**goes to and fro** — awamurpok.

**goes to do something** — suliarpok.

**goes to see if s.o. coming** — -sai-*.

**goes where there are some** — -lijar-*.

**gold** — kanosak.

**good-bye** — tâwawutit, tagvawutit.

**good** (is) — pitsiartok, piktauyok.

**good** (morally g.) — idluartok, akkaôyok, pioyok.

**good for nothing** — atungitok, suinnak.

**good to taste or smell** — mamartok.

**good for you !** — anerta !

**goose** (canadian grey) — nerlerk, tingmiark.

**goose** (blue or white) — kanguk.

**gospel** — tussarnartut; Jesusib okrausingit.

**gossips** v. — okrarayukpok.

**government** — issumatavit.

**gown** (woman's) — arnangodjutit.

**grace,** consolation — saimarnerk.

**grammophone** — tussarnarut.

**grandfather** — atâtatsiark.

**grandchild** — erngutak, ernrutak.

**grandmother** — anânatsiark.

**graniteware** — mamâlik.

**grasps** v. — tigusiyok, tiguyok.

**grass** — ivik.

**grateful** (is) — kuyaliyok.

**gratis** — akkikangitok.

**grave,** tomb — illuverk.

**grave** (puts in a grave) — illuverpok.

**grave-yard** — illuvertalik.

**gravel** — tuwapak.

**gravy** — immerark, kayok.

**grease,** lard — punernerk.

**great** (is) — angiyok.

**greatness** — -aluk-*, -djuark-*, -apik-*.

**green** — tunguyortok.

**Greenlanders** — Kalâdlit.

**grey hair** — krê, siarnak (for animals).

**grindstone,** whetstone — ipiksaut, sidlît, agiut.

**grindstone** (uses g.) — ipiksarpok.

**groans** — ipkolukpok.

**grotto** — kaertok-illutuyok.

**ground** — manerar, nuna.

**grounded ship** — ikkariktok.

**ground-drift** — natteroviktok.

**group** — kattimayut.

**growing** (is) — perorsaiyok, perortok.

**growling dogs** — kattingolartut.

**grows** v. — agliwok.

**grows no more** — aglisuertok.

**grub** (food for travelling) — takoak, takoaksak.

**grumbles** — okrardlukpok.

**guards well** — papatsiwok.

**guardian** — mianersiye.

**guardian angel** — minanersiye, ikayorte.

**guess (try and guess)** — nellaurgiarit.

**guesses** v. — nellautpok.

**guest** — tuyurmiangoyok.

**guide** — krauyimatauyok.

**guides by the hand** — tessiorpok, tassiorpok.

**guilty** (is) — idluilutaôyok.

**gull** (sea g.) — nauyak.

**gum** (chewing g.) — tamuatuar, sirkrortak.

**gun** — sirkotidjut, kokiut.

**gun** (shot gun) — miterniut.

**gut** — innaluark, erkravit.

## — H —

**habitually** — -pak-*, -wak-*.

**hails** (it hails) — natakronartok, alikattok.

**hair** — nuya, mitkok or mitkrok.

**hair fallen off** — siak, pilu.

**hair (grey h.)** — krê.

**hair (has grey hair)** — krêlik.

**hair (heavy h.)** — tulroyok.

**hair (losing h.)** — kiaktok, kiasiyok.
**hair (short h.)** — saggatnar.
**hairless** — nuyaîtok.
**half** — nappak, kôpak, abvako.
**hall** (gathering h.) — kaggebviksak, kadgeviksak.
**hammer** — kautauyark.
**hammer** (stone used as h.) — kautark.
**hamstring** — kimmikrok.
**hand** — adgak, aggak.
**hand** (rendered useless) — adgailiyok.
**hand** (lost h.) — adgaertok.
**hands are cold** — adgaiyartok.
**hands (on four hands)** — pamgorpok.
**hand of watch, clock** — titkut.
**handkerchief** — kakiut.
**handle** — tigumibvik, iput.
**handle (or butt of rifle)** — kangiark, kangik.
**handle of drum** — pablu.
**handle of shovel** — pabliak.
**hand-shaking** — tigutinerk.
**handsome** (is) fair — inekonartok.
**hanged** (is) something — nivingayok.
**hangs oneself** — kremikpok.
**happens** v. — nedliutikpok.
**happiness** — kuviasungnerk.
**happy** (is) — kuviasuktok, nakorsartok, alianaigosuktok.
**happy** (renders one happy) — kuvianartok.
**harbour** — kisarviksak.
**hard** (is) compact and solid — sitiyok.
**hard** (is) stern, difficult, oppressive etc. — ajornartok.
**hare, rabbit** — ôkalerk, ukalerk.
**hark** ! listen ! — imâ ! atâ !
**harmonica** — erkrerpallût.
**harmonium,** organ — nakrittaut.
**harness** — anût, anô.
**harp,** mandolin — nokrarsarpallût.
**harpoon,** lance — nauligak, unark, kapût.
**harpoon for fish** — kakkiwak.
**harpoon's point** — sakku.
**harpoons** v. — kapiwok, naulikpok.
**Harrison,** P.Q. — Kraimrut, Inugdjuark.
**has** (possesses) — -talik-*, -kartok-*.
**hastens** v. — tuwawiorpok, erenesukpok.
**hat** (head gear) — nassak.
**hates** v. — mamiatsakpok, mamiasukpok.
**hawk** — unnuarsiutit.
**hay** — ivik.
**head** (anat.) — niakrok.
**headache** — niakrongoyok.
**head (covers one's head)** — nassarpok.
**head (decoration of hood)** — nassarmiutak.
**head** (uncovers one's head) — nassaerpok.
**head wind** — adgo.
**healed skin** — mamittok.
**health** (is in good h.) — kranoengitok, âniangitok.
**health** (is in bad h.) — âniartok, âniargayuktok.

**hears,** listen v. — tussarpok, tussawok.

**hears with difficulty,** hard hearing — siudjarluktok, siudluktok.

**heard** (is) — tussarsauyok.

**heart** (anat.) — ômat.

**heart** (beats) v. — tiglerpok.

**heaven,** sky — krilak.

**heaven** (of the saints) — kuvianartorvik.

**heavy** (is) — okomaitok, iktariktok.

**heel** (anat.) — kimmerk.

**helicopter** — kolimigulik.

**hell** — kappianartorvik.

**helps** v. — ikayorpok.

**helper** — ikayorte.

**hen** — akrigerdjuark, arnaviak.

**herbivorous** (is) — nunatorte, ivitorte.

**here (where I am)** — tagvani, uwani, mâni.

**here** (he was here recently) — uwanikrauyok.

**here** (come here now) — uwanerarlagit.

**here it is** — ubva !

**hesitates** v. — kollârpok.

**hiccups** (has) — simmiktartok, nerretorartok.

**hidden** (is) — tallisimayok, iyersimayok.

**hide and seek** (game) — immuyut.

**hide of walrus skin** — kau.

**hides something** v. — iyerpâ, talikpâ.

**high** (is) — kôtsiktok, pôktuyok.

**highest** — kôdlerpak, kôtsilak.

**hill** — kingarok.

**hill (steep hill)** — imnak, ikpigak.

**himself** — nangminek, ingminek.

**himself** (acts all by himself) — ingmikoarpok.

**hind part,** rear — kingu.

**hinders** v. — agviarpok.

**hinges n.** — âttatik.

**hip bone** — sibverk.

**hits with fist** v. — tiglukpok, tungautiwok.

**hits with one's head** — kassukpok.

**hits with hammer** — kadgutiwok, kadjukpok.

**hits with a stick** — anaurpok.

**hoarse** (has a h. voice) — erenainartok.

**hog,** pig — kûkûsi, kalaktuyuyok.

**holds** v. — tiguyok, tigumiarpok.

**holds between legs** — kromikpok.

**hole** — putu.

**holy** — pioyok, ibjornaitok.

**Holy-Ghost** — Anernerk Pioyok.

**home** — aisimabvik, ainiarvik.

**home (is at home)** — aisimayok.

**home (goes h.)** — ailerpok.

**home (is always home)** — awingnesuitok.

**homeless** (is) — aiviksakangitok.

**homicide** (is) — inuarte.

**homicide (commits homicide)** — inuarpok.

**homonym** — abva, attereit, saunereit (Okk.).

**homonym of father or mother** — âtsiark.

**honest man** — inudluitok, tiglisuitok.

**honey** — mamaksaut, iguptait nerkringa.

**honors** v. — nertorpok.

**hood** — nassak.

**hook** — niksik, kresuk.

**hooked** (is) —niksiktok.

**hook (for fishing)** — kardjuksak.

**hook (used as a brake)** — kresuktaut.

**hooks** (as with a snap) v. — naktikpok, naksitartok.

**hope** — nerriungnerk.

**hopes** v. — nerriukpok.

**hops** v. — kïggertarpok, or kriggertarpok.

**horn of an animal** — nagdjuk.

**horse** — kringmerdjuark.

**hospital** — pijungnaervik, âniarvik.

**hostel** — tuyurmiangosibvik.

**hot** (is) — ônartok.

**hot weather** — okkoanartok, okkô, ikkianaitok.

**hour** (one) — krauyisautib ikarninga atauserk.

**house** (snow h.) — iglu.

**house** (abandoned h.) — igluvigak, igluvinerk.

**house** (builds a h.)—igluliorpok.

**house** (wooden, stone etc.) — iglurdjuark.

**how ?** — kranok ?

**however** — -ralluar-*, -galluar-*, -kalluar-*, kissiani.

**howling dog** — miagortok, miortok.

**humble** (is) — piosuringitok.

**hump-back** — piku, koksuktok.

**hundred** adj. — tadlimat-awatit, kolit-aggait.

**hungry** (is) — kârpok.

**hungry** (very h., starving) — perlertok.

**hunts** v. — angunasukpok.

**hurry up !** — tuwawi !

**hurry** (in a hurry to urinate) — angôrpok.

**hurts** (it) — ânernartok, ânertok.

**husband** — ui.

**hydropic** (is) — tumangayok.

**hypocrite** (is) — piotsertortok, misertok (Padl.), pitsiartsertortok, pingitsertortok (lit. : as if not).

## — I —

**I** (me) — uwanga.

**ice** — sikku, koasak.

**ice on sea (solid)** — tuwak.

**ice for melting fresh water** — nilak.

**ice from drippings** — kussugak.

**iceberg** — pikaluyak.

**ices runners of sled** v. — sermerpok.

**idea** — issuma.

**igloo** (snow house) — iglu.

**igloo (central i.)** — patark.

**igloo footing** — sau.

**ignorance** — -kiak-*.

**ignores** v. — naluyok, krauyimangitok.

**ill** (is) — âniartok, inungayok, kanimayok.

**image**, picture — adjik.

**imitation of** — -ngoar-*.

**imitates** v. — adjiliwok. ajokarsiwok, idjoarsiwok.

**imitates by playing** — pingoarpok, pikattarpok.

**impassive** (is) — ikpirijuitok.

**impatient** (is) — ningarsareitok.

**implements** — atukat.

**imposes hand upon** — tupviriwok.

**impossible** — pilangitok, sappernartok.

**imprisoned,** tied etc. — atungersimayok.

**improves** v. — piosiwallialerpok.

**incense** — issitsiariktok.

**incline to** (is) — -gayuk-*.

**incomplete** (is) — illako.

**increases** v. — agliwayok.

**indebted** — akkiitolik.

**indeed,** truly — ilar, amilar, assogor.

**index (finger)** — tîkerk.

**indian (Cree)** — ûnalerk.

**indian (Chipweyan)** — itkrelerk.

**indicates** (with finger) v. — tikoarpok.

**indicator** — tikût.

**indirectly** — tailamut.

**individually** — atunit, -kraur-*.

**indoor** — itersimaluni.

**ineffective** — pinangitok.

**infallible** — tammajuitok.

**infectious** — assinut ikârnartok.

**inhales** v. — illumut niorsiwok.

**ink** — missuktaut, titeraut.

**inland** — pâni, takpâni.

**inland** (family moving i.) — taggiarput.

**inland peoples** — kangidlit.

**innocent** — passagaeksaungitok.

**inquires** — apersorpok, aperiwok.

**insensible** — ikpirijuitok.

**inseparable** — awisuitok.

**inside** — illu, illua.

**inside** (demonstrative) — illuani, tatkramani.

**inside ourselves** — illuptingni.

**inside (contained i.)** — illulik.

**inside one another** — illulereit.

**inside** (puts inside) v. — illungotiwok.

**inside is empty** — illulikangitok.

**insipid** — tipikangitok.

**inspects** v. — takusaiyok.

**instantly** — tagvainnar, tagvadlaksinnar, tagva-tagva.

**instead** — -dlerk-*.

**instructs** v. — ajokertuiyok.

**instrument** — -ut-*, -siut-*, -sît-*.

**insufficient** — amigartok, inorsartok.

**insult** (they i. themselves mutually) — kanâluktut.

**intelligence** — silatunerk.

**intelligent** (is) — silatuyok, illituyok, pokrittok, kakrituyok.

**intention** — pidjutiksak.

**intentionally** (does i.) — piyâriyok.

**interchanges** v. — taursiwok.

**interdicts** v. — pitailiwok.

**interesting** (is) — sudluarnartok.

**interpreter** — siutak, okrarte, tussaye.

**interprets** v. — siuteriwok.

**intestine** — erkravik, innaluark.

**intestine** (the large i.) — erkluk.

**intestine without the fat** — kaipkut.

**into** — illuanut.
**intoxicating liquor** — angayarnartok.
**invites** v. — kraikoyiyok.
**invokes,** prays — tuksiarpok.
**irascible** — ningarsareitok.
**iris of the eye** — tauturut.
**iron,** metal — sâvik.
**ironing clothes** (is) — maniksarpok, kaersarpok.
**irresolute** (is) — kollakattartok.
**irresponsible** — krauyimangitok, pokreitok.
**is (substantially so)** — -ô-*.
**is (incidently so)** — -i-*.
**is it not true ?** — hili ? sili ?
**island** — kekertak.
**isolated,** alone — inotôwok, kissermiortok.
**issue,** exit — anigorviksak.
**it** — una.
**itches** v. — kômilaktok, kasiliyok, ungilaktok.
**ivory** — tugar.

## — J —

**Jaeger** (bird) — issungnak.
**jam** (edible) — mamaksaut.
**jaw** (anat.) — aglerok.
**jaw (inner)** — kingmark.
**jealous** (is) — kremigosuktok.
**jets** v. (spurts out) — tingmikarpok.
**job** — pilereaksak.
**joins,** meets v. — aporpok.
**jokes** v. — pingoarsinnarpok.
**journeys** v. — ingelrayok.
**joy** — kuviasungnerk.
**judge** — krauyimatauyok.
**jug** — yahoho.
**juggling balls** — iglukitartok.
**juice,** soup — immerak, kayok.
**jumps** v. — missikpok.
**jumps a little** v. — kiggertarpok, kriggertarpok.
**junction** — apornerk, kattinerk.
**junk** — pivinerk, iksinartok.
**justice (in words)** — saglusuinerk.
**justice (in deeds)** — tiglisuinerk.

## — K —

**Kazan river** — Sagvartok.
**keel** — sipiksak.
**keen,** sharp — ipiktok.
**keeps house for others** — nayudlerpok.
**keeps house for own family** — paiyok.
**keg** — kattauyak.
**kerosene** — ikkiyark, orksork.
**kettle** — torklualik.
**key** — ukkuerut, pinnerut, palangaksaut.
**kicks** v. — ittimgiarpok.
**kicks backwards** v. — tukerpok.
**kidney** — tartuk.
**killed (to be** k.) — tokotaeksak.
**kind** — taimannaitok.
**kindles (fire)** v. — ikkaksarpok.
**kindling** — ikkaksaut.
**King William Land** — Orksortôk.
**kingdom** — nalegaunerk.
**kisses v.** — kunikpok.
**kitchen** — igabvik.
**kite** (plaything) — tingmiuyak.
**knee** (anat.) — sirkrok.
**knee-cap** — sirkroat.
**kneels down** v. — sirkromiarpok.

**knife** — pilaut, aktût.
**knife (pocket** k.) — okkutartok.
**knife (table** k.) — papkuyak.
**knife (snow** k.) — panar.
**knife (sharp** k.) — ipiktok, kimâlerk, kînaktok.
**knife** (dull) — ipkiitok, iksarluktok.
**knife** (woman's k.; half-moon shape) — ulut.
**knits** v. — noversarpok.
**knob** — tigumibvik.
**knocks at the door** v. — kassuktorpok.
**knot** — nimervik.
**know** (I know not) — âmai, amiasuk, at'su (Okk.).
**knows** v. — krauyiwok, krauyimawok.
**knows not what ?** — sunakiark ? sunakiak ?
**knuckle** — nabgoak.
**kodak** — adjilerut, adjiliorut.

## — L —

**labor** — senneksak, pileriyaeksak.
**lace** (shoe l.) — singnerk.
**lace** (boot l.) — krepidjutit, ungerutit.
**ladder** — majorautit, tumerautit.
**ladle** — kadlût, kayôktak.
**Lake Harbour** NWT — Kimmerut.
**lake** — tasserk.
**lake outlet** — moriungnerk.
**lake formed in a river** — kamanaugak.
**lake of small size** — tasserark.
**lame (is)** — sibvêtok, tussiattok.
**lamp (electric)** — ikkittartok.
**lamp,** lantern — kodlerk, naneraut.
**lamp with a wick** — iperalik.
**lance,** harpoon — ûnark.
**land** — nuna.
**lands,** sets v. — mîkpok.
**language** — okrauselik.
**language (Eskimo** l.) — inuktut okrarnerk.
**lantern** — naneraut.
**lapidates** v. — millorpok.
**lard** (shortening) — punernerk.
**large** (at large, at sea) — sâviktok.
**larva** — aubverk.
**last** — kingudlerk.
**last** (at last) — -tainnar-*, assoila.
**late** (is) — kingusiktok, -nasar-*.
**late** (it is l.) — abjursaiyok.
**laughs** v. — iglarpok.
**laughs at** v. — iglautiriwok, iyorpok.
**law** — perkoyak, perkoyauyok.
**laxative** — anârnartok.
**lays down** (animal) — akropiyok.
**lays down** (human) — innangayok, nellangayok.
**lazy,** sleepy — salausuktok, erkreasuktok.
**lead** (metal) — akrilrok.
**leader dog** — issorartuyok.
**leads** v. — sivutiksauyok.
**leads** (walks ahead of sled) — kangelrarpok.
**leaf of tree** — okrauyak, atungauyak.
**leaks** v. — ernrartok.
**leaning** (object only) — uvingayok.

**leans** v. — igangayok, padlortok.
**leans forward** — ukkungawok.
**leans one's head** (on side) — naerpok.
**leans on** — pakinikpok.
**leaps** v. — missikpok.
**learns** v. — illiniarpok, illisaiwok, krauyisaiwok.
**learned** (is) — illisimayok.
**least** (the l.) — mikilak, mikiyomiglônit.
**leather** — kresiuyak.
**leaves,** goes away v. — audlarpok.
**left hand** — saumik.
**left-handed** — saumiôyok.
**left** (towards the left) — saumikkut, saumingmut.
**leg** (of animal) — ipigluk, niuk.
**leg** (of human) — niuk.
**legs (has short l.)** — ipiglukiktok.
**length** — takinerk.
**let me see !** — âmi, takulago !
**let us go** — attago.
**lets fall** v. — kataiyok, sapkuyok.
**letter (written** l.) — titirkret.
**level** (is) — manitsiartok.
**lever** — ibjutak.
**lewdness** — anguserinerk, arnaserinerk.
**licence,** permission — perkoyaunerk.
**lichen** (white moss) — niknark.
**licks with tongue** — aluktorpok, alukpok.
**lies** (tells falsehood) — sagluyok.
**lies** (you lie) — saglu, sagluwutit.
**life** — inôserk.
**life (gives life to)** — inoliorpok.
**lifts something** v. — kibvayok, kangatartok.
**lifts up one's head** — arlorpok.
**light** (is not heavy) — ôkrittok.
**light** (is not heavy for him) — ôkrigiwa.
**light** (opposite of darkness) — kraumanerk, krau.
**light producer** — kraumakraut.
**lighter** (instrum.) — ignaut.
**lightning** (flash of l.) — kraumalak.
**like** (he would like to) — -rasuar-*.
**like** (is resembling) — adjigektok.
**lime-stone** — tunnuyak.
**line,** string etc. — aklunak, nimiutak, krepidjut.
**line (all in one line)** — tukilereit.
**line for dog team** — pitu.
**line for harpoon** — alerk.
**line for making figures (play)** — ayarartut.
**line to tie load on sled** — nakritarut.
**line (top line of nets)** — krimiutak.
**lingers** v. — salausuktok.
**link** — ipiutak, numiutak.
**lip (corner of l.)** — erkri.
**lip (superior l.)** — kakiviark.
**lip (inferior l.)** — kasdluk.
**lips are sore** (in corner) — erkreluktok.
**lips closed** — ipummertok.
**lips open** — aitangayok.
**liquid** — kuvisortok.

**little** —
serdlerk, mikitokolungmik, -kolu-*, -nar-*, -ardjuk-*.

**liver** (anat.) — tinguk.

**lives** v. — ômayok, inôyok.

**lives with** — nayorpok.

**living** (livelihood) — inugutiksak.

**load** (on boat or sled) — ussik.

**load (big l.)** — ussituyok, ussiyoâluk.

**load (has a l.)** — ussiyok.

**load (has no l.)** — ussikangitok.

**load (has a small l.)** — ussikiktok.

**loaded** (cache l. with stones) — peroya.

**localization** — -dlerk-*, -vik-*.

**locked up** — pangnersimayok, atungersimayok.

**locust** (grass-hopper) — missiktartok.

**lonesome** (is) — kipingôyok, inuilangoyok.

**long** (is) — takiyok.

**long** (that long) — imanna takitiriyok.

**long time** — akkuniâluk.

**long (not long ago)** — -krauyok-*, owatsiark.

**look !** — taku ! takulerit !

**looks around from high** — nasittok (explores).

**looks fixedly,** stares at — iyeriwok.

**looks forward** (morally) — nerriukpok.

**looks upwards** — arlorpok.

**looking-glass** — tarrartût.

**loon** (bird) — kaksaut, kaglulik.

**loose (is)** — ipersimangitok, assinaitok.

**loose** (tries to get l.) — kalibjarpok.

**lord,** master — issumatark, nâlegak, atanerk (Okk.).

**loses something** — tammarpa.

**loses time** (as watch etc.) — kingusiktok.

**lost** (is) — assiuyok, tammarsimayok, assiwartok (Padl.).

**lot** (things counted) — amisualuit.

**lot** (things not counted) — angiyomik.

**loud** (is) — nippikortuyok.

**louse** — komak.

**loves** v. — naglikpok, ungayok, pinnariyok.

**low** (is) —atsiktok, pôkittok.

**lowers something** — akparpok, pokliwok.

**lowers nets in water** — ningitsiwok.

**lowest** — adlerpak.

**lung** (anat.) — pubvak, puvak.

**lung trouble** — pubvaleriyok, puvaleriyok.

**lust** — arnaserinerk, anguserinerk.

**lying down** — innangayok, nellayok.

## — M —

**MacKenzie Eskimos** — Kidlinermiut.

**mad** (is angry) — ningakpok.

**mad** (unconscious) — âyok, awârtok.

**madly (speaks m.)** — aivayok.

**maid** (young m.) —niviasar.
**mail** — titirkret.
**main part** (it's m. p.) — timinga, inua.
**mainland** — timâni.
**makes another one act** — -titsi-*, -nar-*, pititsiwok.
**makes something** — -lior-*, -tulli-*.
**male** — angut.
**male animal** — augusadlok.
**male bird** — angutiviark.
**man** — inuk.
**man (becomes** m.) — inungorpok.
**man (the very first man)** — inunraut.
**man (young)** — nukapiark, inôsuktok.
**manager** — angayorkrak, issumatar, audlatitsiye.
**mandolin** — nokrarsarpallût.
**Mansel Island** — Pudjunak, Publurnark.
**many** — amisut, unurtut.
**many (how many ?)** — krapsit ?
**many (how many did you get ?)** — krapsirarpit ?
**many (I know not how many)** — krapsikiak.
**many (not many)** — inuersertut.
**map** — nunangoar.
**Marble Island** — Orksoreark.
**mark** — nalunaikutak.
**mark (land mark)** — inuksuk.
**marks** v. — nalunailiwok.
**marriage** — nulliarengnerk.
**marries** v. — (male) nulliatârpok, (female) uitârpok.
**marrow** (anat.) — paterk.
**marvel (makes one m.)** — nanganartok.
**marvelous,** miraculous — ôpinnartok, tataminartok.
**marvels** (works m.) — nanganartulliwok, kamanartulliwok.
**mask** — kînapak.
**mast** — naparutak.
**mat** — tutiut, tutibviksak.
**match** (to light something) — ikkit (plur.): ikkitit.
**match already burnt** — ikkinikut, ikkiniko.
**mattress** — agvak, adliark.
**me,** pron. — uwanga.
**mean** (is) — kanungayok, angasartok.
**means** (it) v. — tukikartok, tukilik.
**measure,** model — idjoarviksak, oktutiksak.
**meat** — nerkri.
**meat** (fetches m. from cache) — akkoiwok.
**mechanic** (is a m.) — ikkumaleriyeôyok.
**medecine** — idluarsaut, inolisaut, anruark (Padl.).
**meeting of two rivers etc.** — kattinerk, apornerk.
**meets** v. — kattiwok, pârpok, aporpok.
**meets human being** — inuksiwok.
**meets** (goes and meet) — pâreartorpok.
**melted** (soft) —aumayok, akrittok.
**melting ice** (for water) — immiugak.

**melts ice** (for water) v. — immiorpok.
**mends something** — atkrikpok, atkriksorpok.
**mends clothes** — kidlaiyarpok, mapteriwok.
**message (gives m.)** — akkoertuyok.
**message (receives m.)** — akkoertugauyok.
**methylated spirit** — ikkaksaut.
**mica** — kiblereark, kriblereark.
**microscope** — agliut.
**middle** — kriterk, kerkrâ, akkudlerk.
**middle finger** — kriterdlerk.
**middle of flat** — ikkianga.
**midnight** — unnuar kretirarlugo.
**midwife** — angusik.
**migration of deer** — aterput, adgertut.
**milk** — immuk.
**milk in the breasts** etc. — amâmak.
**mind your business !** — kamanak ! issumaringilugo !
**miraculous** — kamanartok, tataminartok, nanranartok.
**mirage** (there is) — puipkartok, uyomereartok, immeriokritartok.
**mirror** — tarratût.
**miscarriage** (has) — aliptortok, avuyok.
**missing** (is) — pitakangitok.
**mist** — mingulertok.
**mitten** — poalu.
**mixes** v. — akkutsiyok. akkutsiwok.
**mixes** (sugar in tea) — ingularpok.
**mockery** — mitautiksak.
**mocking** (is) — mitarpok.
**model** — ajokarviksak, idjoarviksak, adjoribviksak.
**model for netting** — irkaluyak.
**moderates** — palartok.
**molar tooth** — erkdlerpak.
**molasses** — malasi (Engl. corr.).
**money** (coin) — kinauyak.
**month** (moon) — tatkret.
**moon** — tatkret.
**moon** (eclipse of the m.) — tatkrersertok.
**moon** (full moon) — tatkresiwok.
**more** — -nersau-*.
**more (no more)** — -erpok-*, -ruer-*,-eruti-*, pitakaruertok, -ungnaer-*.
**morning** — ublar.
**morning (at one moment of m.)** — ublakut.
**morning (daybreak)** — ublarpalluk, ublarpassik.
**morning (waking early in m.)** v. — ublarorpok.
**morning (it is m.)** — ublarôlertok.
**morning prayers** — ublarsiutit.
**mortal** — tokoyuyok, tokoyungnartok.
**mortal poison** — tokonartok.
**mosquitoe** — kiktoreak.
**mosquitoe net** — kiktorealitak.
**moss** — manerk.
**most** (superlative) — -lak-* (vg. angilak the greatest).
**mother** — anânak.
**mother (by adoption)** — anânaksak, arnaksak, anânaktar.

**mother-in-law** — sakki, saki.
**motion** — auladjaknęrk.
**motive** (has m.) — pidjuterilugo, -djutiri-*.
**motor** — ikkuma, ikkumalik.
**mountain** — kingak, kaggak (Okk.).
**mouse** — awingnak.
**mouse** (shrew-mouse) — ugdjutnark.
**mouth** — kanerk or kranerk.
**mouth** (has in mouth) — okkomiarpok.
**mouth** (open your mouth !) — aitaurit.
**mouth-organ** — subluksarutit.
**mouth (close your lips !)** — ipummerit !
**mouth-wash** — erortût.
**moves** — aulayok, -ar-*, -giar-*.
**moves away with family** — audlârtut.
**moves sled to start** — audladjakteriwok.
**moves with difficulty** — audlarjarlukpok.
**much** — -dlorik-*.
**much (too m.)** — -luar-*.
**much (very m.)** — aksuâluk.
**mud** — marrak, issortok, immarsuk.
**mud for sled runners** — ibjo.
**muddy water** — issortok.
**mug** (cup) — ermoserk, ermoseuyak.
**multiplicative** (idea of multiplication is rendered by infixes) — -ertortok-*, -ertartok-*.
**murders** v. — inuarpok, tokotsiwok inungmik.
**muscle** — nuki.
**mushroom** — tunnuksak.
**musk ox** — omingmak, umingmak.
**must** — -yuksau-*.
**mute** (is) — okrajuitok.
**mutilated** (is) — illakungortok.
**mutuality** — -lerek-*, plur. : -lereit-*.
**muzzles dog** v. — ibjaruserpok.
**my** — -ga.
**mystery** — tukisinangitok.

## — N —

**nail** (iron) — kikierk.
**nail-drawer** — kikiangiyaut.
**nails** v. — kikiekpok.
**nails (of fingers)** — kukît.
**naked** (is) — ussertok, ussingayok.
**name** — attierk, atterk.
**name (of the same** n.) — abvareik, saunereik.
**name (his name is)** — attekartok.
**name (gives the name)** — atterarpok, (-pâ).
**name (what is your name ?)** — kranok-attekarpit ? kinaôwit ?
**named** — taiyauyok.
**nap** — naitomik-siningnerk.
**nape** — tunnusuk.
**narrates** v. — unnerpok.
**narrow** (is) — tuertok, nerrokiktok.
**narrow** (is too narrow) — tattokrittok.
**navel** (anat.) — kalaserk.
**nasal mucus** — kaki.
**near by** — kanigiani, senniani.
**near** (is) — kanittok.
**neat** (is) — salumayok.

**necessary** (is) — pidluavinartok.

**neck** — kungasinerk.

**neck-tie** — kungasilitak, kungisilitak.

**necklace** — uyamik, kangiksak (Padl.).

**needs, is used** v. — atortok.

**needs** (explains one's n.) — udjiluktok.

**needle** (sewing n. etc.) —mitkrut.

**needle case** — kapvik.

**needle eye for thread** — nubvidjut.

**needle (pricker for lamp)** — angmarterut.

**needle (round** needle) — koadjuitok, mitkrutuinnar.

**needle (triangular** n. for leather) — koadjulik.

**needy** (is) — ajuksartok.

**neighbours** — nunakattigeit, silalereit, inukattigeit.

**neither . . . nor** — -lonit-*, lonit-* **with negation.**

**nephew or niece** —
uyorok: child of a male's sister.
kangiark : child of a male's brother.
noak: child of a female's sister.

**nerve, strength** — nuki.

**nervous** — parangaitok, uimayartok, atkrigiark.

**nest** (bird's) — upluk.

**nets** (fish) —
mattitautit, nulluat, nulludjet (Okk.).
kobviait (Net.).

**never** — kangaluktar **with negation** following.

**never mind !** — kuyanna, suwaunit (Padl.).

**new** (is) — nutarôyok.

**next** — tuglia, tuglerk.

**nice !** (excl.) — adja, akkânga, pitsiark ! -tsiark-*.

**niece,** cf. nephew.

**night** — unnuar.

**nine** adj. — kolingiluartok, kolikangituinnartok.

**nine (at cards)** — kritit
uar.

**nine o'clock** — sukkatervik (vg. time to wind up).

**nipple** — millût or mîlût.

**nit** — itkrerk.

**no** — nakka, nauk, aukka, nagga.

**no** (negation is rendered by infix) — -ngi-*.

**no one** — inukangitok.

**noisy** (is) — perpaluktok.

**no more** (does it n. m.) — -jungnaertok-*.

**none** — pitakangitok, sutaitok.

**north** — kannernark.

**north wind** — kannernarktok.

**nose** (anat.) — kringak.

**nose (exterior part** of n.) — takpak.

**nose (interior part** of n.) — sorlok.

**not** (negation) — -ngi-*.

**nothing** (it is n.) — sunaungitok.

**nothing** — sutakangitok sumik.

**noticed** (it is not n.) — terliarpok.

**Nottingham Island** — Tibjalik.

**now** — manna, mannakut.

**now (from now on)** — mannamit.

**numbers** n. — naisautit.

**nun** — nayak; Plur. : nayait.

**nurse** (graduated) — idluarsaiyekoluk.

## — O —

**oakum** — upserutiksak.

**oar** — iput.

**oats** — alugaksak, katseogak (Padl.), alugak.

**obedient** (is) — nâlaktok, ôpalortok.

**obese** (is) — naartok.

**obeys** v. — tussartok, nâlaktok.

**obeys quickly** — annuarsorpok.

**objects,** things — tigukat.

**obliges** v. — perkoyiyok, pititsiyok.

**observes law** — nâlatsiartok, atuarsiyok.

**obstacle** — idluilutak, igvikutak.

**obstacle** (hits an obstacle) v. — tullurpok.

**obtains** (vg. five) — (tadlima)-rartok-*.

**obturated** (is well) — upsiktok, simmiktok.

**obturates** v. — upseriwok.

**occasion** — pibviksak.

**occupied by** — -ler-*, -seri-*.

**occurs** v. — nedliutikpok.

**offering** (makes an o.) — illiyiyok.

**offspring** — kinguvangit.

**often** — -kattar-*, gayuk-*.

**oil** — orksok.

**oil** (black drippings of oil) — anârviut.

**oil** (coal oil) — orksok, ikkiyark (Padl.).

**ointment** — adlarterut, orksorterut.

**O.K.** — nâmaktok.

**old thing** — pitokrak.

**old person** — ôtôkrak.

**old** (how old are you ?) — krapsinik ukkiukarpit ?

**old woman** — arnakoaksak.

**omoplate** — kiasik.

**once upon a time** — taipsomani.

**once (all at once)** — tagvadlaksinnar, erneinnar.

**once** (he did it once) — atauseartok.

**once more** — -kanner-* -mi-*, -ki-*, tamattomani, attilukannerk.

**one** adj. — atauserk.

**one after the other** — tuglilereit, kingulereit.

**one whole** — atautsit.

**one's self** — ingminek, nangminek.

**only** — kissiani.

**only one does it** — piyotuar, -tô-*.

**only (does only that)** — -innar-*.

**opened eyes** (has) — uitayok.

**opener** — angmarterut, angmartaut.

**opening** — angmark.

**opening in the ice** — kupnerk, ajurark.

**opens cover,** book etc. — makperpok.

**opens** — erkpakpok.

**operator of radio** — nalekte.

**opinion** — issuma.

**opponents** — akkirareit.

**opposite** — akkiani.

**orange** (fruit) — paunrak-koksortok.

**order,** commandment — -ko-*, perkoyak.

**order** (is in good order) — atkriktok, ikpariktok.

**order** (puts things in order) — ikpariksaiyok.

**organ,** harmonium — nakrittaut.

**organ (mouth-organ)** — subluksarutit.

**organist** — nakrittarte.

**origin** — pigiarnerk.

**orphan** — illiyardjuk.

**other** — assia, pikattar, aipa, ingnerattar (Padl.).

**other (on the other side)** — iglungadlerk.

**out,** outdoors — silami.

**out** (comes out of) — niuvok, nuivok.

**outlet** — anigorviksak.

**outside** (poss.) — silatâ.

**outside** (looks outside) — itsuarpok.

**outstretched,** tight — sukkangayok.

**over on the other side** — akkiani.

**over that** — unwatani, ungatani.

**over there** — tâwani, awani, tapkonani.

**overcast** (is) — nuvuyayok.

**overcoat** — koliktar.

**overcomes** v. — salaksarpok.

**overdue** (is) — nipamayok.

**overflows** v. — ulipkartok, singortok.

**overheated** — ônadluartok.

**overseas** — tareub akkiani.

**owl (white)** — okpik, okpikdjuark.

**owl (small)** — kiggavik.

**owner** (is) — nangmineriwa.

**oyster,** clam — uviluk, orvilrok.

## — P —

**packed (in a crowd)** — pangmiortut.

**paddles,** rows v. — paurpok.

**paddles** (using double paddle) — opakpok.

**pail** — kattak.

**painful** (is) — ânernartok.

**paint** — mingoarut.

**paint (already dried)** — mingût.

**paint-brush** — mingaut.

**paints** v. — mingoarpok.

**pair** — iglugeik.

**pair** (one of a pair) — igluinnar.

**pair** (one of a p. without the other) — igluitok.

**palate** — krilak.

**palm of the hand** — ittimak.

**palmiped** (web-footed) — iksangualik.

**palsy** (has) — aulasuitok.

**pants** — âtartar (cf. karlik : breeches).

**paper** — alelayok, sikuksayak (Okk.).

**paper (sand-paper)** — okroiyaut.

**paper (toilet-paper)** — erkroiyaut.

**paper (wrapping paper)** — immutiksak.

**paper (writing paper)** — titerarviksak.

**parcel** — kidlartak.

**parents** — angayorkrak.

**part of** — illanga.

**part** (is part of) — atayok.

**participates** v. — illauwok.

**participates** (does not p. in food distribution) — miktauyok.

**partners** — illageit, illamareit.

**partridge** — akrigek.
**partridge** (bush p., ptarmagan) — akrigevik.
**passes ahead** v. — kangerpok.
**passes beyond** — ingiarsiwok.
**passes that way** — apkosarpok.
**passes far off** — salrosiwok.
**Passion instruments** — ânertitaudjutit.
**passive form of verb** — -tau-*, -yau-*.
**past form of verb** — -laur-*, -sima-*.
**patches** v. — illârpok, mabliarpok.
**patient** (is) — ningasuitok.
**pauses** v. — nutkarpok.
**pays** (he pays it) — akkiliwa.
**peak of a steeple, tree, etc.** — papik.
**pearls,** beads — sungauyait, sappagnait (Okk.).
**peat** — ibjo.
**pecks** v. — pokumalukpok.
**peeling skin** — kâglaertok.
**peg** — tuputak.
**Pelly Bay** NWT — Arviligdjuark, Kuraryuk.
**pelvis** (anat.) — kutterk.
**pelvis bone** — makkiserk.
**pen, pencil** — titeraut, iksiraut, aglaut (Okk.).
**penetrates** v. — pulawok, mangukpok.
**penetrated by rain** — sitsertok.
**penetrated by wind** — suvertok.
**penguin** — akpak.
**penis** (anat.) — ussuk.
**pepper** — kangaksaut.
**perfect** (is) — pitsialuaviktok.
**perforator** — putuksaut.
**perfume** — tîpaksaut.
**perhaps** — i-kai, ingoyunar, ingonalrear (Padl.), -yuksauwok-*, wadlaiwok (Okk.).
**perishes at sea** — iagattok.
**perishes** (frozen) — kekrarmago.
**peritoneum** (anat.) — kaniwaut.
**permanent** — kayusiwok, kangaluktar piyok.
**perseveres** v. — kayusiwok, sangusuitok.
**perspires** v. — aumidjaktok, kiagortok.
**perspiration** — ailak, ailattok.
**phalanx of fingers** — inugak.
**phalarope** (red bird) — sauvrak.
**picture,** image — adjik, adjingoark.
**picture (to look at)** — tautuganark.
**pictures (takes p.)** — adjiliorpok.
**pie** — akkulroalik.
**pieces** — illakuit.
**pieces** (falls into p.) — asselroyok.
**pieces** (puts to pieces) — sirkropterpok.
**pig,** hog — kûkûsi, kalaktuyuyok.
**pigeon of the sea** — pitsiolak.
**pike (fish)** — siulik.
**pile,** accumulation — kalereit.
**pillow** — akkiserk, akkiterk.
**pin** n. — tuputauyak.
**pin** (safety pin) — kakidjut.
**pincers** — kîjautit.
**pinches with fingers** — pudjuarpok.
**pinches** — kiggitsiwok.
**pious** — tuksiarayuktok.

**pipe** (smoking p.) — puyulettit.
**pipe** (stove pipe) — igalerk.
**pipe (smokes the p.)** — puyuletsiyok.
**piper** (sand-piper, bird) — siggiarialik.
**pitches** (boat p.) — pôkartok.
**pitiful** (is) — naglingnartok.
**pity** (has pity) — nikâyok, nagliktok, nâpkigosuktok, illabjuridlartok.
**place** — inik, iniksak, -vik-*.
**place** (no more pl.) — nimmiolertut.
**places** v. — illiwok, illiorkraiwok.
**places one's self** — ingniwok.
**plain, country** — natternak.
**plaits**, weaves v. — pilkrarpok, pilkraiyok.
**plane** (tool) — sennerarmik, saviarut.
**plane**, airplane — tingmisût, kangatayût.
**plank** — kreyuksak, igluksak.
**plate**, dish — pogutak, awapsilak.
**playful** — uiritsaktok.
**playing-cards** n. — pattait, kritkutit, sipietsit.
**plays** — kritikpok, pingoarpok.
**plays cards** v. — pattakpok.
**plays drum** — kattukpok.
**plays organ** — nakrittarpok.
**plaything** — pingoark, kritidjutiksak.
**please** — -laur-*.
**please let me have** — -mik-*.
**plenty** — pitaliâluk.
**pliers** (tool) — kîyautit.
**plucks feathers off** — eretarpok.
**plug** — tuputak.
**plunges through the air** — auksarpok, auksararpok.
**plunges into water** — aglorpok.
**point** (sharp) — kak, nubvuk.
**point (on the point of)** — -ler-*.
**pointed** (is) — kakituyok.
**poison** (deadly) — tokonartok.
**pole**, post (vertical) — napayok, napareak.
**police** — pôkertalik, polisi (Engl. corr.).
**polishes**, irons, etc. — kaersarpok.
**polisher**, iron — kaersaut, kaersautit.
**politeness (term of p.)** — -laur-*.
**Pond Inlet** NWT — Tunnunerk.
**poor** (is) — akluyok, piitôyok.
**poorest** — aklulak.
**porch** — pâk, torksok.
**porcupine** — kidjakatsik.
**pork** — kûkûsi.
**portage** — itibjak.
**portages** v. — itivikpok.
**portion of** — illanga, illainnanga.
**possession** (in p. of) v. — pigiwâ.
**possibility** — -ungnar-*, -yuyok-*, -djar-*.
**possible** (is p. to him) — piyungnartok.
**possible** (does his possible) — pinasuktok.
**possible (not possible)** — piyunangitok.
**pours liquid** — kuviwok.
**powder for rifle, gun etc.** — ariek.

**powder (baking p.)** — illaksaut, publurterut.
**powerful** — sangiyok, pidguyok.
**practices** v. — illisaiyok.
**praise** n. — nertût; plur. : nertûtit.
**praises** v. — nertorpok.
**prayer-book** — tuksiutit.
**prayer place** (church) — tuksiarvik.
**prayer-stool** — sirkomiarvik.
**prayer** — tuksiut.
**prayer for some one** — tuksiutinerk.
**prays** v. — tuksiarpok.
**preaches** v. — ajokertuiwok.
**precedes** v. — imgiarpok.
**predicts** v. — nellautpok.
**prefers (in love)** — pinnariwok.
**preferred (is) in love** — pinnariyauyok.
**pregnant** (is) — singaiyok, nutaraksakartok.
**prepares to leave** v. — parnakpok, akteriwok.
**present** (is) — illauyok, tagvaôyok.
**presses to harden** v. — sitiktitsaiyok.
**presses against self** — tatiwok, tatiriwok.
**presses with hand** — natkrikpok.
**pretty,** fair (is) — inekonartok.
**prevention against** — -aikutit-*.
**price** — akkinga.
**pride** — piosurinerk.
**priest** — iksirardjuark.
**priest** (becomes priest) — iksirardjuangortok.
**primus-lamp** — iktutût, kôdlerk.
**prisoner** — atungersimayok, pangnaersimayok
**privation of** — -sui-*, -jui-*, -î-*, -gar-*.
**prize** — aituserk.
**probably** — -onar-*.
**proceeds** — pituinnarpok.
**professional** — -ye-*, -te-*.
**progresses** v. — pitsiarpallialertok.
**prohibited** (is) — perkoyaungitok.
**prohibited by shaman** — tirenartok.
**prohibition** — -pangni-*, -taili-*.
**projector (for films)** — tarraiyaut.
**projects films** v. — tarraiyarpok.
**promise** — angeruserk, angerut.
**promises** v. — satuiyok.
**pronounces badly** — okranelukpok.
**pronounces name** etc. — angortorpok.
**pronounces well** — okratsiarpok.
**propeller** — angûta.
**prophesies** v. — nellautaiyok, nellautpok.
**prophet** — nellautaiye.
**prospectors** — uyaratareat.
**prostitute** (meretrix) — arnâluk.
**prostrated (physically)** — pâmaktok.
**prostrated (morally)** — kevittok.
**protection against** — -aikutit-*.
**protects** v. — sapputiwok.
**protects one's self** — ulureasukpok.
**protestant** — ajokertuyemiutak.
**protests** v. — naggarpok.

**protests by shaking head** — illikritamarpok.

**proud** (is) — piosuriyok, pioyoriyok.

**proves** v. — nalunailiwok.

**pry** — ipjutak, ibjutak.

**pubescent (boy)** — nullianiktok.

**pubescent (girl)** — uiniktok.

**pulls towards self** v. — amuyok, nutsukpok.

**pulls line of canoe from shore** — okamarpok.

**pulls straight ahead** — arvarkrorpok.

**pulls one's self up** — kagverpok.

**pulley** — aksaludjak.

**pulsation** (has) — tiglerpok.

**pump** (air pump) — publurtaut.

**pump (for liquid)** — immaiyaut.

**punishes** v. — pidlarpok.

**pup** (dog) — kringmiluardjuk.

**purchases** v. — pitârpok, nioverpok.

**pure water** — kakiaktok, akkusimangitok sumik.

**purgatory** — utatkribvik, kakiarsarvik.

**purposely (acts p.)** v. — piyâriwok.

**pursues** v. — mallikpok.

**pus** (anat.) — makri, pûnerk.

**pushes** v. — pingowok, ajaurpok.

**pushes something** v. — kaibluarpok.

**pushes (dog sled)** — ajakomiarpok.

**puts on clothes** — attiyok.

**puts aside** — apsarpok.

**puts in its place** — tutkorpok, pôrpok.

**puts to pieces** — igupterpok.

**puzzle** (chinese p.) — ikperititak, atkrisugak.

## — Q —

**quadruped** — sitamanik-niulik.

**quakes** v. — sajukpok.

**quarrels** v. — aivayok.

**quarter** adj. — sitamangat.

**queen** — issumatavik-arnak.

**queen** (at cards) — arnangoark.

**question** n. — apersût, aperiyaeksak, aperkut.

**questions** v. — aperiwok, apersorpok.

**quick !** — tuwawi !

**quickly (acts q.)** v. — tuwawiorpok, erenesukpok.

**quiet** (is) — palartok, pakadlangitok.

**quilt** — krepik.

**quite all** — tamatkerkasaktok, -kasak-*.

**quits** v. — areowok, pianiktok.

**quivers** v. — ôlikpok, sajukpok.

**quotidian,** daily — krau-tamat, ublurât.

## — R —

**rabbit** — ôkalerk or ukalerk.

**race,** running etc. — -kisar-*, -kasaur-*.

**race** (they r.) v. — pialakisaurtut.

**rack for drying skins** — initak, inigvik, pautorvik.

**radio receiver** — nâlaut.

**radio operator** — nâlekte.

**rag** (to wipe anything) — adlarutiksak, ibgut.

**rainbow** — katauyak, ajagutak.

**rains** v. — makuktok, nipaluktok.

**raises** v. — napaiwok. makitayok.

**rapid** (is) — sokalayok.

**rapids (of a river)** — sagvak, kôrluktok.

**rare** (not many) — inuisertut.

**rasp** (tool) — ikkût.

**ration** (receives r.) — nerkreitorpok.

**ration** (receiving time for r.) — nerkreitorvik.

**raven** — tullugak, koakoak (Padl.).

**raw meat** — mikkigak.

**raw bannock** etc. — aipayok.

**razor** — umgiyaut.

**reads (with eyes only)** — titirkrekrewok.

**reads loud** — okralimarpok.

**ready** (is) — pituinnarealik, paknaksimayok.

**ready** (is getting r.) — parnakpok.

**really** — -marik-*, -luavik-*.

**reaps,** collects v. — kattersiwok.

**rear** — kingu.

**reason,** motive — pidjutiksak, -djutirilugo.

**rebounding** (is) — piksiktok, piglertok.

**recently** — -sar-*, -kammer-*, -lisar-*, -krauyok-*.

**receives** v. — pibviriyauyok, tunisibvioyok.

**receives food** — payuktauyok, nekreitorpok.

**receives gift** — tunitsiviuôyok.

**receives work to do** — imitauyok.

**reciprocates** v. — akkiliwok.

**recognizes** v. — illitarsiwok, sokoersiwok.

**red** — aupaluktok, aupârtok.

**redeems** v. — piuliwok, akkiliutiwok.

**redeemer** — piuliye.

**reef** — ikkariktok, ikkalrut.

**refectory** — nerrebvik.

**reflects,** thinks v. — issumaksasiorpok.

**refuels** v. — orkserterpok.

**refuses** v. — krepilukpok, krepariwok.

**regrets** v. — ogguarpok.

**regretful** — oggornartok.

**rejoices** v. — kuviasuktok.

**related ones** — illageit, kattangutigeit.

**relation** (parenthood) — -gek-*, -kut-*.

**religion** — tuksiarkattaunerk.

**remains of,** shavings etc. — pinnikuit, amiakuit.

**remedy,** medicine — idluarsaut, inôlisaut.

**remembers** v. — aulayiyok, puigungitok.

**reminder,** souvenir — erkraumalerutiksak.

**demonstrates** v. — sukkorpok.

**renewed** (is) — nutangortok.

**repairs** v. — atkrikpok, illârpok.

**repeats** v. — akkiorpok, immiatsiyok (echo), -alayok-*.

**replaced (in succession)** — inangertauyok.

**replies,** answers v. — akpikpok, kiowok.

**reports** v. — unnerpok.

**reprimands** — suakpok, sukkorpok.
**Repulse Bay** NWT — Nauja, Aivilik.
**repulses** v. — ajakpok, ajaurpok.
**repulses** (as a rifle), v. — tunerktuyok, sitertok.
**reputation** — pitsiarnerartaunerk.
**requires too much** — sivuranartok.
**reservoir for oil** — orksôsibvik, orksût.
**residence** — aisimabvik.
**resistance (makes no res.)** — manigutiwok, maniwok.
**rests** v. — takrerserpok, mingoerserpok.
**resumes** v. — pikannerpok, kayusiwok.
**resurrection** (Easter) — makkibvia (Jesusib).
**resuscitates** v. — ômagiwok.
**returns home** — angelrauwok.
**reveals** v. — krauyititsiwok.
**revenges** v. — akkiliwok, kiglukpok, akkerartorpok, akkisartorpok.
**revenged** (is) — akkerauyok.
**revenge** (incline to rev.) — akkimayok, akkiyomayok.
**reverses** v. — pussittok.
**revolver** — iglupinnarsût.
**rewards** v. — akkiliwok.
**rib** (anat.) — tullimak.
**rib of a canoe** — tikpit.
**rice** — kopilrouyak, komauyar.
**rich** (is) — akluitok.
**richest** — akluilâk.
**rid of** (to be r. of.) — iksinartok.
**riddle** — ajorsitaut.
**rides** v. — ikkimayok.
**ridge** — kingarôk.
**rifle** — sirkotidjut, kokiut.
**rifle cover** — þitiksitak.
**right** (is morally r.) — pitsiartok, nâmaktok.
**rigid** (is) — kregatayok.
**ring (of annular finger)** — mikilerarut.
**ring (of middle finger)** — kriterdlerut.
**rings the bell** — sivanerteriwok, sâviarpalukpok.
**rises** — kungmuarpok.
**rises early** v. — ublarorpok.
**river** — kurk, kôrk.
**river** (big river) — kurdjuark.
**rivet** — ôriungnerk.
**road,** path — apkut.
**roaring** (is) — perpaluktok.
**robs** v. — tiglikpok, arktayok.
**rock** (solid) — kaertok.
**rock** (boulder) — uyarasugdjuk.
**rock** (rolling) — uyarak.
**rocks** (chair) v. — nivertarpok, aulakattarpok.
**rocking chair** — aulakattaut.
**rolls,** vg. snow balls — aksaliksiwok, aksaluawok, aksalikpok.
**rolls a cigarette** — immutsiwok.
**roof** — kôlâ, kollâ.
**room for sleeping** — sinnigvik.
**room** (plenty room) — inikortuyok, iniksalik.
**root** — mângut, amâk.
**root (edible)** — airark.
**rope** — aklunak.
**rope (for jumping)** — kiggertartaut.

**rope (jumps the rope)** — kiggertartok.
**rotten** (is) — igunartok.
**rotten (smells or tastes)** — igunasunittok.
**rotten (shed to keep r. meat)** — igunausibvik.
**rough,** bad boy — angatuyok.
**rough (to touch)** — maniitok, kidjaktok.
**rough ice on sea** — ikkalrok, maniilrok.
**round** (is) — ulamertok, angmaloriktok.
**row** or paddle — paut, pautit, iput.
**rows or paddles** v. — parorpok, iputpok.
**rubbish** — narroniko, aktako, iksinnartok.
**rubs** v., vg. with ointment — niogarpok.
**rubs feet on mat** — alorluiyarpok.
**rudder (boat r.)** — paperorsût.
**rug** or mat — tutikviksak, alorluiyaut.
**rugged** (is) — maniitok.
**ruined** (is) — soriuktok.
**rule,** measure — ôktoraut.
**rump,** buttocks — erkrok, ôpatik, mimerk.
**runs** v. — akpattok, udlaktok.
**runs (like this . . .)** — imanna illingayok.
**runners of sled** — pilrar.
**runway** (for airplane) — mîbviksak.
**rushes** v. — parlaiyok.
**rust** — okkrok, okkok.
**rusty** (is) — okkroktok, pekartok.

## — S —

**sacrament** — idluarutiksak, inudjutiksak.
**sad** (is) — annuttok, alroyok, nikadlortok.
**sail** (of boat) — tingelrautak.
**saliva,** spittle — nuvak, nôvak.
**salt** — tareor.
**salty** (is) — tareorsunniktok.
**same size** — -kosar-*.
**sand** — siorak.
**sand-paper** — okkroiyaut.
**sauce** (gravy) — immerark.
**savage** (not domesticated) — nûdyuartok.
**saves** v. — piuliwok.
**saviour** — piuliye.
**saw** n. — ulûtit, kipisidjut.
**saws** v. — uluarpok.
**saying (it is a s.)** — okrauseôyok.
**says something** — niplerpok, okrarpok.
**scale,** balance — ôktût.
**scales of fishes** — amerait.
**scar** (has a s.) — mabjulertok.
**scarce** — pitakaluangitok.
**scattered** (are) — apsimayut.
**school** — illiniarvik, ajokertusibvik.
**scissors** — kipyautit, aglerouyait.
**scorned,** left alone — illiyarsortauyok.
**scow** (flat bottom) — ikârsiorut.
**scowls** v. — kriksimigarpok.
**scraper for skins** — serleriyaut, erktorsit, issikrut, kiliutak.
**scrapes skins** v. — sakkuwok, mabjarpok.
**scratches,** hooks v. — kresukpok.

**screw-driver** — kaibjarsit, pitiksiliut.

**sculptures** v. — sennengoarpok.

**sea** — tareor.

**sea divinity** — (Myth.) takannâluk-arnâluk.

**sea people** — tareormiut.

**seal** — netjerk, netserk.

**seal** (big, square flipper s.) — udjuk, ugdjuk.

**seal** (black spotted s.) — kassigiak.

**seal's breathing hole** — aglu.

**seal** (jumping seal) — kaerolik.

**seal (kills a s.)** — netjerpok.

**seal skin** — kresik.

**seal (smelling s.)** — tiggak.

**seal (young s.)** — netsiark.

**seat** — iksiwautak.

**seat of a canoe** — ikterut.

**seated** (is) — iksiwayok.

**seated (be** seated !) — iksiwagit ! iksiwalerit !

**seed** (garden s.) — kangaksaut.

**seeks** v. — kenerpok, ivârpok, -sior-*.

**seems** v. — -uyar-*.

**seen** (is) — takuksauyok.

**sees** v. — tautukpok, takuwok.

**sees for the first time** v. — takunrarpok.

**self** — ingminek, nangminek.

**selfish** (is) — nerdlingoyok, uwangamiutaôyok.

**sells** v. — nioverpok.

**sender** — tilliye.

**sends s.o.** v. — tilliwok, tillidlerpok.

**sent** — tilliyâ, tilliyanga.

**senior** — angayodlerk.

**sensitive to the cold** — pattangayok.

**separates apart** v. — apsikpok.

**servant** — ikayorte, pileriye, kibgak (Okk.).

**sets** v. (bird or airplane) — mîkpok.

**seven** adj. — malronik-arvinilli.

**sews** (clothing etc.) — merksorpok.

**sews badly** — kiluklukpok.

**sewing,** seam — kilu.

**sewing, seam protector** — kilurut, kilugutak.

**sextant** (instrum.) — sikrinrut.

**shade, shadow** — tarrak.

**shakes** v. — sajukpok.

**shakes hand** v. — tigutiwok.

**shakes snow off self** (dog) — ipsorpok.

**shall or will** — -niar-*, -omar-*, -lar-*.

**shallow water** — ikattok.

**shaman,** conjuror — angatkro.

**shame** — kangusungnerk.

**sharp** (is) — ipiktok, kînaktok.

**sharpens** v. — ipiksarpok, kîneksarpok.

**sharpening stone** — kînaut, ipiksaut, sidlît.

**shaves one's self** — umgiarpok.

**shawl** — ôlikattar, nigdjielik.

**shed,** storehouse — serdloark.

**shed, blubber-shed** — igunausibvik.

**shelf** — katterservik, kôleruyak.

**shell** (ammunition) — kardjuk.

**shell** (empty s.) — pôko.

**sheltered from wind** (is) — okkoarmisiortok.

**shield** — tallikut, talluak, tallugak.
**shines bright** v. — kiblariktok.
**ship** — umiardjuark.
**shivers** v. — ôlikpok.
**shivers (from emotion)** — paumnartok.
**shoe** (short s.) — kamik, ittigamak.
**shoe** (snow-shoe) — tadluk, mauyasiutit.
**shoe** (top of shoe) — ittik.
**shoe** (from stores) — kamâluk.
**shoots** v. — sirkrorpok, sirkrotikpok.
**shore** — sidjak, sîna.
**short** (is) — naitok.
**shortens** v. — nailiwok.
**should be** — -yuksau-*, yaeksau-*, -ksa-*.
**should it happen** — -lerai-*.
**shoulder** — tuik, eriek.
**shoulder** (carries on s.) — erksukpok, nangmarpok.
**shouts** v. — erealârpok.
**shovel** — poagrê, nivaôtak.
**shovel (for ice chips)** — illaut.
**shovels** v. — poagresarpok.
**shown** (is) — takuksauyok, sakkrertok.
**shows** v. — takutitsiyok, sakkrertipok.
**shrew-mouse** — ugdjutnar.
**shrubs** — okpigait, okpit, awalakret.
**shrubs (used as mattress)** — iksutit.
**shuts well** — umiktok, umiksimayok.
**shy** (is) — illerasukpok, adlauyarpok.
**sick** (is) — âniartok, kanimayok, inungayok.
**sick** (is often s.) — âniarayuktok.
**side** — sennerark, makutsiak.
**side by side** — sennelereit.
**side** (more on one side) — iglusiktok.
**sighs** v. — ânersaumiwok, ânersarpok.
**sight** (on rifle) — ulurnerk.
**sight** (has bad s.) — takpiitok.
**sight** (has good s.) — takpiktok.
**sign** — nalunaikutak.
**signs** (makes s.) — nullorarpok, nudluartorpok.
**signs** (one's name) v. — atterminik titerarpok.
**signal** — nalunaikutak.
**silence !** — nippaitit ! nipjarnak !
**silence** (imposes s.) — nippangertipok.
**silent** (is) — nippaitok.
**silex** — kukiksak, ignerk.
**similar** (is) — adjigêktok.
**simply** — -miar-*, -mar-*, -tuinnar-*.
**sin** — piunginerk, idluinerk, ajorneâluk.
**sin (legal s.)** — sujungnerk.
**sin (commits s.)** — piungitulliwok, idluitulliwok.
**sin (takes s. away)** — piunginêrutiwok.
**sinner** — piungitulliye.
**sinew** — uliusinerk.
**sinew thread** — îvaluk.
**single** (not married) — aipaitok.
**single** (only one) — atausetuar.
**singing** (is) — pissikartok, pissartok.

**sings Eskimo songs** — ayayarpok.
**sings hymns** — imnierpok.
**sinkers for nets** — iktakutit.
**sinks in water** v. — kiviwok.
**sister of female** — elder, angayok; younger, nukak.
**sister of male** — nayak, naya, naja.
**sister-in-law** — sakkiak.
**sits down** v. — iksiwayok.
**sits on heels** v. — akrovikpok.
**six** adj. — arvinilli.
**six (o'clock)** — kaivattok.
**six (playing cards)** — kamut.
**sixth** — arvinrat.
**size (same)** — aktikusartok.
**skates** v. — salriyarpok.
**skates** n. — salriyautit.
**skeleton** — sauniinait.
**skis** — siturakutit, siturautit.
**skilful** — sennetuyok.
**skin** — amerk.
**skin (drying)** — sermertok.
**skin (of sea animals)** — kresik.
**skin (for icing sled)** — sermersit, piaksaut.
**skin (thin surface of s.)** — mami.
**skin (whitened by air)** — naluak, kakertak.
**skinning** (is) — ârktorpok.
**skinning-knife** — ârktût.
**skinny**, thin (is) — sadluyok.
**skipping rope** (is) — aterartarpok.
**sky** — krilak.
**sky (s. is clear)** — adlartok.
**slack** (is) — kassungayok.
**slanders** v. — okrautiksarpok.
**slaps in the face** v. — patikpok.
**sled** — kamotik, kramotik.
**sled (on the move)** — kremuksit, kremukserark.
**sleep** n. — sinnik.
**sleeps** v. — sinnikpok.
**sleeps at neighbour's home** — tutkuyok.
**sleeps far from home, camping** — sinniktarpok.
**sleeping-bag** — sinnigvik.
**sleepy** (is) — sinnigosuktok, uinrartok, nayagartok.
**sleeve** — aek.
**sleeve-protector** — aengilitak.
**slides** v. — situyok.
**slides (many times)** — siturartok.
**sling (to throw stones)** — idlok.
**slips** — koiyarkrikpok.
**slippery** (is) — piaktok, koiyarkrinartok.
**slippery** (anti-slippery device) — koiyanaikutit.
**slope** — uvinganerk.
**sloth** — sappernerk, erkreasungnerk.
**slow** (is) — pialaitok.
**slow going** — salausuktok, nakiitok.
**slow** (how slow !) — warayar ! maikattar !
**small (is)** — mikittok, -kik-*, -koluk-*, -nar-*, -ardjuk-*, -kli-*.
**small (too** s.) — mikidluartok.
**smell** — tipi, -sunnik-*.
**smells good** — tipiariktok, tipaksaut (perfumes).
**smiles** v. — kunwaktok, kungutortok.
**smith** — saviliorte.
**smoke** n. — isserk.

**smokes** (it) — issertok, pujortok.
**smokes the pipe** v. — pujuletsiyok.
**smooth and soft to touch** — nerromiktok.
**snake** — kopilrok, nimereak.
**snap** n. — niksittartok.
**sneezes** v. — tagiortorpok.
**sneezing tobacco** — tagiorksaut.
**snipe** (bird) — siggutût.
**snores** v. — kamguyok, kripsiyok.
**snow** (spread out) — aput.
**snow-beater** — anautak, tiluktût.
**snow-beating** (is beating snow) — tiluktortok.
**snow block** (for building) — auverk.
**snow drifting** (it is drifting) — perksertok.
**snow** (first snow fall) — apingaut.
**snow** (for melting into water) — aniuk, anio.
**snow is hard** — sitidlorak.
**snow-house** — iglu.
**snow knife** — panar.
**snow (like salt)** — pokaktok.
**snow (mixed with water)** — massak.
**snow (newly drifted)** — akelrorak.
**snow** (on clothes, boots etc.) — ayak.
**snow (is soft)** — mauyak, mauyaôlertok.
**snows** (it) — kannertok.
**so** — taima.
**soaked** (is) — immitsersimayok.
**soaks in water** — missukpok.
**soap** — ermiut.
**sobs** v. — kudviortok.
**sock** — alertik.
**sock** (short) — pinnerak, ikkinroat.
**soft** (is) — akrittok.
**soft,** supple (is) — kretuttok.
**softens skins** (with teeth) v. — angulawok.
**soldier** — unatartuksak.
**sole of shoes** — alark.
**soles (has new** s.) — alatarpok, atungerpok.
**soles (not yet sewn)** — atungaksak.
**solid, hard** (is) — sitiyok.
**solitary** (is) — kissermiortok.
**some** (there is some) — pitalik, pitakartok.
**something to do** — pilereaksak.
**something to eat** — nerkriksak, îyaeksak.
**sometimes** — illâni, kakutikut.
**son** — ernerk.
**son-in-law** — ningauk.
**son (only son)** — ernetuar.
**song** — pisserk, pissik.
**soon** (in the future) — -sali-*, -katnar-* (Padl.).
**soon** (in a very short time) — krilammi.
**soot** — pauk.
**sore** (is) — ânernartok.
**sorry** (I am) — oggornakuni, ogguarpunga.
**soul** — tarnerk.
**sound,** voice, noise — nippi, perpaluktok.
**soundings** (makes) — niktarpok.
**sounding stick for snow** — saubgut.

**sounds like** — -paluk-*.
**sounds loud** — kokernartok.
**soup, juice** — immerark.
**sour** (is) — sernartok.
**Southampton Island** (Coral Harbor) — Sadlerk.
**souvenir** — erkraumalerutiksak.
**spare** (is) — nautiyomayok.
**spares** v. — illipayok.
**spark** — aumergark.
**spatula** — mômiksidjut.
**speaks** v. — okrarpok.
**speaks harsh** — okralukpok.
**speaks in a low voice** — issibjuktok.
**speaks very much** — okradloriktok.
**spears** v. — naulikpok.
**spectacles** — îdgak, îggak.
**spectacles** (wears s.) — îdgalik, îggalik.
**speeds** v. — nakkersartok.
**spends money** — kinauyêrutiwok.
**spider** — nanuyak, assiwak, tuktuyak.
**spills water** etc. v. — kuvisiwok, kameriwok.
**spinal column** — kremerdluk.
**spinal column (upper)** — areark.
**spits** v. — ôriarpok, sikerarpok, kretserarpok.
**spittle** — novak.
**spittoon** — ôriarvik, sikerarvik etc.
**spleen** (anat.) — mapsak.
**splinter** (in skin) — kakiusersimayok.
**split** (has a split) — koblurnilik, sîgsimayok.
**splits** v. — koblurpok.
**spoils** v. — sorarpok.
**spoken** (is spoken to) — piyauyok.
**spoon** — alût, brviuyak (Padl.).
**spoon** (mixed with s.) — alukiorsimayok.
**spoon** (uses s.) — alukpok.
**spoon** (something to be eaten with a s.) — alugaksak.
**spot** — tarkserk.
**spots** (on top of dog's eyes) — iyerutit.
**spreads seeds** — kangarsuiwok.
**spring** — peringayok.
**spring** (season) — ôpinraksak, ôpinrar.
**spring (of watch** etc.) — peringayouyak.
**square** (is) — kippariktok.
**square angle** — erktuartok.
**square** (carpenter's s.) — kippariksaut.
**squeezed (in a crowd)** — pangmiortut.
**squints** v. — nakungayok.
**squirrel** (ground s.) — siksik.
**squirts** v. — tingmikartok.
**stain** — tarkserk.
**stainless** (will not rust) — okkroksuitok.
**stake** (at stake) — nugluktok.
**stake** (puts at s.) — imârkpok.
**stalactite** — kussugak.
**stalagmite** — kuttungnerk.
**stammers** v. — kutakpok.
**stands** v. — nangerpok, nikovikpok.
**stands** (tired of standing) — alungodlarpok.
**star** — ublureak.
**star (polar** s.) — nûtjuitok.

**stares** v. — iyeriwok.
**starts** v. — audlarpok.
**starving** (is) — perlertok.
**starving place** — perlerviksak, kârkvik.
**state of** — -gak-*.
**stays still** — nûtsuitok.
**steals** v. — tiglikpok.
**steams** v. — pujortok.
**steel** — iyariyartok.
**steep hill** — imnak.
**steeple** — nubvugusik, sivanerterausibvik.
**steers boat** v. — paperorpok.
**steps on** v. — tutiwok.
**steps,** walks v. — pissukpok. ablorpok.
**sterile woman** — ernesuitok.
**stick** — kreyuardjuk.
**stiff** (is) — kregatayok.
**stiff dead** (is) — tigittok.
**still (stands** still) v. — nutkangayok.
**stingy** (is) — nerdlingoyok, tutkuitok, erligosuktok, annoardlertok.
**stocking** (inner) — alertik.
**stocking** (outer) — kamikpak.
**stomach** — akrearok.
**stomach envelope** — kresaroak.
**stomach (is full)** — akreatorpok.
**stomach** (second stomach of deer) — nerrokak.
**stone** — uyarak.
**stone age fire making** — ignakpok.
**stool,** ladder — tumeraut.
**stoops** v. — pungawok.
**stops** v. — nutkarpok.
**stops all day** — ubliwok.
**store** (trading s.) — niovervik.
**storehouse** — serdloak.
**stormy sea** — atkonartok, madlernartok.
**stormy drift of snow** — perksertok.
**story,** fable — unipkartuar.
**story telling** — unipkartok.
**stout,** strong — sangiyok, pidguyok.
**stove** (furnace) — aumaliorsibvik.
**stove** (cooking s.) — îgak.
**straight** (is) — tikortok.
**straight** (goes s.) — toratsiarpok.
**strait** — pittak, ikerk, amittok.
**strangers** — adlait, takungartut.
**straw** — ivik.
**strength** — nuki, pidgunerk.
**strength** (motive of his strength) — pidgukotauyok.
**strength** (takes away by strength) — âksarpok.
**strength** (with all your strength) — nukiluktatsiagnut.
**stretches skin to dry** v. — pauktorpok.
**stretches arms** — issangayok.
**strikes** v. — anaurpok.
**string,** line — aklunak, ipiutak.
**string** (game figures) — ayarautit.
**string of beads** — nuviyauyut.
**string of handle** — adgiak.
**stripes** n. — pokerk.
**strong** (is) — nukilik, sangiyok, pidguyok.
**stronger (getting** s.) — nukitarpalliawok.
**strongest of all** — sangilâk, piguyortak, pidgulâk.

**strongly** — -dguyok-* (Padl.).
**stubborn** (is) — angutiriyok.
**stumbles** v. — nârpok.
**stupid** (is) — illitsuitok, akritomayok.
**submarine** — atkasût.
**submits** v. — manigutiwok.
**succeeds** (accomplishes his purpose) — pitorarpok, kayusiwok.
**sucker,** nipple — millukaut.
**sucks the breast** — amâmakpok.
**suddenly** — tagvainnar, erneinnar.
**suffering** (exclam !) — a'a !
**suffering** (is) — ânertok.
**sufficient** (is) — nâmaktok.
**suffocates** v. — ibjangoyok, ipiyok, tupittok.
**sugar** — siorauyak, auksereartok.
**suggests** v. — issumaliutiwok.
**summer** (season) — auyark, auyak.
**summer clothes** — auyaksiutit.
**summer (spends s.)** — auyaksiorpok.
**summit** — kratkrak.
**summit of a tree** etc. — papik.
**sun** — sikrinerk.
**sun (eclipse** of s.) — sikrinersertok.
**sun hidden by clouds** etc. — sikrinêrtok.
**sun-ray** — akkisuktok.
**sun rises** v. — sikrinaksarpok.
**sun sets** v. — sikrinerk nipingmat.
**sun shines** v. — sikrinaktok.
**sunday** — sennektaili.
**superior** — issumatar, angayokrar.
**superlative** (is rendered by infixes) — ʳyoktau-*, -lâk-*.
**supper** (meal) — unnuromitarvik.
**sups** — unnuromitarpok.
**supples** v. — kretulisarpok.
**supply** (food) n. — pagetaeksak.
**suppurates** v. — makreiyok.
**sure** (certainly) — sokaima ! tauka ! (Padl.), amilar, ahalu-una (Okk.).
**surface** — kâ, kânga.
**surprise (taken by s.)** — ôpingaiwok.
**surprised** (is) — koksadlakpok, koasarpok.
**surprises** v. — opingarpok.
**surprising** (it is not surprising) — ôpinnarani.
**suspects** v. — passagosukpok.
**suspenders** — uyatsiutit.
**swallows** v. — îwok, niorpok, -tor-*.
**swan** (bird) — kudgjuk.
**sweats** v. — aumidjakpok, kiagorpok.
**sweeps** v. — sannerpok.
**sweets** (candies) — okkomiakattar, nunguserark.
**swells** v. — puviyok.
**swift team of dogs** — sukkaurtut.
**swift** (is), quick — pialayok, ôkrilayok.
**swims** v. — iperartuarpok, nalugalarpok, immarpok.
**switch (electrical)** — audlalik.

**swollen** (is) — puvittok, tumangayok.

**symbol** — nâlunaikuta.

**syrup** (edible) — mamaksaut.

**syrup** (cough s.) — novaksiut.

— T —

**table** — adlerark, adlerauyak.

**table-cloth** — mangiptark, akkiutark.

**taboo** (follows t.) v. — aglerpok, tiregosukpok.

**taboo** (time of following t.) — aglervik.

**tacks** v. (sailing) — irkroitarpok.

**tag** (play) — âmakitartut, âmak.

**tail** — pameok.

**tail** (bob-tail) — papikattok.

**tail** (has a) — pameolik.

**tail of birds** — papik.

**tail of fishes** — sarpiuyark.

**tail of shirt** — akko.

**tail of whale** — sarpik.

**tails up !** (dogs) — pameiyut.

**takes away** v. — perpok, tiguwok.

**takes with self** — -lijar-*.

**tale, fable** — unipkartuar.

**talks** v. — okrarpok.

**talks much** — okradlakpok.

**tall** (is) — takîyok, angiyok.

**tallow** — tunnu, pûnernerk.

**tame** (is) — kremajuitok.

**tank** — immausibvik.

**tar** — kûtsok.

**task** — piyaeksak.

**tastes,** tries v. — ôksiwok, ôksitarpok.

**tastes** (has taste for) — -guk-*.

**tastes, smells** — -sunnik-*.

**tattooes** v. — kakidjakpok.

**tattooings** — tumnit.

**tattooings around the mouth** — erkrerutit.

**taxes (receives)** — piksaterpok.

**tea** — tî (Engl. cor.).

**tea-thirsty** (is) — tîgukpok.

**tea-pot** — tîliorut.

**teached** (is taught) — ajokertugak.

**teacher** — ajokertuye, illiniartitsiye.

**teaches** v. — ajokertuiyok, illiniartitsiyok.

**teaching** n. — ajokertuserk.

**tears** v. — aliktorpok, kiktorarpok.

**tears easily** — aliksuartok.

**tears with teeth** — iguarpok.

**tear in :lothes** etc. — kidlak, aliktornerk.

**tears** n. — kudviornit.

**tears (is shedding** t.) — kutviortok, kreayok.

**teasing** (is) — tappasuktok, kanogasartok.

**teeth** — kigutit.

**telephone** — okralût.

**telescope** — krinrut.

**television** — nâlautit-tarraiyautit.

**tells s.o.** — okrautiwa.

**temperature** — sila.

**temple** (anat.) — erksak.

**temple** (is hit on the temple) — erksartauyok.

**temple** (church) — tuksiarvik.

**ten** adj. — kolit.

**tendency** — -gayuk-*.

**tender** (is) — akrittok.

**tenor voice** — kateitok.

**tent** — tûperk.

**tent-frame** — sokrark.

**tent (of skins)** — umît.

**tent (people of the same t.)** — tûperkattigeit.

**tent** (place of old time tents) — tûpervivik.

**tent** (puts up the t.) — tûperpok.

**tent** (puts down the t.) — tupkrerpok.

**tern** (arctic t.) — immetkrotailak.

**terrible** (is) — kappianartorâluk.

**testicle** (anat.) — idjuk.

**thanks !** — kujannamik, mat'na, nakorami.

**thanksgiving prayers** — kujasiutit.

**thanks** v. — kujariwok.

**thaws** v. — auksertok, aulertok.

**then** — taima.

**the one I speak of** — imna piyara.

**there is** — -lik-*, -talik-*, -kartok-*.

**there between** — tungâni.

**thereby** — tagvûna.

**thermos bottle** — niglisuitok.

**these** — tamadja.

**thick** (is) (for a solid) — ibjoyok.

**thick** (is) (for a liquid) — kinersiyok.

**thief** — tiglikte.

**thigh bone** — koktorak, sibviark, sivurak.

**thimble** — tîkerk, pudjortok.

**thin** (is t. as paper) — sârtok.

**things** — pit, tigukat.

**thinks** v. — issumawok.

**thinks,** remembers v. — erkrarpok, erkraiyok, erkraiwok.

**thinks,** tries to remember v. — erkrasarpok.

**thinker** — erkraidguyok.

**thirteen** adj. — kolillu-pingasullu.

**thirsty** (is) — immerukpok.

**this one** — ûna.

**this way** — imanna.

**thistle** — kakidlarnerk.

**thorax** — kapilrok, kattigait.

**those above** — pikka.

**thou, you** — igvit (sing.), illipsi (plur.).

**thought** n. — issuma.

**thought** (of the same t.) — issumakattigeit.

**thread of sinew** — ivaluk.

**thread from store** — ivaluyak.

**thread bobbin** — ivaluksaut.

**threatens** v. — kappiasarpok.

**three** adj. — pingasut.

**three by three** — pingasukosartut.

**three** (third) — pingasuat.

**three (TRINITY)** — pingasuliôyok.

**threshold** — manu.

**throat** — idgiark, torkluark.

**throughout** — tamêni.

**throws** v. — êgitpok, iksikpok.

**thumb** — koblu.

**thumbless** — kobluitok.

**thunder** — kadluk, iktulortok.

**thus** — imanna, teat'na (Padl.).

**tibia** — kanak.

**tibia** (second t.) — amilreak.

**tickles** v. — kuinakpok.

**tide is low** (falling) — tiniktok, tiningoyok.
**tide is high** (rising) — ôliktok, ôlingoyok.
**ties** v. — kellakpok, pitukpok, krepikpok, nimerpok.
**ties dogs** v. — iperpok.
**ties** (place to tie dogs) — ipervik.
**ties** (line to tie with) — ipiutak.
**tied** (is) — ipersimayok.
**tight** (is) — nokrarsimayok.
**timber** — kreyuksak, igluksak.
**time to** — -viksak-*, pibviksak.
**time (killing time,** doing nothing) — alrarsaiyok.
**time** (it takes long t.) — akkuniâluk.
**time (long ago)** — immâluk, taipsomani.
**time is short** — akkunikiktok.
**time** (short time ago) — -krau-*, immasar.
**time** (from time to time) — kakutigut, illâni.
**times (so many times)** — -ertortok-*.
**timid** (is) — illerasuksareitok.
**tin** (sheet of tin) — savigayak, amertak.
**tips over** v. — kinguyok.
**tired** (is) — takrayok, minrusuktok.
**tiresome** (is) — takranartok.
**tobacco** — tîpak.
**tobacco** (cut t.) — sennelik.
**tobacco** (chewing t.) — tamuaksak.
**tobacco pouch** — senneliusibvik, ignavik.
**toboggan** — piatsinit.
**to-day** — ublumi.
**toe (big toe)** — putugôr.
**toe (walks** on tip t.) — nikopjarpok.
**toes (walks toes turned inwards)** — kôtuyok.
**toes (walks toes turned outwards)** — sarpituyok.
**together with** — -katt-*, -katta-*.
**together** — atautsikut.
**together** (they are t.) — kattimayut.
**toilet paper** — erkroiyaut.
**toilet room** — anareartorvik.
**tomb,** grave — illuverk.
**to-morrow** — akrago.
**to-morrow** (is leaving t.) — akragorpok.
**to-morrow** (day after t.) — akragoago.
**tongue** — okrark.
**tonsils** — krinerksit.
**tonsure of Eskimo** — kabjerutit.
**tools** — sennetit.
**tooth** — kîgut.
**tooth** (eye-tooth) — tullureak.
**tooth** (false tooth) — kîgusertait.
**tooth** (front tooth) — sivuak, sivudjet.
**tooth (good and strong)** — kîgudjariktok.
**tooth (holds between teeth)** — kîngmiartok.
**tooth (sore** t.) — kîguseriyok.
**tooth (wisdom** t.) — kamorayak.
**top** (cover) — koli, kola, matu.
**top (boat without top)** — kolaitok.
**top** (on top) — kangani.
**top** (on top of one another) — kâlereit.

**top** (a plaything) —**kaiptark, ungomiark.**

**tosses about** v. — **uvertartok.**

**totally** — **tamatkertok, tamarmik.**

**touch** n. — **aktornerk, kalituarnerk** (K.)

**touches** v. — **aktorpok, kalitpok.**

**touches bottom** (with boat) — **ikkariktok, tipiyok.**

**touches ground** — **tutpok.**

**touches shore with boat** — **tullakpok.**

**touchwood** — **ôtak, aumaliark.**

**towards** — **-mut-*.**

**towel** — **adlarutiksak, ibgut.**

**tows** v. — **kallitpok.**

**track** (footprint) — **tumik.**

**track** (of a sled) **inik, plur. : init.**

**track** (finds t.) — **tumisiwok, inisiwok.**

**track** (follows t.) — **tupjarpok, initigut piyok.**

**track** (loses t.) — **inerserpok.**

**trades** v. — **nioverpok.**

**trade goods** — **niovgutiksak.**

**trade (goes and trade)** v. — **nioverеartorpok.**

**trade** (far away) — **kangmalerpok, kablunadjarpok.**

**train** (railroad) — **nunakorutialuit.**

**translates** — **tukiliorpok.**

**trap (deer trap)** — **ublisaut.**

**trap (fox trap)** — **tireganiersiut, mikigiark, pudlat.**

**trap (wolf trap)** — **amakroniut.**

**travels** v. — **ingelrawok.**

**travels far away** — **niovgroyok.**

**travels** (more than one day) — **sinniktarpok.**

**travels** (makes the trip in one day) — **ingmerpok.**

**tree** — **napârtok.**

**trees (forest)** — **napârtolik.**

**tribe** — **-miutak-*, -geit-*.**

**tries** v. — **pinasuktok, -nasuk-*, oktorpok.**

**tries it** — **ôktorpâ.**

**trigger** — **mitingidjut.**

**trouble (is cause of t.)** — **idluilutaôwok.**

**troubles (makes t.)** — **idluiksartok.**

**troublesome** (is) — **piugartok.**

**trout** — **irkaluk.**

**trout** (black) — **idlorak.**

**trout** (red) — **îvitaruk.**

**true** (is) — **saglungitok.**

**trumpeting** (is) — **kokoalarpok.**

**trumpet** — **kokoarut.**

**tube, pipe** — **sublulik.**

**turns back home** — **utterpok.**

**turns his head** — **keviarpok.**

**turns his back** — **tunnukpok.**

**turns upside down** — **mômikpok, pussitpok.**

**tusk** (walrus t.) — **tûgar.**

**twelve** adj. — **kolillu-malroglu.**

**twenty** adj. — **awatit, malrok-adgait.**

**twice** — **malroertarluni.**

**twins** — **kakresareik, karesareik.**

**two** adj. — **malrok.**

**two by two** — **malrokosartut.**

**two bands** — **malroilugit.**

**two with one shot** — **tappereik.**

**two (obtains** two) — **malrorarpok.**

**typewriter** — **titeraut-nâkritaut.**

## — U —

**ubiquity** — naniluktarminerk.

**ugly** (is) — inekonaitok.

**ultimate** — kingudlerk.

**umbilical cord** — mikliark.

**unable** (is) — sappertok, ajortok, pijunangitok.

**unaware** (is) — krauyimangitok.

**uncle** —
father's brother : atkak.
mother's brother : angak.

**unclean** (physically) — salumaitok.

**unclean** (morally) — piunginilik, piktaungitok.

**unconscious** (is) — awârtok, krauyimangilertok.

**unconscious** (almost) — tartikpok.

**unction** — minguartaunerk.

**under** — atâni.

**under-feet** — alornerk.

**underground** — nunab-illuani.

**underneath** — atâni.

**underneath** (is) — adliôyok.

**understands** v. — tukisiwok.

**understands** (hard to understand) — nalunartok.

**understands** (not understandable) — tukisinangitok.

**understands well** v. — sokoerpok.

**undertakes** v. — pigiarpok.

**underwear** — illupâk, uvinersiut.

**undesirable** — ataneluktok.

**undoes** v. — sirkropterpok.

**undresses** (completely) v. — usserpok.

**undresses** (takes off coat) — târpok, koliktaerpok.

**undresses** (takes off shirt) — mattarpok.

**undulation on snow** — kremugdjuk.

**unended** (is) — pianingitok.

**unequal** — aktikosangitok.

**uneven** — maniitok.

**unexpected** (is) — nerriunangitok.

**unfolds** v. — issivikpok.

**unfortunately** — anertaima, mamianamik.

**ungrateful** (is) — kujasuitok.

**unharnesses** v. — mattarpok.

**unhooks** v. — naktingilertok.

**unique** (is) — -tuar-*, assikangitok.

**unites** (joins) v. — illautiwok.

**unkind** (is) — nagliktaitok.

**unknown** (is) — krauyiyaungitok.

**unless** — kissiani.

**unloads** v. — nioraiyok.

**unlocked** (is) — pangnersimangilertok.

**unmoved** (is) — aulatitaungitok.

**unoccupied** (is) — suleringitok.

**unpaid** — akkiliyaungitok.

**unsewn** — kiluartok.

**untied** (loose dog etc.) — assinaitok.

**unties bundle** etc. v. — immudjarpok.

**unusual** — illitkoseungitok.

**unwilling** (is) — piyomangitok.

**unworthy** (is) — nâdlerkotaungitok.

**up** — kungmut.

**upside down** — kutjangayok, pussingayok.
**upstairs** — kôlani.
**urgent** (is) — tuwawinartok.
**urinates** v. — koiyok, kuiyok.
**urine** — itterok, kui.
**us** (we) — uwagut.
**used** — atortok, atulik.
**useful** (is) — suksauyok.
**useful (what is the use ?)** — suksauwâ ? suksak ?
**useful but not necessary** — pilitak, attukattak.
**uses,** habits etc. — illitkroserk, illitkrosit, pitkrosit.
**uvula** (anat.) — nerreliktak.

## — V —

**vacant** (is) — inukangitok.
**vacuum bottle** (thermos) — niglisuitok.
**vagabonds** v. — awamurtok.
**valley** — ittersak, naternak.
**vapour** — puyok, puyortok.
**vapour (makes** v.) — puyortok.
**various** — adjigengitut.
**vast** — innikortuyok.
**veil** — talligutak.
**vein** — takrark.
**verge** (extreme edge) — sîna.
**vernacular** — okrausermigut.
**vertebral spine** — kremerdluk.
**very much** — aksuâluk.
**vibrates** v. — sajukpok.
**vicious** (is) — kanungayok.
**victim** (is) — piyauyok.
**victorious** (is) — salaksartok, salariyok.
**village** — iglurdjuartalik.
**violent** — -dguyok-*.
**violent invasion by dogs** — itârtauyok.
**violin** — agiarialik.
**virgin** (voluntary) — uinigomasuitok.
**virtue,** quality — illitkosetsiak.
**visible** — takuksauyok.
**visibility (good)** — niptâtsiartok.
**visibility (poor)** — niptaitok.
**vision** — takunerk, takudjutinerk.
**visiting close by** — uglartak.
**visiting far away** — tuyurmiangoyok.
**visiting and expecting food** — aimerpok.
**visiting trap line** — pulasarpok.
**voice,** sound — nippi.
**volume** (book) — titirkret ibjoyut, makpertak.
**vomits** v. — merearpok.
**vomits** (about to vomit) v. — mereangoyok, sittokitartok.
**votes** v. — anneriwok.
**vulva** (anat.) — uttuk, angmalerk.

## — W —

**Wager Inlet** — Utkosiksalik.
**wagon** — aksalualik.
**waistband** — tapsi, tireksiutit.
**waits** v. — utatkriwok.
**waits quietly** — nikpartok.
**wait a minute !** — owatsiaro.
**Wakeham Bay** — Kangerdlukdjuark.
**wakes s. o.** — ittersarpok tupatitsiyok.
**walk** n. — pissungnerk.

**walks** v. — pissukpok.
**walks (ahead of the dogs)** — kangelrarpok.
**walks** (for walking) — pissuinnarpok.
**walks** (in water) — iperarpok.
**walks** (on sidewalk) — pissubviksamipiyok.
**walks** (tired of walking) — ablorangorpok.
**walrus** — aiverk.
**walrus (big male w.)** — timertik.
**walrus (mature w.)** — naktivilik.
**walrus (first year w.)** — okkomitalik.
**walrus (new born w.)** — nutara.
**walrus (second year w.)** — ipiksaulik.
**walrus (tusk)** — tûgar.
**wandering wolves** — kadzait.
**wants** v. — -suar-*, -oma-*, piyomawok.
**war** — unatarvik.
**warehouse** — serdloark.
**warm** (is) — ônartok.
**warms up** — ônarsiyok.
**wart** (anat.) — unguk.
**washes** v. — ermikpok.
**wash basin** — ermibvik.
**washing solution** (soap) — ermiut.
**watch, clock** — krauyisaut, silauyak (Padl.).
**watches** v. — mianersiwok.
**watchman** — mianersiye.
**water** — immerk.
**water of the sea** — immark.
**water** (fetches water) v. — immektarpok.
**water (comes out of w. on solid)** — kaksimalerpok.
**water (enters in boots)** — kadlutiyok.
**water (flows under snow)** — moriuktok.
**water (is melting snow for w.)** — immiorpok, immiugak.
**waterproof** — sitsuitok, iptadjangitok.
**wave** — mallik, plur. : mallit.
**waves (are small)** — ingiuliktok.
**waves on snow drift** — krimugdjuk.
**wavy** (it is) — atkonartok, madlernartok.
**way**, path, road — apkut.
**way (gets out of** the way) — agvaerpok.
**ways of doing** — illitkosit, pitkosit.
**we** — uwagut.
**weak** (is) — nukikatsiangitok, pidguitok.
**weather** — sila.
**weather is bad** — silaluktok, silataungitok.
**weather is good** — silatsiartok, silatauyok.
**weather (what kind of weather ?)** — kranoitok sila ? sutô-sila ?
**weed** (sea weed) — kerkoak.
**week** (one) — sennektaili-akkuningani.
**weeps loud** v. — kreawok.
**weights for nets** — okkomaidjutiksait; kitkatit.
**well** (this is w.) — pitsiark, -tsiar-*.
**well** (in good health) — kranoengitok.
**well** n. — immerktarvik.
**west** — wagnark, uwagnark.

**west wind** (it is ww) — wagnartok, wawartok.

**wet** (is) — krausertok, kenepayok.

**wet snow** — massaktok.

**wets** v. — kinikpok.

**whale (black)** — arverk.

**whale (baleen)** — sokrark.

**whale (blubber)** — orksok.

**whale (fin)** — angok.

**whale (food)** — iglerark.

**whale (kills a w.)** — arverpok.

**whale (skin)** — maktar.

**whale (white : beluga)** — kenalugak, kelalugak.

**whale (killer-whale)** — ârluk.

**wharf** — iksarvik, nioraibvik.

**what ?** — sûna ? kisuk ? (Okk.).

**what do you want ?** — sûsiorpit ? sûwit ? sûwa ?

**what do you want to do with that ?** — sûyat-una ?

**what is he doing ?** — sûyok-una ?

**what is the use of this ?** — sûksak ûna ?

**what is it ?** — sûna ûna ?

**what relation have you with . . .** sûriviuk ? kigiviuk ?

**wheat** — akrekoyaksak, adgiksaksak.

**wheel** — aksaluak.

**when ? (in the past)** — kranga ?

**when ? (in the future)** — krakugo ?

**when, during** — -tillugo-*.

**where ?** — nani ? namut ? nakit ?

**whether** — -mangat-*.

**which ?** — nelliat ?

**which of them ?** — nellit ?

**which of us ?** — nellerput, nellipta ?

**which of you ?** — nellerksi ?

**while** — -tillugo-*.

**whiskers** (beard) — umerk, umik.

**whiskers** (side w.) — atayorutit.

**whip** (long) — iperautak.

**whip** (short) — tiggarut.

**whips** v. — iperartorpok, tiggartorpok.

**whispers** v. — issibjukpok.

**whistles** v. — uvingiartok.

**white (colour)** — kakortok, kraudlortok.

**white goose** — kanguk.

**white man** (opp. Eskimo) — kablunak.

**white part of egg** — kakorninga.

**white part of the eye** — koversak, kovertik.

**whitened skin** — naluark, kakertak.

**who ?** — kina ?

**whoever** — kinatuinnar.

**whole** — illuikak, illuitok, tamaluktar.

**whole** — illunat (Okk.).

**whose is it ?** — kia ûna ?

**why ?** — sôg ?

**why** (I know not why) — sôkiak.

**wick of a lamp** — iperak.

**wick-trimmer** (Eskimo) — tatkut.

**wide** (is) — siliktok, nerrotuyok.

**widow** — uikangilertok, uigarneôyok.

**widower** — nulliakangilertok, nulliitok.

**wife** — nulliak.

**wig** — nuyanguit.
**willing** (is) — angertok, piyomayok.
**will** (as he w.) — issumaminik.
**will** (as I will) — issumamnik.
**will** (as you will) — issumagnik (sing.); issumapsingnik (plur.).
**winch** — amulrut.
**wind** — anorê.
**wind (ahead)** — adgo.
**wind (behind)** — okkomut.
**wind (carried by** the w.) — tiktauyok.
**wind (falling)** — kassutpok.
**wind (great)** — anorêtuyok.
**wind (small)** — anorêkiktok.
**wind (N.E.)** — kannernark.
**wind (N.W.)** — wagnark, uwagnark.
**wind (is out of wind)** — anromiyok.
**wind protector** — adgoilitak, okkôtak.
**wind (S.E.)** — niggierk.
**wind (South)** — pinangnark.
**wind (wall protector)** — okkôtak.
**winder** (spring etc.) — sukkaterut.
**winds (clock** etc.) v. — sukkaterpok.
**window** — igalak.
**window protector** — alumitak.
**winks** v. — kablursorpok.
**winter** — ukkior.
**winter (long** w.) — ukkiuktak.
**wipes** v. (face, hands etc.) — ivikpok, adlaterpok.
**wiper** — ibgut, adlarutiksak.
**wire** — savigauyak.
**wishes** v. — tussuwok, ikligosukpok.
**wishes (how I wish !)** — tussunnark ! kranoktôk !
**wishes (makes one wish)** — tussunartok.
**wishes (much)** — tussuyuyok.
**witness** — pikattauyok, takkukattauyok.
**with** — -kattau-*.
**without** — -karani-* (he) or (she).
**wolf** — amarok.
**wolf-trap** — amakroniut.
**wolverine** — kâpvik.
**woman or female** — arnak.
**wondering** — -omangat-*.
**wood** — krejuk.
**wood** (hard w.) — sittaktok.
**wood (lumber)** — igluksak, krejuksak.
**word** — okrauserk.
**word of authority** — okralruserk.
**work to be done** — piyaeksak, suliyaeksak.
**works at** — -lior-*, senneyok.
**works** — senneyok, senneksakartok, senneksorpok, pileriwok.
**workman** — pileriye, senneye.
**workman** (good w.) — sennetuyok, pilerigajuktok.
**workmen's tools** — sennetit.
**world** — silaruark (Okk.).
**worm** — kopilrok.
**worm** (tape w.) — kromak.
**worm** (white little w.) — kretedrodlerk.
**worries** v. — niviorpok.
**worse** — -nersauyok-*, piluarnersauyok.

**worships** v. — tuksiarkattauwok.
**worthy of** (is) — nâdlerkotauyok.
**would (conditionally)** — -nayar-*, -rayar-*.
**wound** — ikit, kilersimayok.
**wound (at surface only)** — padgertok.
**wound healed** — kilerok, mamittok.
**wound made by bullet** — tûdlak.
**wounds self** v. — kilerpok.
**wrapper** — immutiksak.
**wrapper for wounds** — matutiksak, immutiksak, aumitiksak.
**wrestles** v. — pâyok.
**wrings** v. — sibvortorpok.
**wringer** — sibvortorsiut.
**wrist** — adgaut.
**wrist-bracelet** — adgaumik.
**writes** v. — titerarpok, aglarpok (Okk.).
**writing paper** — titerarviksak, aglarviksak.
**writings (receives** w.) — titerarviûyok.
**wrong** (is) — tammarsimayok.

## —X Y Z—

**X-ray** (instrum.) — adjiliorut.

* * *

**yawns** v. — aitaurpok.
**year** (winter) — ukkior.
**year (last** y.) — alrani.
**year (next** y.) — alrago.
**years (has so many years)** — ukkiulik . . .-nik.
**yellow colour** — koksortok.
**yells** (human) v. — erealarpok.
**yells** (dog) v. — mâlarpok.
**yelps** (dog) v. — krelukpok.
**yes** — î, îma, aksût, âmilar.
**yes, maybe** — î'kai, î'ngôyunar, wadlaiwok (Okk.).
**yes** (says yes) — angertok, î-lartok.
**yesterday** — ikpaksak.
**yesterday** (day before y.) — ikpaksani.
**yet** — sulli.
**yoke** (to fetch water etc.) — immertaut.
**yolk of an egg** — iktik, ikterk.
**you** (plural) — illipsi.
**young** — makôktok.
**young girl** — niviasar.
**young man** — nukapiak, inuosuktok.
**yours'** (plur.) — illipsi ukkua.
**youth** — makôktut.

* * *

**zealous** (is) — assiminik nagliktartok.
**zoo** — nerdjutit kattimabvia.

## PART II

# ESKIMO-ENGLISH

# PART II

# ESKIMO-ENGLISH

## — A —

### Introduction to Eskimo words beginning with the letter A

Several words beginning with the letter A, are formed in imitations of natural sounds, or onomatopoeia :

**a'a,** excl. of suffering.
**âyok,** falls unconscious.
**âniartok,** is ill.
**a'agnerk,** squaw duck.
**anrayortok,** is out of breath.
**aitaurpok,** v. yawns, etc.

Some words beginning with the letter A, are derived from the root "Ar", which means movement :

movement from : **aniyok,** goes out; **ârktorpok,** v. , skins v.
movement towards : **adgiarpok,** carries in his hand; **aktorpok,** touches.
movement of dispersion : **apsimayut,** are scattered; **aput,** snow covering the ground.
movement of life and heat : **auma,** fire; **aok,** blood; **audlarpok,** goes away.

## — A —

**a'a !** — Expression of pain.

**abgorpok** — divides into parts.

**abjursâyok**—it is becoming late.

**ablangavok** — astrides, makes a step.

**ablorak** — step.

**ablorangorpok** — is tired of walking.

**ablorpok** — makes a step.

**abva** — homonym.

**abvako** (napako) — one part, one half.

**abvareik, abvakoreik** — two of the same name.

**adgaertok** — has lost one hand.

**adgailiyok**—has a useless hand.

**adgaiyartok** — has cold hands.

**adgak** (anat.) — hand.

**adgakpok, adgasarpok** — digs with hands or paws.

**adgaumik** — wrist bracelet.

**adgerk** — cooked under ashes.

**adgerput** — migration of deer, etc.

**adgertitartok** — peeping in and out (vg sun.)

**adgiark** — string or line on handle.

**adgiarpok** — brings in his hands, carries.

**adgiksak,** adgesak — flour.
**adgo** — head wind.
**adgoilitak** — protection against head wind.
**adgomut** — facing the wind.
**adgopartarpok** — sails and tacks with head wind.
**adgorpok** — travels against the wind.
**adja !** (Aiv) — how nice !
**adjigêktok** — is similar, like.
**adjik** — picture, image.
**adjilerut** — kodak, camera.
**adjiliorpok** — takes pictures, draws, etc.
**adjiliwok** — imitates.
**adjiutiyok** — copies from a model.
**adjortok** — is different, is disguised.
**adjumiyok** — desires to imitate.
**adlak,** pl. : adlait — different, foreigners, etc.
**adlartok** — clear sky.
**adlarteraut, adlarutiksak** — towel, wiper, etc.
**adlarterpok** — wipes.
**adlarterut** — ointment, etc.
**adlauyartok** — is shy, timid before strangers.
**adlerk** — the one below, underneath.
**adlerark** — table, board, etc. (lit. put underneath).
**adlerparmiut** (Padl.) — the dead people.
**adliark** — mattress.
**adliôyok** — is beneath, underneath.
**adlit** — those things under.
**aek** — sleeve.

**aengilitak**—protect
**aggai,** agga — no (
nakka).
**aggerput, adgerput** —
towards sea (deer).
**agiark** — file.
**agiarpok** v. — files.
**agiardjuk**—small kind of du
**agiarealik** — violin.
**agidjakut** (pl. : -kuit) — iron filings.
**agiut** — grind-stone.
**aglait** — braidings, (writings, Okk.).
**aglakpok** — braids, (writes, Okk.).
**aglât** — even so (cf. -lônit-*).
**aglaut** (Okk.) titeraut — pen, pencil, etc. (Okk.).
**aglernartok** — causes to observe taboo.
**aglernertorpok** — follows taboo.
**aglerok** (anat.) — jaw.
**aglerolarpok** — gnashes teeth.
**aglerouyait,** (kipjautit) — scissors.
**aglerpok** — obeys to shaman, abstains.
**aglervik** — time to follow taboo.
**aglilerpok** — is growing, increasing.
**aglingortok** — is tired of following taboo.
**aglisiwok** — is growing.
**aglisuertok** — grows or increases no more.
**agliut** — microscope.
**aglok** (anat.) — whale jaw.
**aglorpok** — dives into the water.
**aglu** — seal's breathing hole in ice.

**agluwak** — fishing hole in ice.
**agvaerpok** — hinders no one.
**agvak**—mattress made of skins.
**agviarpok** — hinders others.
**ai** — brother-in-law.
**aijuktok** — is wet.
**aijukterut** — device to wet something.
**aiklerpok** — fetches something.
**aikoluk** ! (excl.) — deception !
**ailak** — perspiration.
**ailattok** — is wet with perspiration.
**aimerpok** — visits expecting to receive food.
**ainiarvik, aisimabvik** — one's home.
**aipa** — other, companion, partner, spouse, bride.
**aipaitok, aipakangitok** — spinster, maid, without companion.
**aipaksauyok** — commits adultery.
**aipaksauyuitok** — faithful in matrimony.
**aipanganik** (sulli) — once more.
**aipariktok** — has good partner.
**aipayok** — not well cooked.
**airark** — white root (eatable).
**aisimayok** — is at home.
**aita ! aitarâluk !** — dirty !
**aitaliyak** — Eskimo ball, little sand bag.
**aitangayok** — has his mouth open.
**aitarpok** — opens one's mouth.
**aitaurpok** — yawns, is sleepy.
**aitorniarnerk** — promised gift.
**aitorpok** — gives, makes a gift.
**aitortungiark** — very young birds, (lit. beak open).
**aitukomittok** — loses its colour.
**aituserearpok** — seeks gifts.
**aitût,** aitutiksak — gift.
**aivayok** — he quarrels.
**aiverk** — walrus.
**aiverniut** — walrus harpoon.
**aiwok** — goes home.
**ajagarpok** — plays ajagak.
**ajagak** — a game (bone with holes and a needle).
**ajagutak** — post supporting tent, etc., rainbow.
**ajak** — snow on clothes.
**ajakattak** — chequers, etc.
**ajakattarpok** — plays chequers, etc.
**ajakoluk**—aunt (mother's sister).
**ajakomiarpok** — helps dogs pushing sled.
**ajaksaut** — kind of fork.
**ajaktarsinnarealik** — rifle "44".
**ajamerpok** — repulses with hand.
**ajararpok** — makes figures with string.
**ajarautit** — figures made with string.
**ajaupiyark** — crutches.
**ajautak** — support.
**ajokarsiyok** — imitates a model.
**ajokertorpok** — teaches.
**ajokertugak** — pupil, one teached.
**ajokertuserk** — instruction, teaching.
**ajokertuye** — teacher, Protestant Minister.
**ajokertusibvik** — school (lit. where teaching is done).

**ajoribviksak** — model to imitate.
**ajornartok** — difficult.
**ajorneâluk** — sin (cf. piunginerk, etc.).
**ajorneiyarnerk** — forgiveness of sins.
**ajorsartok** — is in need.
**ajorsitaut** — riddle, mystery, difficulty.
**ajorteoyok** — is no good.
**ajortok** — is unable.
**ajurak** — opening in the ice.
**ajurakangitok** — almighty.
**ajuwak̂** — abscess, boil.
**ajuwalik** — leper, etc., has an abscess.
**âkka**, aukka — no.
**akkâ** ! — attention ! get out of the way !
**akkak** — uncle (father's brother).
**âkkakpok** — flatters.
**akkânga** ! (Aiv.) — how well ! how nice ! etc.
**akkaôwok** — is nice.
**akkerareit** — enemies, opponents.
**akkerartorpok** — revenges.
**akkerarpok** — carry (two or more carrying s. th.).
**akkeraut** — litter (carrier).
**akkerauyok**—is carried on litter.
**akkerok** — branch, joint, etc.
**akki** — root word for exchange : equivalent, worth, price, etc.
**akkiani** — on the other side, over.
**akkiarmiut** — those on the other side.
**akkiitoliyarpok** — buys on credit.
**akkiitok** — no fee, no charge.
**akkiksak** (Padl.) — debt.
**akkilereit** — those on both sides.
**akkililerpok** — pays for.
**akkiliksak** — something to pay one's debt.
**akkiliut** — credit (resources adequate to future payment).
**akkiorpok** v. — echoes.
**akkisartorpok** — revenges.
**akkiserk, akkiterk** — pillow.
**akkisuitok** — never answers.
**akkisuktok** — sun ray reflection.
**akkituyok** — expensive.
**akkiutak** — serves as tablecloth.
**akkiwok** — revenges, answers, exchanges, etc.
**akkiyomawok** — inclined to revenge.
**akko** — hind part, tail of garment.
**akkoertugauyok** — receives a message.
**akkoertuyok** — gives a message.
**akkoiyok** — fetches meat caches.
**akkokiktut** — Greenlanders (name given by Canadian Eskimos).
**akkonasuktok** — tries to please both.
**akkorngani** — in between.
**akkorngatigut** — in between us.
**akkorpok** — catches when flying (ball, etc.).
**akku** — middle.
**akkudlerk** — the one in the middle.
**akkulaitok** — close to one another.
**akkuliak** (anat.) — between the eyes.

**akkuliakattar** — point between two bays.

**akkulroalik** — pie.

**akkunaptingni** — in the midst of us, among us.

**akkuni, akkunialuk** — long time.

**akkunikiktok** — short time.

**akkunilutaôyok** — is the reason for which we are late.

**akunigosuktok** — is longing for.

**akkurtuyok** — distant from one another.

**akkutsiyok, akkuyok** — mixes.

**aklark** — brown bear.

**akluilak** — the richest.

**akluitok** — is rich.

**akluitomanerk** — is avaricious.

**aklulak** — the poorest.

**aklunark** — line, string.

**akluyok** — is poor.

**akpak** — kind of penguin.

**akpattok** — steps, walks, runs.

**akpalikitaurtut** — they race.

**akpangorpok** — is tired of walking.

**akpasortok** — walks quickly.

**akpatordjuark** — Coats Island.

**akpatorardjuk** — Walrus Is. (near Southampton).

**akpik** — kind of yellow berry.

**akpikutit** — stem of yellow berry.

**akpiusarpok, akpikok** — replies, answers.

**akrago** — to-morrow.

**akragoago** — day after to-morrow.

**akragoinnarpok** — postpones departure.

**akrark** (anat.) — second birth.

**akreark** — soft part of belly near ribs.

**akrearok** — stomach.

**akrearoksiut** — medicine for stomach trouble.

**akrearornerk** — Duke of York Bay, (Southampton).

**akreatorpok** — ate his fill.

**akreatusukpok** — is no more hungry.

**akridgek** — partridge, ptarmagan.

**akridgevik** — bush ptarmagan.

**akrilkriyok** — puts into small pieces.

**akrilrok** — lead (soft metal).

**akrilrouyak** — bread.

**akrilrouyaksak** — flour.

**akrittok** — is soft.

**akrittungayok** — has no sense, is stupid.

**akrittorartok** — has diarrhoea.

**akrivok** — places something in position.

**akromorpok** — stoops to approach game.

**akropiyok** — lies down (as a dog).

**akrotarpok** — drags itself (wounded game).

**akrovikpok** — sits on heels.

**aksak** — ball.

**aksakrok** (anat.) — upper arm, (outside of upper arm).

**aksaliksiyok** — rolls snow balls, etc.

**aksalikpok** — rolls.

**aksaliksidjut** — small roller.

**aksaluark** — wheel.

**aksalualik** — wagon.

**aksaluayok** — the wheel turns.

**aksaludjak** — pulley.
**aksarnerk** — aurora borealis.
**âktok** v. — skins.
**aktok** — adult.
**aktorpok** — touches.
**âktorpok** v. — skins.
**âktût** — skinning knife.
**alak** — sole of shoe.
**alaksauyartok** — bannock.
**alârpok**—turns head, not to see.
**alatarpok** — has new soles put on shoes.
**alegor** — glass, bottle.
**alelayok** — paper.
**alerk** — harpoon line.
**alertik** — inside socks.
**alianai** ! (excl.) — fortunately, cf. kujannamik, etc.
**alianaiitok** — is unfortunate.
**alianaigosuktok** — is happy, cheerful.
**aliasuktok** — is frightened by unknown cause.
**aligertok** — is tearing.
**aligortarpok** — shines.
**aligekkut** — seam protector.
**aliguartok** — tears easily.
**alikattok** — hail.
**alikpok** — is tearing.
**alikridjut** — glass cutter.
**aliktornerk** — a rent, a rip.
**aliptortok** — has miscarriage.
**alorluiyaut** — mat.
**alorluk** — dust or snow under feet.
**alornek** (anat.)—sole of the foot.
**aluk, allua** — bottom of sea, etc.
**alorluiyarpok** — rubs one's feet on mat, etc.
**aluksak** — grease.
**alugaksak,** alugak — to be eaten with spoon.
**alukiorpok** — mixes with spoon.
**alorluiyarvik** — mat (to rub one's feet).
**aluilitak** — sole (added over).
**alukpok** — eats with a spoon, licks.
**aluktorpok** — licks.
**alumerarpok** — licks one's lips.
**alungordlartok** — is tired of standing.
**alurut** — sole of foot.
**alût** (orviuyak) — spoon.
**alrago** — next year, year.
**alragoago** — in two years from now.
**alragokartok** — is . . . years old.
**alrak** (Padl.) — second.
**alrani** — last year.
**alraroserk** — second stomach of deer.
**alumitak** — protector for Eskimo window.
**amai** (Aiv) — I do not know (maybe yes, maybe no).
**âmak !** — tag ! (when playing tag).
**amâk** — root.
**amakroniut** — wolf-trap.
**amâmak** — milk, breast.
**amâmakpok** — sucks milk.
**amâmaktipok** — suckles her child.
**amaoligak** — snow bird.
**amarkraut** — basket, etc. to carry.
**amarok** — wolf.
**amaronilik** — remains of slaughter by wolves.

**amârpok** — carries baby in the amaut.

**amaulik** (mitivik) — eider duck.

**amaut** — kind of pouch in women's hood.

**amerark** — fish scale, bark of trees.

**amerk** — skin.

**amerluktok** — has desease of the skin.

**amêrpok** — has lost its skin.

**amertak** — tin; sheet of metal.

**âmi !** — let me see !

**amiakut** — remains of anything.

**amiasuk** (Padl.) — I do not know, cf. amai.

**amigaitut** — plenty.

**amigalartok** — insufficient for all.

**amigartok** — insufficient.

**amikikpok** — is too small.

**âmilar** — truly, surely.

**amilrait** — very many.

**amilreak** (anat.) — second tibia.

**amisut** — many.

**amittok** — strait, narrows.

**amma** — once more, again.

**ammut** — downwards (vertically).

**amuakattaut** (instrm.) — crane; also amulrut.

**amuarpok** — pulls towards self.

**amuyakattar** — drawer of table.

**amuyok** — pulls.

**ânana !** — beautiful !

**anânak** — mother.

**anângierk** — fly.

**anârk** — excrement.

**anârnartok** — laxative.

**anârnittok** — smells excrement.

**anârpok** — evacuates .

**anârsitauyok** — is very annoying.

**anârtortok** — contradicts.

**anârviut** — black oil drippings.

**anauligark** — ball (players').

**anautark** — snow beater; also tiluktût.

**anaurpok** — hits the ball, etc.

**ânernangerpok** — breathes his last, expires.

**ânernartok** — it hurts.

**ânernasartok** — holds his breath.

**anerneâluk** — Great Spirit, God.

**anernerk** — breath, angel, spirit, ghost.

**anernerk Pioyok** — Holy Ghost.

**anerpanarmik !** — good for you (pessimistic).

**ânerpok** — gets hurt.

**ânersarpok** — sighs.

**anerta !** — fortunately !

**anertaima** — now I understand why.

**anerteriyok** — breathes.

**ânertitaudjutit** — instruments of Christ's Passion.

**angagnerk** — first age unconsciousness.

**angak** — uncle (mother's brother).

**angâr !** — exclamation of surprise.

**angatkro** — shaman, conjuror, medecine man.

**angayarnartok** — intoxicating liquor.

**angayarpok** — is drunk, intoxicated.

**angatuyok** — is rough, bad boy.

**angayok, anrayok** — elder of the same sex.
**angayokrak** — superior, parents.
**angayudlerk** — eldest.
**angayuyok** — is dull.
**angelrarpok** — comes back home.
**angerlerittartok** — shakes head as if affirming.
**angerpok** — says yes, affirms, consents.
**angeruserk** — promise, kind of promise.
**angerut** — promise made, object of promise.
**angidlortak** — curve of a river.
**angiinarpok** — comes back without any success.
**angiuyak** — head of pin, of nail, etc.
**angiyortak** — the biggest.
**angiut** — triangular needle.
**angmak** — opening.
**angmaloriktok** — is round.
**angmaloriksaut** — a pair of compasses
**angmalerk** (anat.) — vulva (also: uttuk).
**angmalik** — has an opening.
**angmartaut** — can opener.
**angmarterut** — needle for primus lamp.
**angmarpok** — makes an opening.
**angmayok** — has an opening.
**angna** — that, (which is visible).
**angok** — whale fin.
**angornikut** — egg (outside nest).
**ângorpok** — is in a hurry to urinate, etc.
**angortorpok** — pronounces a name, etc.
**ânguark, anruark** — amulet.
**anguauyak** — medecine.
**angudjarêktuk** — two husbands exchange wives.
**angulayok** — softens skin with teeth.
**angusadlok** — adult male animal.
**angusik** — midwife.
**anguseriyok** — a lewd woman.
**angusuktok** — is good hunter.
**angut** (pl: angutit) — male.
**angût** (pl: angutait) — propeller, fish fins.
**anguyaksak** — game.
**angutiksak** — finger or toe, adopted father.
**angutiriyok** — holds his own.
**angutiviark** — male of any bird.
**anguyok** — catches game.
**âniarayuktok** — is often ill.
**âniarpok** — is ill, sick, etc.
**âniarvik** — hospital.
**aniarsuitok** — is never ill.
**anibvik** — place and time of birth, birthday.
**anigorpok** — finds an outlet.
**anik** — brother of a woman.
**aniksak** — adopted brother of a woman.
**aniuk** (anio) — snow for melting into water.
**aniusarpok** — dog eats snow.
**aniyok** — goes out, is born.
**aniyauksak** — exit, outlet.
**annaiwok** — hunter loses game.
**annakpok** — is not caught, is still free, escapes.

**riwok** — chooses, wants to keep.

**nnerosukpok** — does not want to give.

**annorark** — clothes.

**annorarpok** — puts on his clothes.

**annuarsorpok** — obeys, listens well.

**annudlakpok** — is very sad.

**annutpok** — is sad.

**annudlaksaiyok** — hits or whips to correct.

**annunsingorpok** — sulks.

**anorartok** — it is windy.

**anoreâluk** — great wind.

**anorê** — wind.

**anorekiktok** — very light wind.

**anoretuyok** — it is windy.

**anromiyok** — is out of breath (after running).

**anût** (ano) — harness.

**anuwok** v. — harnesses.

**aok** (anat.) — blood.

**aokannerpok** — thaws, blood circulation re-established.

**aokpok, aonarpok** — bleeds.

**aokserpok** — is thawing.

**aoksireartok**, siorauyak — sugar.

**aoksorpok** — mixes, deals cards.

**aolerpok** — it thaws.

**aomaliorsibvik** — stove.

**aomayok** — melted, soft.

**aomidjaktok** v. — sweats.

**aonartok** — bleeds much.

**aonerk** — is rotten.

**aonialertok** — will thaw and rot.

**aopaluktok, aopartok** — red.

**aopayartok** — almost red, pink.

**aopilaktok** — very young fawn, (reddish colour).

**aorpok** — crawls.

**aotitsiyok** — makes something thaw.

**aoyok** — wound that opens.

**apa** (Ǩid) — father.

**apadlerpak** — last dog (has shortest line).

**apâpakpok** — eats (childish expression).

**aperiyok** — questions, asks.

**aperiyaeksak** — question to be asked.

**apersorpok** — questions many times.

**apersorutiksak** — a question.

**aperkut** — object of a question.

**apiktuark !** — big thing !

**apingaut** — first snow.

**apiyok** — covered with snow.

**apkalawok** — devours like dogs.

**apkarpok** — devours.

**apkosarpok** — passes by that way.

**apkosinerk** — way, path, etc.

**apkut** — path followed.

**aporaktak** — deer (left over on hunting ground).

**apornerk** — meeting of rivers, etc.

**aportinrait** — sand waves on shore.

**aporpok** — passes there, meets.

**apsarpok** — puts aside, spread out.

**apsikpok** — separates from others.

**apsimayut** — are scattered.

**apterput** — spread out.

**aput** (general use) — snow.

**aputaerpok** — cleans off snow.
**aputaitok** — there is no snow.
**aputainnarôwok** — has much snow on clothes, etc.
**arêodjarêkput** — exchange wives for few days only.
**arêoyok** — has finished, sulks.
**ariaksak** — coal.
**arialinerk** — ashes.
**arialineusibvik** — ash tray.
**ariyaut** (ariaut) — powder horn.
**ariyek** — gun powder (black or grey).
**arkadluark** — brother (younger than one's sister).
**arklungertarpok** — swings on a rope.
**arksak** — ball to play with.
**arksârpok** — takes away by force, etc.
**arktayut** (Okk.) — thieves.
**arkteriyok** — gets ready to leave.
**ârktorpok** — skins.
**arliarpok** — expects a gift.
**arlorpok** — lifts up eyes and head.
**arluk** (arlo) — killer whale.
**arnak** — female, woman.
**arnakoaksak** — old woman.
**arnaksak** — adoptive mother.
**arnaksiut** — articles for woman.
**arnalerivok** — preoccupied with women.
**ârnaluk** — bitch.
**arnâluk** — prostitute, meretrix.
**arnangoark** — queen (a playing card).
**arnaseriyok** — a lewd man.
**arnarvik** (arnabvik) — aunt (mother's sister).
**arredjakut** — filings.
**arsliorpok** — flame agitated b[y] wind.
**arvadlerk** — the one to the right.
**arvak** (anat) — palm of the hand.
**arvarkorpok** — pulls to the right.
**arverk** — black whale.
**arverniut** — whale harpoon.
**arverpok** — kills a whale.
**Arviark** — Eskimo Point NWT.
**Arviligdjuark** — Pelly Bay NWT.
**arvinrat** — sixth.
**arvinilli** — six.
**âsiwak** — spider.
**âsorpok** — subject to epilepsy.
**asselroyok** — falls into pieces.
**asserortok** — is out of use, broken, etc.
**asseruiyok** — breaks.
**assia,** (possessive of assi) — another.
**assiangorpok** — becomes totally different.
**assianuarpok** — goes elsewhere.
**assikangitok** — unique.
**assilrerpok** — is reduced to pieces.
**assimiutak** — always elsewhere.
**assinaitok** — untied, free (dog, etc.).
**assinik okrarpok** — is delirious.
**assirorpok** — destroys.
**âssit !** — this one again !
**assiuyok** — is lost.
**assiwartok** (Padl.) — is lost.
**asso** — enough.
**assogor** — I do tell you.
**assoila** — this is what I expected.

**assoiyutit !** — here you are !
**ata** — lowest part.
**atâ !** (excl.) — hark ! listen !
**atailitak** — women's dress.
**ataluktar** — often.
**atamanna** — all the more reason.
**atanerk** (Okk.) — boss, lord, master.
**atangertok** — separated.
**ataneluktok** — is undesirable.
**atâni** — underneath.
**atârpok** — family moving towards sea.
**atarutak** — yard for sail (lowest one).
**atâtak** — father.
**atâtaksak** — adoptive father.
**atâtatsiak** — grandfather.
**atatau !** — be careful ! danger!
**atauk** — certainly well, cf. tauka, sokaima.
**atausearluni** — he . . . once.
**atauserk** — one
**atautsikut** — together.
**atautsit** — many together.
**atayok** — all in one piece, adheres, makes one with.
**atayolik** — one piece garment.
**atayomik** — always.
**atayorutit** — side whiskers.
**aterak** — calf of leg.
**atertak** — bear cub.
**aterput** — deer migration.
**aterartarpok** — skipping the rope.
**atkark** — uncle (father's brother).
**atkarpok** — comes down.
**atkasût** — submarine.
**atkonartok** — it is wavy.
**atkranilik** — over ten.
**atkrearok, akrearok** (anat.) — stomach.
**atkrigiark** — nervous, never quiet.
**atkrikpok** — is arranged, fixed up.
**atkriksorpok** — he is fixing it.
**atkrok** — bottom of a boat, at the rear.
**atla** (Padl) — different, stranger.
**atniyak** — carp.
**atsiark** — homonym of one's father or mother.
**atsikpok** — is low.
**at'su** (Okk.) — I do not know.
**attago !** — let us endeavor.
**attarneluktok** — is not solid, almost broken.
**attak** — aunt (father's sister).
**âttatark** — pants.
**âttatik** — hinges.
**atterkarpok** — has the name of...
**attereit** — of the same name, homonym.
**atterarpok** — gives a name.
**atterk** — name.
**attî, attai** — go on, it is time.
**attikiktok** — small or pointed base.
**attigi** — inside shirt (hair inside).
**attilukannerk !** — once more !
**attirark** — waterproof deer skin boots.
**attituyok** — has a large base.
**atortok** — useful.
**atortugak** — something borrowed.
**atortuinnartok** — borrowed.
**atuarsiyok** — follows tracks.

**atugak** — has been used, not new.
**atungaksak** — skin for soles.
**atungauyak** — small leaves to be mixed with tobacco.
**atungerpok** — sews new soles.
**atungersimayok** — locked up in prison, etc.
**atunit** — each.
**aubverk** — larva.
**audlalik** — switch.
**audlateriyok** — moves sled to start.
**audlarpok** — leaves, goes away.
**audlat** — family on the move.
**augarpok** v. — leans forward.
**augiauyak** — brick.
**audlatsiariktok** — moves with facility, skilful.
**audlardjarluktok** — moves with difficulty.
**augiak** — coagulated blood.
**auksararpok** v. — diving through the air.
**auktartok** — takes colour of blood.
**aulakattarpok** v. — uses rocking chair.
**aulakrut** — flag.
**aulalayok** — never quiet.
**aulasarpok** v. — fishing with line.
**aulasaut** — fishing line.
**aulaiyiyok** — pays attention, remembers.
**aulayok** — moves one's self.
**auma** — fire.
**aumaliark** — touchwood, amadou.
**aumalikpok** — gets on fire.
**aumaliorsibvik** — furnace, stove.
**aumagertaut** — spark.
**aumagertarvik** — battery (electric).
**aumarorpok** — takes fire.
**aumerk** (aumitit) — bedding
**aumergerk** — spark.
**aumidjakpok** v. — sweats.
**aumiserpok** — dresses a wound, etc.
**aumitauvok** — is wrapped up.
**aumitiksak** — bandages for wounds, etc.
**auvarpok** — goes deer hunting.
**auverk** — snow block.
**auyak** — summer.
**auyaksiortok** — spends summer.
**auyaksiut**—summer clothes, etc.
**avioyok** — has buzzing in the ears.
**awa** — far away.
**awadlerk** — to the extremity.
**awadlerpok** — goes far away.
**awalakret** — shrubs.
**awaliarutak** — circle around the moon.
**awalikpok** — river separates in two.
**awaluk** — frame of picture, etc.
**awalukpok** — goes around.
**awalut** — footing of wall.
**awamurpok** — goes to and fro, far.
**awapsilar** — plate.
**awapsilarekut** — device to stop edges of garment from rolling.
**awârpok** v. — loses consciousness.
**awat, awatit** — twenty, (lit. : limbs, hands and feet).
**awatâni** — around.

**awatâ** — a circle.

**awatiptingni** — all around us.

**awikpok** v. — separates, divides, divorces.

**awiksarpok** v. — cuts blocks of snow.

**awinesuitok** — is always home.

**awingark** — mouse, lemming.

**awingayet,** (pussi) — cat.

**awisuitok** — inseparable.

**ayaiya** — Eskimo singing with drum.

**âyok** — is unconscious, has a fit, etc.

**âyuwak** — abscêss, boil, etc.

**âyuwalik** — leper.

## — E —

### Introduction to Eskimo words beginning with the letter E

Most of these words are derived from the root words : **egitpok, erkriwok, erkrarpok,** having the following meaning :

**egitpök,** projecting far away, extraction from, throwing, casting.
**erkriwok,** folding, curling up, etc.
**erkrarpok,** remembers, pays attention, etc.

The root ER meaning privation, separation, is also used in some derived words beginning with E, as : eresaraitok, easily loses its feathers, etc.

### — E —

**edlok** — sling, (to throw stones).

**egitpok** — throws away.

**ei ?** — is it not true ?

**eiei** — almost.

**erealârpok** — yells, cries out.

**erenainartok** — has a hoarse voice.

**erenesuktok** — is in a hurry.

**eresaraitok** — easily loses hair or feathers.

**eretak** — down (after feathers are fallen).

**eretarpok** v. — plucks off feathers.

**erevittok** — is tired, exhausted.

**eriê** (anat.) — shoulder blade.

**erklerpak** (anat.) — molar tooth.

**erkluk** (anat.) — large intestine.

**erkpakpok** — opens, blossoms, etc.

**erkranartok** — prepares to travel far away.

**erkrarpok** — remembers.

**erkraidguyok** (Padl.) — is inventive.

**erkrarte** — arbitrator.

**erkrarsautit** — souvenir.

**erkravit** — intestines.

**erkre** — commissure of the lips.

**erkreanartok** — tiresome, makes one sleepy.

**erkreanaitok** — keeps one busy, awake, sprightly.

**erkreasukpok** — is lazy, feels sleepy.

**erkreangoyok** — sulks.

**erkredjut** — barrel circle.

**erkreluktok** — sore lips.

**erkrerpalût** — harmonica, mouth organ.

**erkresulingayok** — has curly hair.
**erkrikpok** v. — embraces.
**erkrivok** — curls up.
**erkrirutit** — tattooings around the mouth.
**erkrok** (anat.) — rump, buttocks.
**erkroiyaut,** erkrûtit — toilet paper.
**erkrortok** — sharp shooter.
**erkromayok** — is awake.
**erksak** (anat.) — temple.
**erksartauyok** — is hit on the temple.
**erksiriwâ** (irksiriwa) — is afraid of him.
**erksiwok** — is afraid.
**erksinartok** — makes one afraid, is dangerous.
**erksukpok**—carries on shoulder.
**erktorsit** (instrum.) — skin scraper.
**erktuartok** — is square, diamond (playing cards).
**erligosuktok** — is stingy.
**erlikpok** — is attached to own belongings.
**ermibvik** — washing basin.
**ermikpok** — washes.
**ermiut** — soap.
**ermoserk** — cup, mug, glass, chalice, etc.
**ernerk** — son.
**erneinnar** — all at once.
**ernetariwâ** — has taken him for his son.
**ernetuar** — only son.
**ernibvik** — time or place of birth.
**ernikpok** — gives birth to.
**erniorpok** — lays eggs.
**ernisuitok** — barren woman or female.
**ernisukpok** — is about to give birth.
**ernrartok** — leaks, drips.
**ernrutak** — grandchild.
**erotartok** — loses its colour on other.
**erortorpok** v. — washes mouth.
**erortût** — mouth wash.
**eruitok** — emptied deer body.
**ertortok** (infix) — so many times.

## — I —

### Introduction to Eskimo words beginning with the letter I

N.B. The letter I is pronounced "ee".

The letter I at the beginning of a word means "to be", that is any modification of being :

Here are a few ideas suggested by the words beginning with I :

idea of : heat, fire : **ikkitit,** matches.
idea of : laughing, mockery : **iglartok,** laughs; **iyortok,** mocks.
idea of : wound, cut : **iki,** wound: **ikkiarpok,** cuts into layers.
idea of : attention : **itkraumayok,** remembers.
idea of : different ways of being in a place : **iksiwayok,** is seated; **inangayok,** is lying down; **issangayok,** is outstretched, etc.

## — I —

**i, îma** — yes.

**iagattok** — is lost with his boat.

**iak !**—exclamation of deception.

**ibgut** — wiper, towel, etc.

**ibjangoyok** — is choking, (from lack of air).

**ibjaruserpok** v. — muzzles.

**ibjo** (sermerk) — black mud for sled runners, peat.

**ibjornaitok** — holy, saint, pure.

**ibjorsiyok** — puts black mud on sled runners.

**ibjoyok** — is thick.

**ibjutak** — lever.

**ibleriwok** — is stingy, prefers.

**iblungayok** — has crooked legs.

**idgak** — eye glasses.

**idgalik** — wears eye glasses.

**idgiak** (anat.) — throat.

**idjuk** (anat.) — testicle.

**idjuyak** (anat.) — ovary.

**idjuarsiwok** — imitates.

**idjortok** — coagulated blood.

**idlaerpok** v. — combs.

**idlaerut, idlaerutit** — comb.

**idlalik** — is entangled.

**idlerdjuareik** — two who should never name one another.

**idleriwok** — mixes with.

**idlok** as idluk, ibluk — sling.

**idlorak** — big black fish, fresh water fish.

**idluarsaiye** — medical doctor.

**idluarsaiyekolu** — nurse.

**idluarsaut** — medecine, medicament, drug.

**idluarsaiyok** — nurses.

**idluarsiwalliayok** — improves in health.

**idluartok** — is good.

**idluartulliwok** — does a good action.

**idluarutiksak** — that by which one is improved.

**idluigosukpok** — is envious.

**idluiksarpok** — gets others in trouble.

**idluilutaowok** — is the cause of trouble.

**idluinerk** — sin, something bad.

**idluitok** — is bad.

**idluitulliyok** — acts badly.

**igak, igabvik** — stove, cooking range.

**igalak** — glass, window, etc.
**igalauyak** (anat.) — eardrum.
**igalerk** — stove pipe, etc.
**igangayok** — is leaning forwards.
**igasimayok** — is cooked.
**igavik** — kitchen.
**igawok** v.— cooks.
**igaye** — cook.
**igiak** — throat.
**iglangorpok** — is tired of laughing.
**iglarosukpok** — is about to laugh.
**iglarpok** — laughs.
**iglautiriyok** (-wâ) — laughs at.
**iglerark** — kind of gelatine, whale food.
**iglerk** — bed.
**igliark** — uterus.
**iglikpok** — is in bed.
**igliorpok** — makes his bedding.
**iglua** — the other of a pair.
**iglugeik** — both of the pair.
**igluinnar** — one of a pair.
**igluitok** — has lost one of a pair.
**iglu** — snow house.
**iglukattigeit** — all those of the same house.
**iglukittartut** — juggling balls.
**îglukpok, îdlukpok** — is snow blind, has sore eyes.
**igluktût** — uses both hands or feet.
**igluligardjuk** — Chesterfield, NWT.
**igluliorpok** — builds a house.
**iglungadlerk** — on the other hand.
**iglupinnarsût** — revolver.
**iglurdjuark** (-ruark) — wooden or stone house.
**iglurdjuartalik** — gathering of houses, village.
**igluserpok, iglusiktok** — shifted more to one side, (load, etc.).
**iglutârpok** — the house is built, ready.
**iglutorpok** — uses both hands.
**igluvigak** — old house, abandoned house.
**igmerpok**, ingmerpok — makes the whole trip without camping.
**igmerk**, ingmerk — self, end, goal.
**igminek**, ingminek — oneself.
**igmekorpok, ingmegorpok** — does as he pleases.
**ignakpok** — makes fire with flint.
**ignavik** (ignaviut) — tobacco pouch.
**ignaut** — lighter.
**ignerattar** (Padl.) — companion (cf. pikattar).
**ignerk** — flint or spark.
**ignerpok** — takes fire.
**igsak** — cooked.
**iguarpok** — tears with teeth.
**igubjarpok** — disentangles.
**igumiktok** — is entangled.
**igunarnittok** — tastes or smells rotten.
**igunartok** — is rotten.
**igunausibvik** — blubber shed.
**iguptak**, iguppak, igupsak — bee.
**igupsiwok** — opens bundle.
**igupterpok** — takes to pieces.
**i'guyunar** — yes, maybe.

**igvikotak** (Okk.) agvâkotak — obstacle.

**igvit** — you (sing.).

**iiwok** — swallows.

**ikadjet**, ikat — elevated cache.

**ikayorpok** — helps.

**ikayorte** — helper.

**ikerk** — strait.

**ikayusiarpok** — carries with frontal band.

**ikayût** — frontal band to carry.

**ikârsiorut** — scow.

**ikârpok** — crosses over.

**ikertinerk** — water between land and ice.

**iki** — wound.

**ikinroak** — short socks.

**ikka** — there it is, a little lower.

**ikkat, ikadjet** — elevated caches.

**ikkaksarpok** — kindles fire.

**ikkaksaut** — kindling (methylated spirit).

**ikkalrok** — rough ice.

**ikkariktok** — boat grounded on reef.

**ikkarvik** — ford.

**ikkattok** — shallow water.

**ikkerasar** — strait.

**ikkii** — it is çold weather.

**ikki** — root word of most words : meaning heat.

**ikkîanartok** — it is cold weather. (lit. : it makes one without heat).

**ikkiânga** — layer (poss.).

**ikkiarpok** — cuts into layers.

**ikkidlerpok** — is wounded.

**ikkîerpok** — feels cold.

**ikkimayok** — embarked.

**ikkisaraitok** — gasoline.

**ikkit** (pl. ikkitit) — matches.

**ikkitinikut** — matches already burnt.

**ikkittartok** — electric lamp, flash-light, etc.

**ikkitokoluit** — not very many.

**ikkiyark** (Padl.) — kerosene.

**ikkiyalik** — kerosene lamp.

**ikkiyarsit** — funnel.

**ikkiyok** — is on fire.

**ikkualarpok** — is in flames, on fire.

**ikkualarsarpok** — sets on fire.

**ikkualausibvik** — stove, furnace, etc.

**ikkublawok** v. — wind falls.

**ikkubliartok** — wind begins to fall.

**ikkuma** — fire.

**ikkumabvik** — electric switch.

**ikkumaleriye** — mechanic, engineer.

**ikkumalik** — engine, motor.

**ikkumalinerk** — place where there has been a fire.

**ikkumâluk** — big fire, hell.

**ikkumayark** (Padl.) — candle.

**ikkupikpok** — supplies food, etc.

**ikkurpok** — bores a hole.

**ikkûserk** (anat.) — elbow.

**ikkuserpok** — ties one leg of dog to neck.

**ikkusemigarpok** — leans on elbows.

**ikkusiarpok** — pushes another with the elbow.

**ikkût** — wooden rasp.

**ikkûtak** — brace and bit.

**iklervik** (Okk.) — box, coffin, casket.

**ikligosukpok** — desires much.
**iklinnamik !** — how I wish !
**ikpaksak** — yesterday.
**ikpasagoâluk**—a long time ago.
**ikpaksani** — a few days ago.
**ikpanartok** (Net.) — amiable.
**ikpariksarpok** — places things in order.
**ikpeardjuk** — pocket, bag, etc.
**ikperititak** — jig saw puzzle.
**ikperiyok** — feels.
**ikpigak** — steep hill.
**ikpik** — steep.
**ikpinartok** — causes one to feel something.
**ikrarte** — hair worn very short.
**ikritkrok** (anat.) — little finger.
**iksangualik** — palmiped, web-footed.
**iksaumikpok** — wastes last cartridge.
**iksarlukpok** — dull knife.
**iksarvik** — wharf.
**ikserk** (Okk.) (kadluk)—thunder.
**iksikpok** — leans forward.
**iksinartok** — rubbish.
**iksirardjuark** — priest.
**iksirardjurâluk** — bishop.
**iksirardjuarâpik** — pope.
**iksirardjuakasak** — deacon.
**iksirardjuaksak** — future priest.
**iksiradjuangosibvik** — day of ordination.
**iksirardjuarpok** — priest celebrates mass.
**iksirarpok** (Padl.) — writes.
**iksiraut** — pen, pencil, etc.
**iksirkrekreyok** — reads with eyes only.
**iksirkret** — writings.
**iksiwautak** — seat.
**iksiwayok** — is sitting.
**iksuk,** iksua (Okk.) — handle of snow knife.
**iksutit** — shrubs.
**iktakuserpok** (-pâ) — puts nets into water.
**iktakutit** — net sinkers.
**iktak** — curved front part of sled.
**iktariktok** — is heavy.
**ikterut** — seat of a canoe.
**iktik** — yolk of an egg.
**iktititsiyok** — melts fat.
**iktok** — old person.
**iktorak** — elder of the camp.
**iktortok** — goes out to see if someone is coming.
**iktsuarpok** — often goes out to see if someone is coming.
**iktulorpok** — it thunders.
**iktumiyok** — makes noise.
**iktutût** — primus lamp.
**ikublayok** — is moderate.
**ikuigarpok** — expands skin by scarping.
**ikuvrark** — base, stool, cf. tungavik.
**ila-suwit** (Padl.) — never mind.
**ilar** — indeed, truly.
**ilarli** (Okk.) — indeed.
**illa** — partner, friend, related.
**illaksak** — something with which to mend.
**illaksaut** — baking powder, cf. publurterut.
**illarnerk** — remains, shavings.
**illârpok,** illatorpok — repairs, adding piece.
**illaut** — device to clean hole in ice.

**illagektut** — are related, friends, associates.
**illaksiorpok** — seeks associates, addresses s.o.
**illaksiwok** — lives with.
**illakungorpok** — is mutilated.
**illamar** — associate.
**illangiutiyok** v. — participates.
**illâni** — sometimes.
**illatuyok** — has many friends, relatives.
**illautiyok** — joins together.
**illauwok** — goes with the party.
**illayokartok** — there are circumstances.
**illeranaitok** — makes every one at ease.
**illeranartok** — makes one uneasy.
**illerasukpok** — is shy, timid, ashamed.
**illerksi** — those among you.
**illersarpok** — opens a cache of meat.
**illigeik** — two who should never name one another.
**illikritamarpok** — shaking head sideways.
**illimasukpok** — is on the watch, suspects.
**illingartok** — is broken.
**illingnerk** (Okk.) — loin of an animal, cf. tartuk.
**illingayok** — is such, runs so.
**illiniarpok** — learns.
**illiniarvik** — school.
**illiniarte** — disciple.
**illiniartitsiye** — teacher, professor.
**illiniartitsiyok** — teaches.
**illiorkraiyok** — distributes, throws his card.
**illiornerk** — action.
**illiorût** — drill, cf. ikkutak.
**illipsi** — you (pl.).
**illisautit** — first notion, alphabet, etc.
**illisaiyok** — does exercises to learn.
**illisimayok** — is learned, scholar.
**illitariyok, illitarsiyok** — recognizes.
**illitjuitok** — cannot learn anything.
**illitkoserk** — habits, uses, ways of doing.
**illituyok** — learns easily, intelligent.
**illiviark** — wooden box, handy box.
**illiwa (kr nok ?)** — how has this happened ?
**illiyak, illiyardjuk** — orphan, abandoned child, etc.
**illiyarsortauyok** — is scorned, left alone.
**illiyiyok** — makes an offering to the ghosts.
**illiyok** v. — puts.
**illu** — inside.
**illudlerlugo** — filling it.
**illudlit** — inside garments, underwear, etc.
**illuikak, illuitok** — the whole, complete.
**illungotiwok** — puts inside.
**illutorpok** — digs.
**illulereit** — one inside the other.
**illulik** — content.
**illulikangitok** — is empty.
**illumut** — towards the inside.

**illunat** (Okk.) — all; cf. tamarmik, tameta.
**illungertorpok** — endeavors.
**illupak** — underwear.
**illupkut** — bird's crop.
**illuptingni** — in ourselves.
**illusikpok**, manusiyok — caves in (iglu wall caving in).
**illutorpok** — is concave.
**illutuyok** — contains much.
**illûverk** — grave, tomb.
**illûvertalik** — grave yard.
**illûverpok** — puts in a grave, under stones.
**ilravit** (anat.) — intestines.
**ima, î** — yes.
**imagpok** — is full.
**imailiwa** — answers so.
**imâk !** — hark ! listen !
**ima-kra** — I think so.
**imâkpok** — gambling stake.
**imanna** — this way, thus.
**imat'nar** (Padl.) — it is of no importance.
**imitauyok** — receives work to be done.
**imgiarpok**, ingiarpok — precedes, goes ahead.
**imgorpok**, imigorpok — snow house falls.
**immaertok**—emptied container.
**immagorpok** — follows close to water.
**immaiyaut** — pump.
**immakiktok** — small container.
**immâluk** — a long time ago.
**immânîtok** — is in the water.
**immark** — sea; great water.
**immarsuk** — mud.
**immârpok**—falls into the water.
**immasar — not long ago.**
**immerak** — juice, soup, etc.
**immerk** — water.
**immekangitok** — is empty (of liquid or solid).
**immekaut** — recipient, receiver, container.
**immerkrotailak** — tern of the arctic.
**immerkrotak** (anat.) — groin.
**immerluk** (Okk.) — strong liquor, alcohol.
**immerolik** — dropsical.
**immerpok** — drinks.
**immertarpok** — fetches water.
**immertarvik** — watering place
**immertaut** — yoke to carry water.
**immertût** — scraper to dry deer skins.
**immêrutiwok** — is completely empty.
**immerukpok** — is thirsty.
**immiatsiyok** — repeats as echo, cf. akkiorpok.
**immikpok** — crumbles completely.
**immiorpok** — melts snow or ice (for water provision).
**immitserpok** — is soaked into water.
**immiugak** — snow (to be melted into water).
**immoriktok** — is curled up (as a dog).
**immosiuyak** — cup, cf. ermoseuyak.
**immudluk** — wrinkle.
**immudjarpok** — unties a bundle.
**immuk** — milk.
**immulerpok** — curls up.

**immuserpok,** immuyiyok — wraps in a bundle.

**immutiksak** — wrapping paper, skin, etc.

**immût,** immûtâ — envelope, cover.

**immuyaeksak**—cigarette paper.

**immuuyak** — butter.

**immuuyartok** — cheese.

**immuyiyok** — rolls, (vg. cigarette).

**immuyut** v. — they play "hide and seek".

**imna** — the one I speak of.

**imnak** — steep slope.

**imnierpok** — sings.

**imniutit** — hymns, songs; hymn book.

**inekonartok** — is fair, pretty.

**inersimayok** — is finished.

**inerterpok** — corrects, scolds.

**ingelrayok** — travels, by boat or sled, etc.

**ingertarpok** — walks to and fro.

**ingiuliktok** — very smalls waves on water.

**ingiarpok** — finishes, goes ahead.

**ingiarsiwok** — passes beyond.

**ingmek** — alone, by one's self.

**ingmikoartok** — all by himself.

**ingminek** — himself, herself.

**ingmerpok** — makes the whole trip without camping.

**ingnaut** — lighter.

**ingniarattar** (Padl.) — another, companion, etc. (cf. pikattar).

**ingniwok** — takes place in iglu, tent etc.

**ingnorêk** — canvas or skin under load.

**ingularpok** — mixes, (vg. sugar in tea).

**ingorkortok** — yes, perhaps.

**ingutak,** enrutak — grandchild.

**inna** — entrance of boat.

**innaluak** (plur. innaludjet) — intestine.

**innangavok** — is lying down.

**innangerpok** —takes another's place.

**innangertauyok** — is replaced, beaten, conquered.

**innark** — adult, grown up.

**innarktok** — is in bed.

**innatauyok** — is companion of action.

**innekonaitok,** inekonaitok — is ugly, not pretty, nor fair.

**innererpok** — corrects.

**inneriyok** — talks to.

**innertok** — is completed, finished.

**innersertok** — loses tracks of sled.

**innibvik** — board used to dry small skins.

**innik** (pl: innit) — tracks of sled.

**innitak** — drying net (in iglu).

**innolisaut** (Okk.) — medecine.

**innorpok,** innorsarpok — does not reqch goal.

**innua** or **înua** — possessor, master, etc.

**inuarpok** — murders.

**inudluitok** — honest person.

**inuerutiyok** — people are gone.

**inugak** — phalanx of fingers.

**inugaruvligak** — dwarf.

**inugiak** — crowd.

**inuguserk** — evil person.

**inuilak** — no people there.

**inuilangonartok** — makes one lonesone, cf. kepingonartok.
**inuilitiriyok** — seeks to be alone.
**inuisartut** — they are not many people.
**inuk** — man, Eskimo.
**inukatti** — neighbour.
**inuinnark** — human being.
**inukangitok** — empty house, empty egg, etc.
**inuktariwa** — he killed him, he took him as servant.
**inukat**, inukatti — neighbour.
**inukka** — my hand (playing cards).
**inukpak** — giant.
**inukpakpok** — lives long, is old.
**inuksarpok** — does not reach goal.
**inuksiwok** — meets, finds human being.
**inuksuk** — land mark, beacon.
**inuktigut** — we the Eskimos.
**inuktut** — in Eskimo language, as an Eskimo.
**inulervik** — place and time of birth.
**inuliorpok** — procreates.
**inumarik**, inuminak — real man, the Eskimo.
**inungayok** — is ill.
**inungorpok** — becomes man.
**inungoark**, inuyak — doll.
**inunraut** (Myth. Omangitok and Akuludjosi) — very first man.
**inuosuktok**, nukapiak — young man.
**inuotipok** — was made man, Jesus Christ.
**inuôvok** — is a man, a human being.
**inuserk**, inoserk — life.
**inuyok**, inôyok — is living.
**ipakpok** — is dirty, unclean.
**ipariktok** — is in good order.
**iparsiwok** (Okk.) — understands easily, intelligent.
**iparluktok** — is crooked, knotty.
**ipârpok** — cleans, licks, etc.
**iperainnarpok** — abandons, puts aside, etc.
**iperalik** — lamp with wick.
**iperak** — wick.
**iperarpok** — gets in water, walks in water.
**iperartuarpok** — swims.
**iperauserk** — waterproof boots.
**iperautak** — long Eskimo whip.
**iperiktipok** — replaces in order.
**iperk, ipak** — dirt, uncleanliness.
**iperpok** — ties, (dog etc.).
**ipersimayok** — is tied, not loose.
**ipervik** — a place to tie.
**ipgut**, ibgut — wiper.
**ipiark** — braids to hold boots.
**ipiaruserpok**, ibjaruserpok — muzzles dogs, etc.
**ipigluk** — legs.
**ipiglukiktok** — has short legs.
**ipiiyarpok** — cleans.
**ipiksaiyok** — sharpens.
**ipiksaut** — whetstone, grindstone.
**ipiktok** — is sharp.
**ipiut**, ipiutak — line, string, etc.
**ipjutak**, ibjutak — lever.
**ipkîtok** — is not sharp, dull.
**ipkolukpok** (Padl.) — whines, complains.
**ipka** (poss. of ipu) — its handle.
**ipkrittok** — is clean.

**iplaut** (anat.) (iblaut) — embryo.
**ipsorpok** — shakes one's self.
**iptadjangitok** — is waterproof.
**ipteriyok** — is dry.
**ipterk,** iptinga, immerak — juice.
**ipu** — handle, lance etc.
**ipualik** — frying pan.
**ipubvik** — place of the oars on side of boat.
**ipuitok** — tin can, etc. (lit.: has no handle).
**ipummertok** — has lips closed firmly.
**ipummiyok** — has not eaten since a long time.
**iputtok** — uses oars, rows.
**iput** — oar.
**irk !** (exclam.) — attention ! danger ! stop !
**irkralerark** (Okk.) — corner, angle, (cf tiretkroak).
**irkadliarpok** — goes fishing.
**irkraluk** — fish.
**irkralût** — fish owned by someone.
**irkraluyak** — model for network.
**irkraumalerutiksak** — souvenir.
**irkranertok** — something finished.
**irkrark** — bottom of river etc.
**irkrisulingayok,** (erkri...) — has curly hair.
**irkroitartok** — tacks (naut.)
**irpadlakpok** (erp.) — swallows with noise.
**issa** — bird fat, heavy.
**issangayok** — has arms stretched.
**issark** — fathom.
**issarok** — wing, branch.
**issarutak** — branch, walrus flipper.
**issarpok** — outstretches arms.
**issaruksorpok** — spreads out wings.
**issausimayok** — at arms length.
**issautiyok** — lifts at arms length.
**issavrayok** (Padl.) — examines something.
**isserartok** — is foggy, smoky.
**isserk** — smoke.
**isserlukpok** — makes smoke to chase flies.
**issetsiariktok** — incense, (lit.: nice smoke).
**issibjukpok** — speaks in low voice.
**issikrut** — skin scraper.
**îssimayok** — is swallowed.
**issiterpok** — scrapes and stretches skin.
**issivikpok,** issivingayok — expands, stretches out.
**issortok** — opaque liquid, muddy water.
**issorartuyok** — leader (dog), pulls hard.
**issubjuk** (anat.) (Okk.) — articulation of shoulder.
**issuk** — end, seven at cards or 7 o'clock.
**issudlerpak** — the furthest.
**issukangitok** — has no end: eternal.
**issuma** — thought, idea.
**issumadguyok** (Padl.) — intelligent, great thinker.
**issumadjutauyok** — is the reason of one's thought.
**issumaerutiwok** — out of his head, is brainless.

**issumariwâ** — thinks of it.
**issumariyaungitok** — left alone, no one thinks of him.
**issumariyungnaerpok** — forgets, forgives.
**issumakattigeit** — of the same opinion.
**issumaksak** — object of thought.
**issumaksasiorpok** — reflects.
**issumaksorpok** — does as he pleases.
**issumaliorpok** — gives advice, influences.
**issumaminik** — as he pleases.
**issumanartok** — gives motive of reflection.
**issumatark** — chief, one who thinks much.
**issumayok** — thinks.
**issungnark** — gull, Jaeger.
**issurkriyok,** tîgiktok — tea is strong (not clear).
**itaknartok** — easily broken.
**itârpok** — dog breaks in tent, iglu, etc.
**itauyartok** — line stretched for games.
**iterpok** — enters.
**itertsitsinerk** — entrance.
**itibjak** — portage (ittibjak).
**itivittok** — makes portages.
**itiyok** — is deep.
**itjangiarpok** — mild weather.
**itkranartok** — makes one reflect.
**itkranayarpok** — makes preparations to leave.
**itkrerk** — nit.
**itkrelerk** (pl. : -lit) — Chipweyan indian.
**itkrômik !** (excl.) — more or less pleasing !
**itkrorutit** — white spots on women trousers.
**itkrok** — rump, buttocks.
**itnerk** — channel.
**itsak,** itsarnitak — very long time ago.
**itserk** — yolk of an egg.
**itsuarpok** — goes out to see if s.o. coming.
**ittak,** iktak — curved front of sled.
**itterok** — urine.
**ittersak** — valley.
**ittersaliorpok** — digs a hole.
**ittersarpok** — awakes someone, shakes him.
**ittierk** (anat.) — anus.
**ittigak** (anat.) — foot.
**ittigakpok** — steps on.
**ittigamak** — low shoes.
**ittik** — top of low shoes.
**ittigarutit** — seal skin shoes.
**ittimak** (anat.) — palm of the hand.
**ittimiarpok** — kicks.
**ittiyok** — deep water.
**ivarpok** — seeks, looks for s.o.
**ivalinerk** — young bird, still without feathers.
**ivalu,** ivalunerk — sinew, Eskimo thread.
**ivaluyak** — thread from stores.
**ivaluksaut** — bobbin.
**ivâyok** — broods.
**iviangek** — breasts, mammae.
**ivikpok** — wipes after eating.
**ivik** — grass, hay, straw.
**ivitaruk** — red trout.
**ivunerk** — accumulation of ice, etc.

**ivuyok** — accumulates.

**ivuyivik** — a place near Wolstenhiolme, P.Q.

**iyailiwok** — has sore eyes.

**îyaeksak** — to be swallowed.

**iyariyartok** — steel.

**iyaroak** (anat.) — pupil, apple of the eye.

**iyakovik**, takuvitnar — pupil, apple of the eye.

**iyarorpok** — loses an eye, wounded.

**iyauservik** (anat.) — orbit of the eye.

**iye, pl.** : iyit (anat.) — eye.

**iyeluktok** — has sore eyes, (idluktok : is snow blind).

**iyerartorpok** — goes and hides.

**iyeriyok** — looks fixedly, stares.

**iyeruserk** (anat.) — opening of the temple.

**iyerutit** — spots on dog's eyes.

**iyersimayok** — is hidden, cannot be seen.

**iyerpok** — hides self.

**iyetornak** (Padl.) — an insect living in water.

**iyorpok** — laughs, mocks.

**iyorayuktok** — teases often.

**iyorosuktok** — mocker.

**iyukarpok**, eyukarpok — falls from high.

## — K —

### Introduction to Eskimo words beginning with the letter K

Eskimos seem to have a preference for words beginning with the letter K. In fact these and the words beginning with A are the most numerous. At times it is difficult to perceive the difference in sound between the usual K and the very guttural K. For convenience, we have written the very guttural K : Kr.

Here are some general ideas expressed by words beginning with K :

**KA** or **KRA** :
idea of surface : **kanga,** it's surface; **kadlerk,** at the very top.
idea of group : **kattimayut,** are together; **kattersorpok,** collects.
idea of light : **kraumayok,** it is a bright light; **kraukpat,** tomorrow.
idea of knowledge : **krau,** forehead; **krauyimayok,** knows.
idea of colour : **kraudlortok,** is white; **krernertok,** is black.
idea of being pointed : **kakiwak,** fish harpoon; **kapiwok,** pierces.
idea of being inside : **kramanitok,** is inside;
**katituyok,** has a bass voice.

**KI** or **KRI** :
idea of heat, and absence of heat : **kiagorpok,** sweats;
**kikreyok,** is frozen.
idea of wound, tearing : **kilerpok,** is wounded; **kidlalik,** has a tear.
idea of neighbourhood : **kiglinga,** its border.
idea of curling up : **kripingayok,** is twisted.
idea of hind part, rear : **kingudlermik,** at last; **kinguani,** at the rear.
idea of person : **kina ?,** who ?; **kinasingingmat,** has not found anybody.
idea of only : **kissiani,** only; **kissima,** only me; **kissimi,** only he or she.

**KO** or **KRO** :
idea of being high : **kôtsiktok,** is high; **konmuarpok,** rises in the air.
idea of surprise : **koarsarpok,** starts (from surprise);
**koglurtuarpok,** is surprised; **koksadlakpok,** is surprised.

**KU** or **KRU** :
idea of imitation of sound : **kukiut,** rifle; **kuertorpok,** coughs.
idea of passing by : **kurk,** river; **kutviorpok,** sheds tears.

## — K —

**ka** (poss. : kanga) — surface colour.

**kabjek** (anat.) (kâbjierk) — crown of the head.

**kabjerutik** — Eskimo tonsure.

**kabjerpok** (kabjarpok) — scrapes off fat from skin.

**kabjutiyok** (Okk.) — stops s.o. just in time.

**kablait** — small black berries.

**kabluk** (anat.) — eyebrow.

**kabluna** — white men (lit. : big eyebrow).

**kablunadjarpok** (-liarpok) — goes and trades at the store.

**kablunartak** — white men's clothes.

**kablursorpok** — winks v.

**kablût** — kind of slippers for iglu only.

**kabverpok,** (kagverpok) (-pa) — hoists.

**kadgek** — gathering house.

**kadgemioyok** — takes part in gathering.

**kadgeviksak** — meeting place.

**kadgitak** — snow trap for deer.

**kadgutiyok** — hits fingers against obstacle.

**kadjukpok**—hammers meat, etc.

**kadjutiyut** — play "who will hit the hardest".

**kadlaktorpok,** koertorpok — coughs.

**kadlerarpok** — water enters over board.

**kadlerk** — scabies, surface.

**kadlinartok** (Okk.) — has skin trouble.

**kadluk** — thunder.

**kadluktok** — it thunders.

**kadlût** — ladle.

**kadlungniut** (Okk.) — small bone in joint.

**kadlupidluk** — bogeyman (kind of ghost).

**kadlutiyok** — water enters boots by top.

**kadyuartok** — hammers with noise.

**kadzait** — wolves wandering and hungry.

**kaerolik** — jumping seal.

**kaersarpok** — polishes, irons clothes, etc.

**kaersautit** — polisher.

**kaertok,** (kaersuk) — solid rock.

**kagattok,** (Okk.); atkonartok — it is wavy.

**kâglaertok** — skin peels off.

**kagliwok** — comes closer.

**kagvartok** — comes up to the surface.

**kagvik** — carcajou.

**kai** (or krai) — I think so.

**kaibluarpok** — pushes in front of self.

**kaiblût** — gun cleaning rod.

**kaibjâyok** — dizzy, turns easily.

**kaipkut** — intestines without fat.

**kaippak** — shirt having no slit on sides.

**kaiptark** (Padl.), ungomiark (Aiv.) — top (plaything).

**kaivattok** — six o'clock.

**kaivittok** — turns on itself.

**kaiwût** — bit and brace.

**kak** (Okk.) — sharp point.

**kakakpok** — carries astride on shoulder.

**kakaksak** — head of nail, bolt, etc.

**kakerluk** (anat.) — under chin.

**kakertok** — iglu snow worn by wind.

**kakersertok** (kakkersertok) — skin exposed to air to bleach.

**kaki** (anat.) — nasal mucus.

**kakiaksaut** (kakkiaksaut) — liquid filter.

**kakiarsarvik** (kakkiaksavik) — purgatory.

**kakiartok** (kakkiaktok) — clear liquid, water, etc.

**kakidjarpok** — tatooes.

**kakidjut** (kakkût) — safety pin.

**kakidlarnerk** — thistle.

**kakikpok** — blows one's nose.
**kakilisartok** — is numb.
**kakinerk** — tatooings.
**kakingayok** — closes one eye to aim.
**kakituyok** — clever, intelligent.
**kakiut** — handkerchief.
**kakiusersimayok** — penetrated in skin.
**kakiviark** (anat.) kakkiviark — superior lip.
**kakiviartok** — white fish.
**kakiviarutit** — mustachio, whiskers.
**kakiwak, kakkiwak** —fish spear. harpoon.
**kakiwok** — comes out of water, to solid ice.
**kakluk** (anat.) — lower lip.
**kakortok**, kraudlurtok — is white.
**kapvik** — needle case.
**kakrayok** — is cheerful, lively.
**kakresareik**, karesareik — twins.
**kaksimayok** — seal on the ice.
**kaksungaut** — diamond (playing cards).
**kakutigut, kakutikut** — sometimes, from time to time.
**kakreakerpok** — converts himself.
**kakverpok** — hoists himself, passes over.
**kakvik** — starving place.
**kâlâdlit** — Greenlanders.
**kalaktuyuyok** — pig, hog.
**kalamiyok, kalawok** — is lying on.
**kalârtok** — it boils.
**kalaserk** (anat.) — navel.
**kalayarpok** — leans on, pressing against it.
**kalealik** — falling hair.
**kalereit** — one on top of another.
**kalertanartok** — makes one shiver with emotion.
**kâlersaut** — helps appetite.
**kaleruat** — exterior breeches.
**kalibjarpok** — dog making effort to get loose.
**kallertorpok** — piles on top one another.
**kalligauyok** (Padl.) — is touched.
**kallikpok** (Padl.) — touches.
**kallitpok** — tows boat, canoe, etc.
**kallût** or kadlût — ladle.
**kalunerk** — fat from cooked fish.
**kamâluk** — white men's shoes.
**kamanak !** — mind your business !
**kamanartok** (Okk.) — is marvelous.
**kamanartulliyok** — works marvels.
**kamanaugak** — lake formed in a river.
**kamaniktuark**, kramaniktuark — Baker Lake, N.W.T.
**kamariyok** — takes interest in.
**kamasukpok** — answers well, obeys, takes interest in.
**kamateitok** — disobedient, takes no interest in.
**kameriyok** (Okk.) — spills water.
**kamertok** — has no boots.
**kamguyok** — snores.
**kamidlartok** — takes off his shoes.
**kamik** — shoe.

**kamikpak** — long exterior socks.

**kamiktorpok**—puts on his shoes.

**kamingartok, kamingayok** — no fire at home.

**kamittok** — the fire is out.

**kammarpok** — calls dogs.

**kamorayark** (anat.) — molar tooth.

**kamotik, kamut** — sled.

**kanâlukput** — they exchange harsh words.

**kanangnark** — North wind.

**kanark** (anat.) — tibia.

**kanerk** (anat.) — mouth.

**kanayok** — kind of small fish.

**kangalak** — deer about to lose its hair.

**kangani** — on the top of.

**kangârtok** — is very sensitive.

**kangarsaut, kangarsût** — pepper, seed.

**kangarsuiyok** — spreads like pepper, sows.

**kangatarpok,** kangattarpok — lifts above the ground.

**kangelrarpok** — walks ahead of dogs.

**kangerdluk** — bay or gulf.

**kangerdlukdjuark** — Wakeham Bay, P.Q.

**kangerdlukadlak** — Wolstenholme, P.Q.

**kangerpok** — passed ahead.

**kangi** — handle, further inland.

**kangia** — butt of rifle.

**kangiark** — nephew, niece, child of two brothers.

**kangiksak** (Padl.) — necklace.

**kangidlit** — those who live further inland.

**kangmalerk** — travelling far to trade, etc.

**kangmark** — kind of dwelling; half tent, half iglu.

**kanguk** — white and blue goose.

**kangunartok** — makes one ashamed.

**kangusukpok**—is ashamed, shy.

**kanguyak** — kind of daisy.

**kanigiani** — not far from it.

**kanigiwok** — carries load ahead of people moving.

**kaniorpok** — accompanies s.o. at departure.

**kanittok** (kaningonartok) — is close by, (undesirably close by).

**kaniwaut** (anat.) — peritoneum.

**kanna** — that one which is lower.

**kannerk** — snow (falling).

**kannerpok** — it snows.

**kannernartok** — the wind is North N.E. (lit. : wind that brings snow).

**kannimayok** (Okk.) — is ill, cf. âniartok.

**kanogasârtok,** kanungayok — is mean, teases.

**kanosak** — gold or brass, (lit. : shining).

**kapiannamik !** kappianamik ! — how frightful !

**kapiannartok** — is frightening.

**kapiannartorvik** — hell.

**kapiartitok** — mirage on sea.

**kapiasarpok** — threatens.

**kapiasukpok** — is afraid.

**kâpik** — coffee, (English corr.).

**kapilanartok** — makes one lonesome.

**kapilrok**—front part of the deer.
**kapitak** — one garment over another.
**kapiyok, kapurpok** — pierces, harpoons.
**kapût** — lance, harpoon, etc.
**kaputiyok** — puts one inside the other.
**kapvik** — wolverine.
**karak, kaggak** (Okk.) — top of a mountain.
**kardjuk** — cartridge, arrow, end of harpoon.
**kardjuksak** — fish hook.
**kardjurauyak** — bullet.
**kardjurautit** — instrument to make cartridges.
**karesareik, kakresareik** — twins.
**karetak** (or : karesak) — brain.
**kaksaut** — loon.
**kargolarpok** — makes noise when eating.
**karklik** — breeches.
**karklutût** — wild duck, (flying high).
**karvik** — starving place or time.
**kârpok** — is hungry.
**karulik** — insect in water.
**kaslalapak** — clubs (playing cards).
**kassigiark** — black spotted seal.
**kassiliyok** — burns, bites, itches.
**kassukpok** — hits one's self.
**kassuktorpok** — knocks at the door.
**kassungayok** — is slack, not tight.
**kassutpok** — the wind is falling down.
**kataiyok** — lets something fall.
**katakpok** — it falls.
**katangutit** — relatives.
**katark** — frame of iglu-door, tent-door.
**katauyak** — rainbow.
**kateitok** — high voice, tenor.
**katituyok** — bass voice.
**katkareik** — two beds facing one another.
**katkariktok** — completely white.
**katkiut**—splinter under the skin.
**katsukpok** — pronounces well.
**katseogak** (Padl.) — rolled oats.
**katsiogiorpok** — mixes with spoon.
**k'atsoak** (Padl.) (anat.) — biceps.
**kattak** — pail.
**kattauyak** — barrel.
**kattersiutiksak** — crop, etc. (to be picked up).
**kattersibvik** — time or place of gathering crop.
**kattersorpok** — is gathering things.
**kattibvik** — shelve, etc.
**kattidgait** (anat.) — thorax, bust.
**kattigarpok,** (krattigarpok) — pierces the thorax.
**kattigiarpok**, parearpok — goes and meet.
**kattik** — bird carcass, bones.
**kattiktalik** — Fullerton, N.W.T.
**kattimabvik** — place of gathering.
**kattimayut** — are together.
**kattinerk** — meeting of rivers, etc.
**kattingolarpok** — dog is grunting.
**kattukpok** — plays drum, drumming.

**kattutiyut,** kattutsiyut — are associates.

**kau** — walrus hide.

**kaugarpok** — crushes.

**kauk** — white part of egg.

**kaukpok** — hits, cuts cards.

**kaulertanerpok** — makes one shiver with fear.

**kauliut** — stick used to soften boots.

**kaupkoark** — device to dry fox skins.

**kausertok, krausertok** — is wet.

**kautak** — stone, etc., used as hammer.

**kautauyak** — iron hammer.

**kautauyarvik** — anvil.

**kaviserk** — scale fish, envelope of heart.

**kavisilik** — fish with scales.

**kayaiyok** — abandons behind.

**kayak** — Eskimo canoe.

**kayauyok** — drowned, lost in water.

**kayok** — reddish colour, brown.

**kayok** — soup, meat juice, reddish colour.

**kayôktak** — Eskimo ladle.

**kayusiyok** — perseveres.

**kawâkpok** — has eaten his fill, is uneasy.

**kekarpok** — is stopped, is idle.

**kekertak** — island.

**kekertaugardjuk** — Bear Island (close to Southampton Island).

**kekrarpok** — freezes to death.

**kekreyok** — is frozen.

**kellakpok, kellaksorpok** — ties.

**kellaksautit** — line, string, etc., to tie with.

**kemmerdluk** — vertebral spine.

**Kemmerut** — Lake Harbour, Baffin Land.

**kemmukserark** — sled on the move.

**kenalogak** (kelalogak) — beluga, white whale.

**kenepayok** — is wet.

**kessertut** — small shrubs, branches.

**keviarpok** — turns one's head

**kevittok** — is discouraged.

**keviok** — hair short like down.

**kia ?** — whose is it ?

**kiakiak**—I know not whose it is.

**kiagorpok** (Padl.) — sweats; syn. : aumidjakpok.

**kiaperok** — part of deer close to the neck.

**kiasik** (anat.) — shoulder blade, omoplate.

**kiasiyok** — loses its hair.

**kibgak** (Okk.) — workman, servant.

**kiblereak, kriblereak** — mica, shining.

**kiblariktok** — is shining.

**kibliktok** — wounded profoundly.

**kiblût,** koblût — crosscut saw.

**kibvatsiyok** — can lift it.

**kibvayok** — lifts an object.

**kidgavik** — small kind of hawk.

**kidjaktok** — is rough to touch.

**kidjakatsik** — porcupine.

**kidlaiyarpok** — mends nets, etc.

**kidlak** — a tearing, an opening, etc.

**kidlauyak** — bay in lower stream.

**kidlernartok** — very sharp, could inflict wound.

**kidlinermiut** — Eskimos of the Mackenzie.
**kidlinerk** — extreme.

**kigluk** — outdoor fireplace.
**kiggertarpok**, kriggertarpok — steps and dances.
**kiggertok** — snow house that drips.
**kiggiark** — beaver.
**kiggierikpok** — tears with teeth.
**kiggitsiyok** — pinches.
**kiglerk**, kidlerk — extreme opposite, edge, etc.
**kiglik** (Okk.) — witness.
**kiglilukpok** — lies.
**kiglukpok**, igluanut piyok — revenges.
**kiglisiwok** (Okk.), unnerpok — gives testimony.
**kiguseriwok** — has teeth trouble.
**kigudjariktok** — has good teeth.
**kigusertait** — false teeth.
**kigut**, pl. : kigutit — tooth.
**kigutaerpok** — has tooth pulled out.
**kiisiwok** — bites.
**kiingmiarpok** — holds with his teeth.
**kiijakattar** — trap, spring trap.
**kikalukpok** — noisy walking on hard snow.
**kikiangiyaut** — nail-drawer.
**kikierk** — nail.
**kikiakpok** v. — nails.
**kikiersit** — sergeant (OIC RCMP).
**kikparpok** — attracts fish with bait, etc.
**kiksaut** — deer fat from intestines.
**kiktorartok** — tears, breaks.
**kiktoreark** — mosquito.
**kiktorealitak** — mosquito net.
**kilerok** (anat.) — scar.
**kilerpok** — wounds himself.
**kilikpak** — coat of arms.
**kiliorsarpok** — removes paint etc.
**kiliutak** — scraper for skins, etc.
**kiluarpok** — unsews, kiluartok, unsewn.
**kilugutak** — seam protector.
**kiluk** — seam, sewed.
**kilulukpok** — sews badly.
**kilurut** — design covering seam.
**kilusikpok** — goes further in the iglu.
**kimalerk** — women's knife (very sharp).
**kimmik** (anat.) — heel.
**kimmikrok** (anat.) — tibia bone.
**kina ?** — who ?
**kînaksarpok** — sharpens.
**kînark** (anat.) — face.
**kînarluktok** — makes a bad face.
**kînaut** — sharpening stone.
**kinauyak** — piece of money.
**kinerk** — front part of Eskimo female dress.
**kinersiwok** — thick as oil.
**kingait** — Cape Dorset.
**kinganerk** — dregs of mug.
**kingark** — mountain.
**kingârok** — hill.
**kingilik** — without teeth.
**kingmait** — inner jaws.
**kingorak** — its rear part.
**kingu** — after that.
**kingudlerk** — the last.

**kingupiusarpok** — falls backwards, steps backwards.

**kinguraiyok** — loses time, is late.

**kinguvak** — line of descendants.

**kinguvasiktok** — is slow, behind time.

**kinguvangokattigeit.** — descendants from.

**kinguyok** — tips over (canoe etc.).

**kinikpok** — wets.

**kiniyiyok** — women following taboo after child-birth.

**kinnark,** kinark — edge of a blade.

**kioyok** — answers.

**kipingoyok** — feels lonesome.

**kipiyok** — cuts.

**kipjautit** — scissors.

**kipkark** — bone for dog to chew.

**kipminak** — red sour berries.

**kippisidjut** — saw.

**kippariksaut** — square (instrument).

**kippariktok** — is square.

**kippark** — has a square end.

**kippudjarektuk** — two men who trade.

**kippukpakpok** — commits adultery.

**kippukpok** — exchanges.

**kippungayok** — cross of St Andrew.

**kipputit,** kurlurtok — cascades.

**kisartok** — is anchored.

**kisaut** — anchor.

**kissermiorpok** — is solitary, alone.

**kissi** — alone.

**kissiani** — only, however.

**kissima** — only me.

**kissitidjutit** — numbers used.

**kissitsiyok** — counts.

**kisuk ?** (Okk.) — what is it ?

**kîta** — just a little.

**kitkatit** (Padl.) — weights for nets.

**kitterodlerk** — little white worms.

**kittorarpok,** kiktorarpok — breaks, (as string, etc.)

**kitunitgarpit ?** — where do you come from ?

**kivadlit** — those people in the south.

**kiviyok** — sinks.

**kîwok, kîsiwok** — bites.

**koadjuitok** — round sewing needle.

**koakdjuk** — triangle.

**koakdjulik** — triangular needle.

**koaiyakrikpok** — slips on ice, etc.

**koaiyanartok** — is slippery.

**koaiyanaikutit** — device to prevent slipping.

**koak** — frozen hard meat (raw).

**koakoak** (Padl.) — raven; syn. tulugak.

**koaktorpok** — eats frozen meat (raw).

**koartait** — small worms in intestines.

**koasak** — new formed ice, (on fresh water lake).

**koarsarpok** — starts (from surprise).

**koayok** — copulates.

**koblorpok** — divides, splits.

**kobluitok** — is without thumb.

**kobluk,** kubluk — thumb.

**koblurnilik** — splitted object.

**kobverinerk** — baptism.
**kobverinayok** — baptizes.
**kobveriyok** — pours liquid on.
**kobvitit, kobvivik** — funnel, tap.
**kobviait** (Net.) — fish nets.
**kodjangayok** — is upside down, head downwards.
**kodlerk** — the highest, the lamp.
**kodlikodliak** — plover.
**koertorpok** — coughs.
**koglureak** (Okk.) — snake.
**koglurpok** — folds lengthways.
**koinaksarpok** — tickles.
**koinaktok**, koinaktuyuyok — tickled.
**koiyok** — urinates.
**kôkak !** — it is but a joke.
**kokârtok** — it is not clear, is fading.
**kokernartok** — loud noise, (hurting ears).
**kokidjut, kokiut** — rifle, gun.
**kôkiktok** — strait.
**koko** — chocolate (English corruption of cocoa, etc.).
**kokoalarpok** — is trumpetting.
**kokoarut** — trumpet.
**koksadlakpok** — starts (from surprise).
**koksukpok** — hump back; syn: piku.
**koksortok** — is yellow.
**kôktok** — has small bottom.
**koktorak** — thigh bone, femur.
**koli**, (kolâ) — top of.
**kolikangituinnartok** — nine.
**kolingiluartok** — nine.
**kolit** — ten.
**kollaitok** — open boat.
**kollangorpok** — passes above, over.
**kollarauyak** — shelve.
**kollarpok** — hesitates.
**kollereit** — one above the other.
**kolligak** — thin snow over trap; syn.: talugak.
**kolliktar** — overcoat.
**komak** — louse.
**komikpok**, kromikpok — itches (has arm inside clothes).
**komilaktok** — it itches.
**komiukpok** — carries something inside clothes.
**kongasinerk** (anat.) — neck.
**kongasinilitak** — handkerchief around neck etc.
**konwakpok** — smiles; syn.: kungotorpok.
**konwasuitok** — never smiles.
**kopanoar** — snow bird.
**kopertok** — has hair divided well.
**kopilkriktok** — has hair well divided.
**kopilrok** — worm (of all kinds).
**koppak, koppako** — one half.
**koppiyok** — divided in two.
**kopput** — milky way.
**kopuangayok** — has eyes slanted upwards.
**kôrvik** — chamber-pot.
**korvertarvik** — rubbish pail, refuse bin etc.
**kotakpok** — stammers.
**kotok** (anat.) — collar bone.
**kotserk** (anat.) — hip bone, pelvis.
**kotsiktok** — is placed high, is high.
**kôtuyok** — walks with toes pointing inside.
**koversak** (anat.) — white of the eye.

**koversertok** — the white of the eye is wounded.

**kowiyok** — pours liquid.

**krainyok**[1] — comes.

**krainkoyiyok** — calls some one.

**krakorpok** — crunches.

**krakugo ?** — when ? (in the future).

**krakugoluktar** — always (in the future).

**kramani** — in there.

**kramaniktuark** — Baker Lake, N.W.T.

**kramguyok** — snores.

**kranga ?** — when (in the past).

**krangaluktar** — always (in the past).

**kranganitak** — a very long time ago.

**kranok ?** — how ?

**kranoengitok** — has no trouble, (all is well).

**kranoetok** — misfortune.

**kraorpok** — breaks off ice adhering to pail.

**krappuk** — foam.

**krapsirarpit** — how many did you get ?

**krapsikiak** — I do not know how many.

**krapsit ?** — how many ?

**krarpok** — it bursts.

**krarsortok** — blistered.

**kraterk** — ivory end of harpoon handle.

**kratkrak** — top of mountain.

**krau (anat.)** — forehead, light, brightness.

**kraudlortok** — is white.

**kraumak** — daylight.

**kraumakraut** — produces light.

**kraumaksarpok** — shows light to s.o.

**kraumalak** — lightning, flash.

**kraumayok** — it is daylight, it is bright.

**kraurut** — frontal band (decorative).

**krausertok** — is wet.

**krau-tamat** — daily, every day.

**krauyimayok, krauyiyok** — knows.

**krauyisaut** — watch, clock, etc.

**krauyisaiyok** — learns.

**krauyiyatuartit ?** — is that all you know ?

**kreanartak** — blue fox.

**kreanartok** — makes one cry.

**kreayok** — cries and yells.

**krerk** — grey hair.

**kregatayok** — is rigid.

**kregertarpok, kiggertarpok** — makes little leaps, hops, etc.

**kregluk** — spinal marrow.

**krejuk** — wood.

**krejukut** — box.

**kreko,** krekut — cement.

**krelanartorpok** — desires intensely.

**krelerpok** — is very thirsty.

**krelukpok** — yelps (dog).

**kreluliyok, kreluyiyok** — has cramps.

**kremaibvik** — cache left behind.

**kremarortartok** — soft ground.

---

[1] The following words beginning with kr could have been written with k instead. The k however would not render the distinctly different pronounciation of these words from all others beginning with k. The Eskimos pronounce them with a much deeper guttural sound very similar indeed to kr.

**kremayok** — flees.
**krematût** — cache.
**kremayarpok** — flees.
**kremawok** — leaves.
**kremereak** — eye-lash.
**kremeruarpok** — looks at pictures.
**kremikpok** — hangs himself.
**kremigosukpok** — is jealous.
**kremukserpok** — leads a dog team.
**kremuksit** — team and sled on the move.
**krenerpok, krenorarpok** — looks for, seeks.
**krenuk** — frost (new) on sea ice.
**krenutuyok** — insistent beggar.
**kreorpok** — cuts tobacco, etc.
**kreorvik** — board to cut tobacco, etc.
**krepariyok** — hates.
**krepanartok** — hateful.
**krepasuitok** — never discouraged.
**krepidjutit** — boot laces.
**krepik** — quilt.
**krepiktok** — is in bed, under quilt.
**krepiluktok** — refuses.
**krepingayok** — is twisted.
**krepingut** (anat.) — appendix.
**krerkra** — its middle.
**krekoa, kerkoa** — sea weed.
**krernermiut** — people of Baker Lake region.
**krernertok** — is black.
**krersorpok** — is epileptic.
**kresaroak** (anat.) — envelope of stomach.
**kresik** — skin of sea animals.
**kresiuyak** — leather.
**kresuk** — hook.
**kresuktautit** — hook used as brake.
**kresukpok** v. — hooks, scratches, etc.
**kretikisautit** — girdle.
**kretulisarpok** — softens.
**kretuttok** — is supple, soft.
**kridlok** — carcass.
**kriksimigarpok** — scowls at s.o.
**kriktorarpok,** kiktorarpok — breaks line or string, tears clothes, etc.
**krilerte** — hair-do with sticks.
**krilak** — palate, sky, ceiling.
**krilaliarpok** — above the horizon, up in the sky.
**krilammi** — soon.
**krilanartok** — is desirable.
**krilarmiutak** — some one in the sky.
**krilarmuarpok** — same as krilaliarpok.
**krilaut** — Eskimo drum.
**kriluak** (Padl.) — net for hare.
**krilulak** — line helping dogs.
**kriluliyok** — has cramps.
**krimiutiksak** — line at top of nets.
**krimukdjuk** — small snowdrifts.
**krinerksit** — tonsils.
**kringalik** — eider duck.
**kringak** — nose.
**kringanartok** — brillant, (makes one contract face).
**kringmerk** — dog.
**kringmerdjuark** — horse.
**kringork** — skin of deer's forehead.
**krinrut, krinrutit** — telescope.

**kripikpok** — ties with a rope.
**kripsiyok** — is in bad humour.
**kriptaerpok** — is well awake, in good humour.
**kritkutit,** pattait—playing cards.
**kritserarpok** — spits.
**krittiraiyok** — is in the middle.
**kriterdlerk** — middle finger.
**kriterdlermigarpok** — despises, (shows it by sign with finger).
**kriterdlerut** — ring of middle finger.
**kritiani** — in the middle.
**kritigutiksak** — toy.
**kritikpok** — plays.
**krittuark** — nine (playing cards), nine o'clock.
**krittongak** — child of.
**kromak** — worm in dear skin, tape worm, etc.
**kromikpok** — holds between his legs.
**kronuyok,** kronutpok — refuses.
**kudlût** — top block of snow house.
**kudvit** — tears from eyes.
**kudviorpok** — sheds tears.
**kuinakpok** — tickles.
**kuiyok** — urinates.
**kujariwok** v. — thanks.
**kujdjuk,** kugdjuk — swan.
**kukik** — claws, finger nails.
**kukiksak** — silex, flint.
**kukilitit** (Padl.) — pins.
**kukiliut** — tooth-pick.
**kikiuyak** — scales of fish.
**kukukpak,** nassauyak — point of hood.
**kukusi** — pig, hog.
**kulavak** — female deer without fawn.
**kumuyok** — has no handle.
**kunerpok** — pulls back in hood.
**kungisilitak** — neck tie, handkerchief, etc.
**kungniarpok** — looks at pictures, etc.
**kungutorpok** — smiles; syn.: kunwaktok.
**kunigor** — short downlike hair.
**kunikpok** — kisses, smells.
**kuniktipok** — forces to converge.
**kunuyok** — refuses.
**kupiktaurpuk** — two having a three legged race.
**kupilruyak** — rice.
**kupnerk** — opening in the ice, crack.
**kupniut** — ripsaw.
**kurk** — river.
**kurkdjuark,** kôrkdjuark — Churchill, Chimo, (lit.: big river).
**kurkluktok** — cascades, Coppermine River.
**kûrliorpok** — digs a ditch, etc.
**kusserk** — drop of liquid.
**kusserpok** — drips.
**kussugak** — stalactites of ice.
**kussuyok** — is a coward.
**kuttik** (anat.) — pelvis bone.
**kuttingnerk** — stalacmite of ice.
**kutsok** — tar.
**kuvianartok** — makes one happy.
**kuvianartorvik** — heaven.
**kuviasuguserk** — gift, received a gift at festival.
**kuviasukpok** -- is glad, happy.
**kuviasungnerk** — happiness.

**kuvisortok** — is liquid.
**kuyariyok** — is thankful.
**kuyana,** kujanna — never mind, no matter.
**kuyannamik !** — thanks ! I thank you !
**kuyannakuni** (Padl., K.) — thanks ! I thank you !
**kuyasiutit** — thanksgiving prayers.
**kuyasuitok** v. — is ungrateful, never says thanks.

## — M —

### Introduction to Eskimo words beginning with the letter M

Here are some ideas suggested by the words beginning with M :

idea of pain : **mâlârpok,** yelling (as a dog); **maikpok,** it hurts.
idea of covering a surface : **mâmi,** thin skin; **manerark,** field.
idea of special place : **mâni,** here; **maniyok,** yields.
idea of good : **mamartok,** tastes good; **mamiarnartok,** is hateful.
idea of root : **mangukpok,** penetrates; **mauyak,** soft snow.
idea of localisation : **mîkpok,** v. lands, sets.
idea of movement : **momerpok,** v. dances.
idea of extraction : **millukpok,** suckles.

## — M —

**mabjarpok** — scrapes a skin, makes it thinner.
**mabjulertok** — scar.
**mabliarpok** — patches (garment, etc.)
**madlernartok, madlertok** — the sea is wavy.
**magperpok** — opens the cover, the book etc.
**mai !** (excl. of admiration) — well !
**maikattar !** — how slow he is !
**maiksuk !** (excl.) — how despicable !
**maikpok** — it hurts when you touch it.
**majorarvik** — stairs, etc., time to go up.
**majorarpok** — goes up.
**majorarvia** — Ascension of O.L.J.C.
**majorautit** — stairs, ladder, etc.
**majorpok** — goes upstairs, up hill, etc.
**makkak** — cranium.
**makkauyak** — basin, bowl.
**makkibvik** — time or place to get up.
**makkitpok** — gets up, resuscitates.
**makkititsiwok** — causes one to get up.
**makkiserk** (anat.) — pelvis bone.
**makôktok, makkoktok** — is young.
**makpatark** — snow block cut on the flat.
**makperpok** — opens cover, book, etc.
**makpertokrak, makpertak** — book.
**makreitok** — is absent, travelling away.

**makreyok** — suppurates.
**makri** — pus.
**makrittok** — carries kayak alone.
**maktark** — whale skin.
**makuktok,** makroktok, nipaluktok — it rains.
**makutsierk** — side.
**mâlarpok** — yells (dog).
**mâlasi** — molasses (English corrupt.).
**malgeyok** (-reyok) — has twins.
**malgoalik** (-roalik) — has two (vg. wives).
**malgoertarluni** — does it twice.
**malgoilugit** — divides them in two groups.
**malgok, malrok** — two.
**malgokosartut** — they are two by two.
**mallik** — wave.
**mallikpok** — follows.
**malliksarpok** — tries to follow vg. game.
**malliktauyok** — is pursued, followed.
**mallugiwok, mallugosukpok** v. — suspects, doubts.
**mamaksaut** — sirup, honey, etc.
**mamâlik** (Okk.) — graniteware.
**mamartok** — is good to taste or smell.
**mamaut** — dug of cow, dog, etc.
**mamautalitak** — apron.
**mamaitok** — tastes or smells bad.
**mameriyok** — hates.
**mamerpok** — revenges.
**mami** (anat.) — thin skin, new skin, etc.
**mamianartok** — it is unfortunate.
**mamiasukpok** v. — hates.
**mamiatsakpok** — has hatred for.
**mamituyok** — has a thick mami, skin.
**manark** — line and bait (still l.).
**manangayok** — holds head leaning on one side.
**manerark** — ground, field.
**maneraungitok** — uneven ground.
**manerk** — moss.
**mangatpok** — flees away (game etc.).
**mangiptark** — table cloth; a covering.
**mangitpok** — tears with teeth.
**mângukpok** — penetrates.
**mângut, mângok** — root, anything half in, half out.
**mâni** — here.
**maningmiyok** — makes no resistance.
**manigutiyok** — flatters to obtain something.
**maniilak,** (-lait) — gear.
**maniilrok** — rough ice.
**maniyok** — is easy to reach, (lit.: stays there).
**manna** — now.
**mannakut** — at the same moment.
**mannamit** — from now on.
**mannik** — egg.
**manniliorpok** — lays eggs.
**mannit** — month of eggs: June.
**manu** — threshold, underchin.
**manuilitak** — drip-flap.
**mapkikpok** — cleans clothes.

**mapkisarpok** — cleans by scraping clothes.
**mapsak** (anat.) — spleen.
**mapteriyok** — sews again.
**marrak** — clay, mud, etc.
**massakpok** — is wet.
**massik** — fish gill.
**massulingayok** — handle not firmly fixed.
**mat'na** (Padl.) — I thank you.
**mattarpok** — takes off clothes, harness.
**mattareikutit** — device to stop dogs from unharnessing.
**mattitautit** — fish nets.
**mattitautitorpok** — visits nets (mattitausiarpok).
**matu** — door, cover etc.
**matuerpok** — opens door etc.
**matuerut** — cover-opener.
**matulik** — has a cover (box, tin, etc.).
**matuserpok** — dresses wounds, covers.
**matutiksak** — wound bandages.
**matuyok** — closes door, puts cover on.
**maukpak** (Net.) — football; also: arksak.
**maulerpok** — hunts at seal holes.
**maunark** — end of fingers.
**maungarpok** — comes over here.
**mauyak** — soft snow.
**mauyasiorpok** — travels in soft snow.
**mauyasiutit** — snow shoes.
**merearnartok** — emetic, induces vomiting.
**merearpok** — vomits.
**merkringayok** — has wrinkled skin.
**merkroiyiyok** — takes off hair from skin.
**merksorpok** — sews.
**miagorpok** — howls (dog).
**mianersiyok** — watches, guards.
**mianersiye** — watchman, guardian.
**mikkakpok** — gnaws.
**mikkigak** — raw meat.
**mikkigiark** (Okk.) — fox trap.
**mikkikpok** v. — bites.
**mikilak** — the smallest.
**mikilerark** — the ring finger.
**mikilerarut** — ring for finger.
**mikiyok** — is small, little.
**mikliark** — umbilical cord.
**mikliwok** — gets smaller.
**mikpok** — sets, (bird or aircraft).
**miksa** — between, miksani.
**miksikarnerk** (Okk.) — truth.
**miktauyok** — does not receive part in food distribution.
**millik** — cover or door.
**millorpok** — lapidates.
**millugiark** — fly.
**milluk** — nipple (of breasts).
**millukaut** — nipple for nursing bottle, lollipop etc.
**millukpok** — suckles.
**mimerk** — buttock.
**minariwok** — carries s.t. home from banquet.
**minerk, minik** — small rain, light rain.
**minguarsit, minguarut** — paint brush.
**mingaut** — paint.

**mingereak** — kind of fish.

**mingoarpok** — paints.

**mingoertorpok** (Padl.) — is tired cf takrayok.

**mingoerserpok, minroerserpok** — takes a rest.

**mingolertok** — small snow drift.

**mingût** — paint.

**minitsiyok** — has no part in food distribution.

**miniyok** — it rains slightly, it drizzles.

**minuk** — light frost.

**miorpok** — howls.

**miperpok** — is late.

**mipkut, mipkô** — dried meat.

**misertok** (Padl.) — hypocrite (cf. pitsiartsertortok).

**missiarpok** — denies, knowing it is true.

**missikpok** — jumps down.

**missuk** — dew.

**missukpok** — soaks in water.

**mitârpok** — mocks.

**mitautiksak** — object of mockery.

**mitaut** — mockery.

**mîterk** — duck.

**mîterniut** — shotgun.

**mîtiglerαut** — flick of the finger.

**mîtingidjut** — gun trigger.

**mîtkrut** — needle.

**mîtsimayok** — is setting on water, etc.

**mitsuktok** — is covered with water, (cf missuktok).

**momerpok** — turns from one side to the other.

**momerpok** — dances the eskimo way.

**mominguarpok** — dances the white-men's way.

**mominguarvik** — dance hall.

**momisidjut** — spatula.

**morjuktok** — water flowing from a lake.

**morjungnerk** — outlet of a lake.

**mulorpok** — is late.

**mungôwok** (Okk.) — is discouraged.

## — N —

### Introduction to Eskimo words beginning with the letter N

Here are some ideas suggested by the words beginning with the letter N :

**Words beginning with NA** expresses the idea of :
place : **nani,** where; **namut ?** where to ?; **nangertok,** is standing.
**Words beginning with NI** or **NERK** expresses the idea of something perceptible by the senses :
by the sight : **niptayok,** is seen; **nipamayok,** is long unseen.
by the hearing : **nippi,** sound of the voice; **nipjarpok,** makes a sound.
by the sense of smell : **niorsitok,** inhales and smells.
by the taste: **nerkri,** meat; **nerrewok,** eats.
by the touch : **nerromiktok,** is smooth to the touch.
**Words beginning with NU** and coming from the **"terminalis case" : NUT** (cf. app. II, 153), express the idea of :
what is seen : **nuya,** hair; **nuvak,** mucus from the nose; **nuiyok,** comes out.
what moves : **nuuktok,** is on the move; **nukterpok,** changes place, moves.

## — N —

**naak** — abdomen, belly.

**naaktok** — is obese.

**naarluktok** — has a belly-ache.

**naarsiut** — medecine for belly-ache.

**nabgoak** — articulation, joint.

**nabgut, nuktak** — crack in the ice.

**nabluartok** — has trouble with one's knee.

**nabluk** — joint of the knee.

**nâdjeriwok** — has abdomen trouble.

**nadjuk** — horn of animal.

**nadlerkotauwok** — is worthy of.

**nadlikartok** — it is time.

**nadlikangitok** — has no equal.

**nadluarpok** — fishes with line.

**naertok** — leans head on one side.

**naertorpok** — keeps dogs quiet during hunt.

**nagga, nakka** — no.

**naggarpok** — says no.

**naggavik** — cribbage board, counter.

**nagligosukpok** — loves, pities.

**nagliktartok** — is very charitable.

**naglikpok** — loves.

**naglingnartok** — is lovable.

**naglingnerk** — love, charity.

**nagvarpok** — finds, (even if not seeking).

**nailiyok** — shortens.

**naimayok, naiyok** — scents, smells.

**naiperkutigeit** — born at about the same time.

**naisarpok** — counts one, two, three.

**naisautit,** ublursiutit — calendar.

**naitok** — is short.

**najak, nayak** — sister of a male.

**najorpok** — lives with.

**nakit ?** — where from ?

**nakka** — no.

**nakkapok** — breaks through, (vg. ice).

**nakkasuk** — bladder.

**nakkasungnark** — calf of leg.

**nakkatak,** (nakatak) — foresight of a rifle.

**nakkertok** — goes fast, quick, far.

**nakkersarpok** — goes faster and faster.

**nakkîtok** — falls close by, not far.

**nakkoriwok** — congratulates.

**nakkorami** (Okk.) — I thank you.

**nakkorsarpok** — is happy.

**nakkoyarpok,** nakroyarpok — despises.

**nâklisimayok** — has empty stomach.

**nakoarpok** — acts well.

**nakpok, narpok** — stumbles on (naarpok).

**nakritarpok** — plays organ, uses typewriter.

**nakritaut** — organ, typewriter.

**nakritarut** — line to tie load on sled.

**nakritpok** — presses (to tie).

**naksak** — valley.

**naksarpok, nerksarpok** — brings with him.

**naksiusarpok** — receives through commission.

**naksiusiwok** — gives commission.

**naksitarpok** — says no, (making sign with nose).

**nakterpok** — hooks v.

**naktikpok** — is hooked.

**nakungayok** — is cross-eyed.

**nâlaut** — radio.

**nâlegak** — lord, master.

**nâlegaunerk** — domination.

**nâlekte** — radio-operator.

**nâlektok nâlaktok** — listens, obeys.

**naluark** — skin, whitened outdoors.

**nalugalarpok** v. — swims.

**nalugpok v.** — swims.

**nalunaikutak** — sign.

**nalunailiyok** — makes signs, approves.

**nalunartok** — is hard to understand.

**nalurterut** — something to guess, riddle, etc.

**naluyok** — does not know.

**nâmaksiyok, nâmaktok** — it is sufficient, enough.

**naneraut** — lamp, lantern.

**nanertak** — bear cub.

**nanganartok, nanranartok** — marvelous.

**nangerpok** — is standing.

**nangianartok** — is dangerous, is to be feared.

**nangiărpok** — is afraid.

**nangmakpok** — carries on shoulder.

**nangmaut** — sack for carrying objects.

**nangminek** — him or her-self.

**nangmineriwâ** — has it for his own use.

**nani ?** — where ?

**nanuyait** — caterpillars.

**nanuk** — polar bear.

**nanurak** — polar bear skin.

**napaiyok** — is erected, strait, (vg. pole).

**napareak** — pole.

**nâpartak**, ikkumayak (Padl.) — candle.

**nâpartarvik** — candlestick.

**napârtok** — tree.

**napârtolik** — forest.

**napayararpok** — with head downwards.

**napayok** — is standing vertically.

**napittartok** — double-barreled shotgun.

**napiyok** — is broken.

**napkigosuktok** — has pity on.

**napkotingitok** — is too weak.

**nappak** — half.

**nappatak** (Okk.) — fox.

**nappu** — cross bar of sled.

**nappuliut** — line or sinew uniting cross bars of sled.

**napsiktok** — breakable.

**nârpok** — stumbles v.

**narreak, narreaksak** — bait for trap, etc.

**narrearpok** — smells the bait.

**narromanerk** — narrowness in river etc.

**narronikut** (-niko) — is put aside, neglected.

**narroyok** — despises.

**narksiktok** — denies with sign of the nose.

**nassak** — head-gear, hood, cap or hat.

**nassarmiutak** — decoration of head-gear.

**nassarpok** — puts on hood or cap.

**nassaerpok** — takes off hood or cap.

**nassauyak** — pointed end of hood.

**nasittok** — exploring from a high place.

**natakrut** (anat.) — cartilage.

**natkosukpok** — has pity.

**natkrikpok** — is hooked.

**natserk or netserk**, netjerk — seal.

**natterk** — floor.

**natternak** — plain; open country.

**natteroviktok** — ground-drift.

**nauk ?** — where ?

**nauk, nakka** — no.

**nauligak** — lance, harpoon.

**nauligarpok** — harpoons.

**nautiyomayok** — is spare.

**nautsertorpok** — pays much attention, explores.

**nauyak** — gull, name of Repulse Bay.

**nauyawak** — large gull.

**nauyeôlertok** — is beginning pregnancy.

**nâvikpok** — empties container.

**nâwok** — it is tinished.

**nayagarpok** — is half asleep.

**nayudlerpok** — keeps house for others.

**nayurpok** — keeps with, is with.

**nayurterut**, nayorterut — The Ark of the Covenant.

**neatut !** — I was joking !

**nedlikartok** — it is time to, has its equal.

**neksartok, nerksartok** — carries with self.

**nektoralik** — eagle.

**nektorark** — line between dogs and sled.

**nellâ**, nellani — facing opposite.

**nellautpok** v. — guesses.

**nellautaiyok** v. — prophesies.

**nellaugiarit** (imp.) — try and guess.

**nellâyok** — is in bed, stretched on floor.

**nellekareik** — two things equal.

**nellerkpta ?** — which one of us ?

**nelliat ?** — which ?

**nellipsartok** — facing opposite.

**nenniyok** — finds after searching.

**nerdleogak** (Padl.) — biscuit.

**nerdlingôyok** — is stingy with food etc.

**nerdlukpok** — is bent.

**nergiut** — land animal.

**nerkeitorpok** — receives food ration.

**nerkri** — food, meat.

**nerkriksak** — food, edible.

**nerkriyaiyok** — takes game.

**nerkritortailibvik** — day of abstinence.

**nerlerk** — goose (canadian).

**nerrebvik** — where one eats.

**nerrek** — hole gnawed by mice etc.

**nerreliktak** (anat.) — uvula.

**nerretailibvik** — day of fasting.

**nerretorarpok** — has the hiccups.

**nerretunerk** — gluttony.

**nerrevikdjuark** — banquet.

**nerreyok** — eats.

**nerriukpok** — hopes v.

**nerriungnerk** — hope.

**nerroadlerpok** — chooses best for self.

**nerrokak** — second stomach of deer.

**nerrokiktok** — is narrow.

**nerromiktok** — is smooth, soft to touch.

**nerrotuyok** — is wide open.

**nertorpok** — praises.

**nertuark** — is strong, powerful.

**netserk**, netjerk — seal.

**netsikutit** — clothes made of seal skin.

**nia'a** (Padl.) — thus.

**niakrok** (anat.) — head.

**niakrongosiutit** — remedy against headache.

**niakrouyak** (Okk.) — bread.

**niakrorut**, niakrût — crown.

**nigapterpok** — is entangled.

**niggielik** — shawl.

**niggierk** — South-East wind.

**niggiet**, nikjet — fringes.

**nigiut** — spider.

**niglasuktok** — weather becoming colder.

**nigliktok** — is cooled.

**niglisuitok** — thermos bottle.

**nigorpok** — goes around to avoid.

**nikadlorpok** — is sad.

**nikayok** — has pity.

**nikipok, nikitartok** — each in turn.

**nikobjarpok** — lifts self on tip of toes.

**nikovikpok** — is standing.

**nikpârpok** — waits at seal holes.

**niksârpok** v. — belches.
**niksiarpok** — attracts towards self.
**niksik** — hook.
**niksiktok** — is hooked.
**niksitartok** — snap.
**niktarpok** — makes soundings.
**nilark, nilak** — ice (to be melted for water).
**nilauyak** (Padl.) — glass.
**nilernait** — beans (baked).
**nimnârpok** — agitated, never quiet.
**nimerk, nimiut** — something to tie with.
**nimniolerpok** — all the place is taken.
**ningarpok** — gets angry.
**ningarsareitok** — irascible.
**ningarsarpok** — makes others angry, voluntarily.
**ningatsuitok** — patient.
**ningauk** — son-in-law.
**ningerpok** — receives result of others' hunt.
**ningimnartok** — girl (not yet pubescent).
**ningiorkoaksak** — old woman.
**ningitsiyok** — lowers nets into water.
**ningoyok** — thick liquid.
**niogarpok** — rubs in, (vg. ointment).
**nioraibvik** — wharf.
**nioraiyok** — unloads a boat.
**niordluk** — eddy of water.
**niorpok** — swallows liquid, sips.
**niortitok** — is bending.
**niovgutiksak** — trade articles.
**nioverpok** — trades v.
**niovervik** — trading store.
**niovgoyok** — travels far.
**nipaluktok** — it rains.
**nipamayok** — overdue.
**nipingmat-sikrinerk** — sun set.
**nipingayok** — adheres, sticks, etc.
**nipiterut, nippiut** — glue, paste, etc.
**nipitjaekut, (nipidjaekut)** — protector against adherence.
**niplerpok** — makes noise.
**nippaitok** — makes no noise, is silent.
**nippangerpok** — silences s.o.
**nippjarnak !** (imp.) — shut your mouth ! be silent !
**nippjartitak** — organ, harmonium.
**nippik** — voice, sound.
**niptaitok** — it is foggy, (poor visibility).
**niptatsiartok** — good visibility.
**niptayok** — can be seen.
**nipterk** — fog.
**niputiyok** — causes one to perish.
**nirknark** — white moss.
**niuk** (anat.) — leg.
**niungayok** — is crooked.
**niuvok, nuivok** — comes out.
**nivaotark** — shovel.
**nivertarpok** — rocks in a chair.
**niverpok** — lean backwards.
**niviasar** — young girl.
**nivingayok** — is hanged.
**niviorpok** — is anxious.
**niviugak** — fly.
**nivralayok** — is lying on his back, in bed, etc.
**noak** — niece: child of a female's sister.

**noatsiyok** (Okk.) — gathers scattered objects.

**nogak, norrak** — fawn.

**nogalik, norralik** — doe with fawn.

**nokarsarpalut** — mandolin.

**nokarsimayok** — is tight.

**noversak** (Padl.) — white men s clothes; kablunartak.

**nubvidjut** — needle hole.

**nubvuarsimayok** — unsharpened point.

**nubvudloriktok** — very sharp point.

**nubvugusit** — steeple.

**nubvuk** — pointed, point.

**nudjuitok** — does not move; polar star.

**nudluartorpok** — points out with finger.

**nuglukpok** — gambles.

**nuilak** — hood fur lining.

**nuitayok** — it appears.

**nuiyakattark** — pull-over, sweater.

**nuiyok** — is seen coming out from.

**nujak** (nuyak) — human hair.

**nukangoreik** — two sisters-in-law (husbands being brothers).

**nukangoreik** — two brothers-in-law (wives being sisters).

**nukapiak** (Aiv.) — young man.

**nukar** — younger person of the same sex.

**nukatokrak** — young deer (one year old).

**nuki** — strength, nerve.

**nukiertok** — is without strength.

**nukilik** — is strong.

**nukiluktarmut** — with all strength.

**nukitarpallialerpok** — is getting stronger and stronger.

**nûkpok** — is on the move.

**nûkterpok** — changes place of dwelling.

**nullernikpok** — steals another man's wife.

**nulliak** — wife.

**nulliakpok** — copulates.

**nulliarêk** — husband and wife.

**nulliarengnerk** — marriage.

**nullikpok** — widower.

**nullorarpok** — makes signs.

**nulluat** (Okk.) — fish nets cf. mattitautit.

**nuna** — land, earth, country, flower.

**nunakattigeit** — of the same country.

**nunaliorte** — Creator of the earth: God.

**nunalikpok** — comes ashore from sea.

**nunatorpok** — herbivorous.

**nunatsiark** — good land, paradise on earth.

**nungilerpok** — takes his time to leave.

**nungukpok** — has finished.

**nungusaiyok** — waning (of the moon).

**nunguserark,** okkomiakattark — candy.

**nunguterut** — eraser.

**nunguyok** — is finished, there is no more.

**nussulingnartomik piyok** — dies of a sudden death.

**nutakreyok** — brings forth child.

**nutangorpok** v. — renews.

**nutarak** (pl: nutakret) — child.

**nutaraksakartok.** — is pregnant.

**nutarakattit** — children of the same age.

**nutar** — new.

**nutiblerk** — birth-mark in face.

**nûtikpok,** nûktikpok — cracks with noise.

**nutkarsuitok** — cannot stop.

**nutkarpok** — stops.

**nûtsuitok** — does not move.

**nutsukpok** — drags, pulls.

**nuûtpok** — is working, moving.

**nuvaerutinartok** — so desirable, lit. : saliva comes to mouth.

**nuvak** — saliva, spittle.

**nuvakpok** — has a cold.

**nuviyiyok** — strings beads v.

**nuvuk** — point.

**nuvuliksak** — lowest costal bone.

**nuvuyak** — cloud.

**nuvuyayok** — it is cloudy.

**nuyaiyaut** — clipper for hair.

**nuyak, nujak** — human hair.

**nuyartuyok** — has long hair.

**nuyaerpok** — cuts someone's hair.

**nûyuartok** — is savage, shuns company.

**nûyuitok** — is domesticated.

**nuyuisertok** — is not frightened (as deer, etc.).

## — O —

### Introduction to Eskimo words beginning with the letter O

Here are some ideas suggested by the words beginning with the letter O :

idea of : weather and seasons : **okkô,** it is hot; **okkiaksak,** fall season.
idea of : clothes : **okkorutit,** clothes; **okkortok,** warm clothes.
idea of : heat in objects : **ônartok,** is warm; **ôyok,** is cooked.
idea of : feelings of the soul, faith : **okpertok,** believes.
idea of : admiration : **ôpinnartok,** is marvelous; **ôpipok,** is astonished.
idea of : hatred : **ômisukpok,** hates; **ôgiartut,** fight as dogs.
idea of : regret : **oggorpok,** regrets; **ogçornartok,** is regrettable.
idea of : coming out of : **ôkrark,** tongue; **ôkrok,** rust.
idea of : spreading easily : **orksok,** oil; **ôlingoyok,** the rising tide.

## — O —

**ôgark** — codfish.

**ôgagiartok** — cooked meat, (ready to serve).

**ôgertok** — is cooked.

**oggoriwok, ogguarpok** — regrets.

**oggornartok** — is to be regretted, causes one to regret.

**ogiarpok v.** — fights (dogs).

**ogitorpok** — filled with cooked meat.

**okamarpok** — from shore, pulls canoe with line.

**okkikpok** — wounds seriously, (skin lifted).

**okkô** — hot weather, temperature.

**okkodjet** — extremity of branches.

**okkodluartok** — leans forward, (is sleepy).
**okkoiyaut** — sand-paper.
**okkojiyok** — is absent minded.
**okkoksak** — clothes.
**okkosiksalik** — Wager Inlet.
**okkoksiorpok** — is sheltered from wind.
**okkoksuitok** — cannot rust.
**okkoktok** — is rusty.
**okkomaigutiksak** — ballast.
**okkomaitok** — is heavy.
**okkomiakattark** — candy.
**okkomiarpok** — has in his mouth.
**okkomikpok** — goes with the wind.
**okkomiutak** — people of the East.
**okkomut** — with the wind behind.
**okkortok** — warm clothes.
**okkorutit** — clothes.
**okkoyok** — temperature is hot.
**okkungayok** — is leaning forward.
**okkungiarpok** — makes signs of approval.
**okkutartok** — pocket knife.
**ôkliwa, ôkpa** — tastes it, tries it.
**okpat** (anat.) — buttock.
**okperkattigeit** — have faith together.
**okperkotit** — believers.
**okpernerk** — faith.
**okperpok** — believes.
**okperuserk** — kind of faith.
**okpigosukpok** — has confidence.
**okpik, okpigdjuark** — white owl.
**okpikattok** — falls head first.
**ôkpok** — tries, tastes.
**ôkradlakpok** — talks much about it.
**ôkradlorikpok** — is a great talker.
**ôkrajuitok** — is mute, cannot speak.
**ôkralimarpok** — reads loud.
**ôkalruserk** — word of authority.
**ôkralukpok** — speaks harsh words.
**ôkrarayukpok** — speaks too much.
**ôkrark** — tongue.
**ôkrarlorluktok** — does not speak much.
**ôkrarluktok** — has sore tongue.
**ôkrarnelukpok** — speaks rashly, pronounces badly.
**ôkrarpaluktok** — sound of words.
**ôkrarpok** — speaks.
**ôkrarte** — interpreter.
**ôkratsiak** — good speaker.
**ôkrauseoyok** — is spoken of.
**ôkrauserk** — a word.
**ôkrautiksarpok** — speaks ill of s.o.
**ôkrauyak** — leaf (lit.: imitation of the tongue).
**ôkrigisertok** — makes little leaps, hops.
**okrigiwa** — he deems it light.
**okrilayok** — is swift.
**okrittok** — is not heavy, light.
**okrok** — rust, cf okkoktok.
**okserk** — ivory device to join dog lines.
**okserterut** — ointment.
**oksitartok** — tries everything.
**oksoreark** — Marble Island.
**oksortok** — King William Land.

**oksuk**, orksuk — oil, blubber.
**oksût, orksût** — oil container.
**oktût** — scale, measure.
**okturaut**, oktoraut — ruler, (measure).
**okturpok, oktorpok** — measures, tries v.
**ôlik, ulik** — blanket.
**ôlikattark** — shawl.
**ôlikpok** — shivers.
**ôlingoyurdjuark** — flood, deluge.
**ôlingoyok** — rising tide.
**olrowok** — falls down.
**ôma** — this one (transitive form of 'una' cf. app. III p. 157.)
**ômagiwok** — is living again, resuscitates.
**ômanerdjuark** — Black Lead Island.
**ômangitok** — Name of the very first man, the other being Akuludjosik (Myth.).
**ômariksartok** — is full of energy.
**ômarsaiyok** — brings s.o. back to life.
**ômat** — heart.
**ômayok** — is living.
**ômikpok, umikpok** — well closed.
**omilarpok** — complains.
**ômingmak** — musk ox.
**ômingmauyait** — young musk ox.
**ôminisarpok** — agitated youngster.
**ônarsiyok, ônartok** — is becoming hot, is hot.
**ônerk**, unerk — armpit.
**ongomiark** — top (toy).
**ôpagiarpok** — is anxious, looks for trouble.
**opakpok** — uses double paddle (in kayaking).
**ôpalorpok** (Padl.) — is obedient.
**ôpaluayarpok** — has bad intentions.
**ôpalungitok** — is disobedient.
**ôpalungnerpok** — ready to obey.
**ôpigosukpok** — admires etc.
**ôpingaiwok**, ôpingarpok — takes one by surprise.
**ôpinnangitok** — this was to be expected.
**ôpinnarani** — this was to be expected.
**ôpinnartok** — is marvelous, miraculous.
**ôpinrar** — spring (season).
**ôpipok** — admires.
**oriarpok** (Aiv.) — spits.
**oriungnerk** — rivet.
**orksingolerpok** — is too fat.
**orksoiyaiyok** — takes off fat from skin.
**orkserpok** — adds oil, refuels.
**orksuartok** — sea is calm.
**orksût**, oksût — oil container.
**ormkartut** — children humming.
**ornikpok** — gets close to.
**oronerk** - partridge intestines.
**orpigak, orpit** — small shrubs.
**orpiuyartut** — play "standing on one leg".
**orvilrok** (uviluk) — clam.
**orviuyak**, alut — spoon.
**ôsimayok** — is cooked.
**ôtark** — amadou, touchwood.
**ôtartok** — is burnt.

**ôternartok** — has fever.

**ôtersortok**—boiling over the top.

**ôtok** — seal basking on ice.

**ôtôkralak** — eldest.

**ôtôkrak** — old man.

**owaliago**—day after tomorrow.

**owanerarlagit** (imp.) — come here.

**owani** — here.

**owanikrauyok** — was here just a moment ago.

**owatago,** ungatago — day after tomorrow.

**owatsiark** — not long ago.

**owatsiaro** (imp.) — wait a moment.

**ôyok** — cooked meat.

**ôyoungitok** — is not cooked.

## — P —

### Introduction to Eskimo words beginning with the letter P

Here are some ideas suggested by the words beginning with the letter P :

**PA** : idea of place, situation, position : **pâ,** entrance of a snow house.
**PI** : very general idea of getting, gets, goes, etc. :
**piyok,** acts; **pitsiartok,** acts well.
**PO** : idea of visibility : **pôktalartok,** it floats.
**PU** : idea of swelling : **publartok,** is swollen; **puyortok,** it smokes.

## — P —

**pâ** or **paak** — porch.

**paarpok** — meets.

**pabliark** — handle of Eskimo shovel.

**pablu** — drum handle.

**padgertok**—is slightly wounded.

**padjalukpok** — is spread out in disorder.

**pâdlakpok** — stumbles.

**pâdlerk** — shrubs.

**pâdlermiut** — people of Eskimo Point district.

**padlorpok** — is prostrated.

**padlungayok** — leaning forward on something.

**pagetaeksak** — food left home for family.

**pagmiorpok** — is packed, is crowded.

**pagnerk** — buck.

**pagvisarpok** — bothers v.

**paiya** (Padl.), **paya** — ghost, bogey.

**paiyok** — keeps house.

**pajukpok** —gives food.

**pakadlakpok** — is noisy.

**pakinikpok** — leans on something.

**palangaksaut** — key.

**palarpok** — is quiet, better.

**palarsiyok** — is getting better.

**palagekkut** — flame distributor (for primus lamp).

**palittok,** palertok — fire goes out by itself.

**palrearpok** — meets.

**palreartorpok** — goes to meet.

**palungatsivok** — has long ears.

**pâmakpok** — prostrates.

**pameodluk** (anat.) — coccyx.
**pameiyut** — dogs have tail up.
**pameolik** — has a tail.
**pameok** — tail.
**pamerpok** — is jealous, envious.
**pamitsiartok** — well educated.
**pamroyok** — mends hole (vg. in pail).
**panak** — snow-knife.
**pangalikpok** — gallops.
**pangna** — the one up there.
**pangorpok** — on four legs (to hide and hunt).
**pâni** — far inland.
**panik** — daughter.
**pannertok** — is dry.
**paomnartok** — nervous through seeing many lice.
**papatsiyok** — keeps well guarded.
**paperkrut** — flesh near fish tail.
**paperok** — tail.
**paperorsût** — rudder.
**paperorpok** — stears a boat.
**papigutit** — leaves of shrubs.
**papik** — tail of bird.
**papikattok** — bob-tail.
**papkuyark** — table knife.
**parangayok** — is concave.
**pareartorpok** — goes and meets s.o.
**parlaiyut** — there is a general rush for something.
**parnakpok** — gets ready to leave.
**parorpok** — rows.
**parpok** — meets.
**passariwa** — suspects him.
**passariyauyok** — is accused of.
**passitiksasiorpok** — seeks an accusation.
**passiyauyungaerutiksasiorpok** — seeks an excuse.
**pâtak** — central igloo.
**paterk** (anat.) — marrow.
**patikpok** — gives slaps with hands.
**patigakpok** — applauds with both hands.
**patitik** — sins against taboo.
**patjarlukpok** — wind that changes easily.
**pattakpok** — plays cards.
**pattangayok** — feels chilly.
**pattait,** patteit — playing cards.
**patu,** pato — frost.
**paubjiyok** — itches.
**paubliyok** — cannot sleep.
**paugaorpok,** pautorpok — stretches skin to be dried.
**pauguserk** — drying net.
**pauk** — soot.
**paut** — row, paddle.
**paunrakutit** — fruit branch.
**paunrak** — fruit.
**paurpok, parorpok** — paddles, rows.
**pauruserk** — way of rowing.
**pautark** (Padl.) — row.
**pautik** — double paddle.
**pâyok** — is wrestling.
**payukpok** — is generous in giving food.
**payuktauwok** — is given food.
**pepsi, pipsi** — dried fish.
**perangaitok** — is nervous.
**perauyait** — fetishes.
**peresimayok** — curbed.

**peringayok** — spring of watch, etc.
**perittok** (pâ) — is folded, (folds it).
**perkârtok** — is rusted, etc.
**perkângayok** — is stiff.
**perkominartok** — is desirable.
**perkoserarpok** — Eskimo dance.
**perkotit** — belongings.
**perkoyak** — commandment.
**perkoyiyok** — commands, orders, v.
**perksiktok, perktok** — it is drifting.
**perlerpok** — is dying of hunger.
**pernerk** — a joint in wood, etc.
**pernikpaktok** — gives little and expects much.
**perornerk** — growing.
**perorsêvik** — garden, cultivated field.
**perorpok** — becomes bigger.
**perorsimayok** — is in cache.
**perortitsiyok** — is farming.
**perotsiark** — flower.
**perowok** (-wâ) — loads with stones, (caches) v.
**peroyak** — cache.
**perpaluktok** — makes a sound.
**pêrpok** — is taken away.
**perrark, pilrark** — plait of hair.
**pertorsiorpok** — travels when it is drifting.
**pertudjukpok** — it is drifting a little.
**peruyak** — cache.
**piagnartok** — is slippery.
**piaksaut** — skin to ice the runners (of sled).
**piaktok** — is smooth, slippery.
**pialaitok** — is slow.
**pialak** — young bird.
**pialakisaurtut** — they race. v.
**pialayok** — is swift, quick.
**pianiktok** — is finished.
**piatsinit** — toboggan.
**pidgalerpok** — runs around.
**pidgukotauwok** — this makes his strength.
**pidguyok** — is strong.
**pidjarpok** — he can do it.
**pidjangitok, pilangitok** — he cannot do it.
**pidjutiriwa** — it is his motive.
**pidlarpok** — punishes.
**pidluarpok** — exceeds.
**pidluavignartok** — is necessary.
**pigârpok** — stays up over night.
**pigâtni** (Padl.) — if you do this.
**pigiarpok** — begins.
**pigingayok, pigittok** — is ready, dressed.
**pigiongautauyok** — is the first to do this.
**pigiorpok** — is a beginner.
**pigiwâ** — it belongs to him.
**piglertark** — bouncing ball.
**piglertarpok** — it bounces.
**piitok** — has nothing.
**piitotuarôvok** — is the only one without anything.
**pijareakiktok** — requires little.
**pijareakortuyok** — requires much.
**pijarealik** — is ready to be done.
**pijominartok** — is desirable.
**pijuksauwok** — should do it.
**pijungnaerpok** — is cured.
**pijungnaervik** — hospital.
**pikalukpok** — is clumsy.
**pikaluyak** — iceberg.

**pikannerpok** — does it once more, continues.
**pikarikpok** — is able to ao much.
**pikattar**, pikatti — companion, partner, the other.
**pikattarput** — children imitating elder person.
**pikattauyok** — takes part in game, etc.
**pikiulak** — sea pigeon.
**pikjuk** — egg (found).
**pikjukpok** — finds eggs.
**pikka** — those above.
**pikrâurpok** — act each for themselves.
**piksarsiwok** — procures.
**piksaterpok** — pays taxes.
**piksitaut** — ejector (of rifle).
**piksikpok** — is thrown away.
**piksukpok** — acts slowly, punishes unjustly.
**piktauyoriyauyok** — has a good reputation.
**piktaungitok** — is bad.
**piktauyok, pioyok** — is good.
**pikudluktok** — is hunchbacked.
**pikuk** — humpback.
**pikungarlaunga** — take me on your back.
**pilaktok** — cuts with knife.
**pilaut** — butcher knife, etc.
**pilereaksak** — work to be done.
**pilerigayuktok** — good worker.
**pileriye** — workman, etc.
**pileriyok** — works.
**pilisarpok** — begins.
**pilitak** — useful.
**pilraiyok**, pilrarpok — plaits, weaves v.
**pilrar** — sled runners.
**pilraut** — comb.
**pilu** (Aiv.) — hair fallen from skin.
**pilu** (Padl.) — lump of earth, etc.
**piluartok** — is excessive.
**piluiyarpok** — brushes clothes.
**piluiyaut** — clothes-brush.
**piluktok** — is poor, has a hard living.
**pimaklerpok** (-pâ) — keeps a stranger with them.
**pimayarpok** — gives.
**pinaimiyok** — holds on (afraid to fall).
**pina ?** — what ? (searching for the proper name).
**pinasuarpok, pinasukpok** — endeavors.
**pinereavinerk** — action in the past.
**pingasuungni** — for the third time.
**pingasuat** — the third.
**pingasulioyok** — Blessed Trinity.
**píngasut** — three.
**pingasuyortok** (Okk.) — six.
**pi'nga** (Padl.) — do this for me.
**pingigarpok** — is anxious, tormenting self.
**pingitsertorpok** — is hypocrite.
**pingitotôvunga** — I am the only one not to do it.
**pingoarpok** — plays, imitates, jokes.
**pingortitsiyok** — creates.
**pingortitsiye** — Creator.
**pingôyok** — pushes s.o. to make him fall.
**pinguyarpok** — pushes s.o. to make him fall.
**piniarsarpok** — exercises.

**pinnak** (imp.) — do not do it.
**pinnariyok** — loves preferably.
**pinnariyauyok** — is loved preferably.
**pinnangnark** — S.W. wind.
**pinneraeksak, pinnerak** — socks.
**pinnerlukpok** — acts badly.
**pinnerut** — key.
**pinnikut** — remains, shavings.
**piomitartok,** piyomittartok — is ambitious.
**piosuriyok, pioyoriyok** — is proud.
**piotsertortok** — is hypocrite.
**pioyok** — is good.
**piosiyok** — is getting better.
**piosiwallialertok** — is convalescing.
**pipkarlutarivok** — hardly succeeds.
**pipkartitsiyok** — calumniates.
**piktaungititsiyok** — calumniates.
**pissârpok** — sings.
**pisserk** — Eskimo song.
**pissiariwok** — acquires.
**pissimayok** — is done.
**pissimaitok** — has not been touched.
**pissualayok** — is a good walker.
**pissuarpok** — wants to, desires to.
**pissupvik** — side-walk, place to walk.
**pissuinnarpok** — takes a walk.
**pissuktit** — land animals.
**pissukpok** — walks v.
**pissungnerk** — walk.
**pit** (poss. : pingit) — things.
**pitailiwok** — abstains from.
**pitakangitok** — there is none.
**pitalik** — there is some.
**pitâromayok** — wants to receive gift.
**pitjuterilugo** — it is his motive.
**pitikserark** — bow for Eskimo bit.
**pitiksik** — bow for arrows.
**pitiksiliut** — screw driver.
**pitiksitarpok** — shoots with bow and arrow.
**pitiksitark** — rifle cover.
**pititsiyok** — has someone do it.
**pitkoserk,** illitkoserk — custom, habit, etc.
**pitsiark** — beautiful.
**pittak** — strait.
**pituak** — support for Eskimo lamp.
**pituk** — line in front of sled.
**pituinnarealik** — is ready.
**pitukotit** — amulets.
**pitukpok** — ties.
**piturarpok** — attains his end.
**pitût,** pitûta — line, string.
**piugarpok**—looking for trouble.
**piuliye** — saviour.
**piuliyok** — saves.
**piunginerk** — sin.
**piunginêrutinerk** — confession, absolution.
**piungitulliyok** — sins.
**piviliktok** — easily moved.
**pivinerk** — formerly of.
**pivigdjuark** — great festivity.
**piwallialerpok** — is more and more active.
**piyarealik** — has to be worked.
**piyarivok** — does on purpose.
**pîyaut** (Aiv.) — eraser.
**piyauyok** — is caught.

**piyominartok** — is desirable.
**piyomayok** — wants.
**poagrek,** poalrek — shovel.
**poagresarpok** — shovels. v.
**poaluk** —.mitt, glove.
**pogutak** — plate.
**pogutalutak** — flat bottom boat.
**pôk, poksak** — container, bag, box, etc.
**pôkattar** — bag.
**pokak** — snow (like salt).
**pôkâkpok** — pitches (as a boat).
**pokerk** — white part of deer skins.
**pokertalik** — police (lit. : wears trousers with stripes)
**pokittok** — is low.
**pokliwok** — becomes lower.
**pokpok** — bends one's self.
**pokreitok** — is not intelligent.
**pokrittok** — is intelligent.
**pôksak** — container for solids.
**poktakut** — net float.
**poktalârpok** — floats. v
**poktuyok** — is high.
**pokuliut** — chisel.
**pokumalukpok** — pecks. v.
**pôkut** — empty cartridge shell.
**pôlik** — insect in water.
**pôrpa** — puts it in container.
**publaksaut,** illaksaut — baking powder.
**publarpok** — is swollen, blown with wind, etc.
**publaut** — air pump.
**pudjurnark** — Mansel Island.
**pubvak** (anat.) — lung.
**pubviark** — bird crop.
**pudjortok** — tailor's thimble.
**pudjuarpok** — pinches with fingers v.
**pudjut** (anat.) — finger tips.
**pudlat** — snow-trap.
**pugutak** — plate.
**puibjarpok** — shows head above water.
**puigorpok** — forgets.
**puigodguyok** (Padl.) — has no memory, forgets easily.
**puigojuitok** — never forgets.
**puipkartok** — mirage.
**puipsarpok** — gives the death blow.
**puiyarpok** v. — shows head above water.
**puiye** — sea animal.
**pujortok** — there is smoke, fog, etc.
**pujulettit** — pipe.
**pujuletsiyok** — smokes the pipe.
**puktok, pungayok** — is bent (to hide from game).
**pullarpok,** uglarpok — visits.
**pullasarpok** — visits traps.
**pullawok** — penetrates.
**pûnerit, pûnelik** — full of pus.
**pûnerk** — pus, etc.
**pûnernerk** — lard, grease, shortening.
**pungattok** — approves by signs of head.
**pungok,** ârnaluk — bitch.
**puruserk** — bag (for meat).
**pussik** — cat.
**pussigarpok** — hits with his head.
**pussittok** — is reversed, upside down.
**putuk** — hole.

**putugor** — big toe.

**putorpok** — braids (with four units).

**putuksaut** — perforator.

**putuliyarpok** — places both hands on hips.

**puvaleriyok** — has lung trouble.

**puvark** (anat.) — lung.

**puverark** — Eskimo bag (made of skin).

**puvittok** — is swollen.

**puyâluk** — earwax, cerumen.

**puyak** — dried oil adhering to one's clothes.

**puyârtok** — is dirty, greasy.

**puyok** — vapour of the sea.

**puyortok** — it smokes, steems.

**puyulettit** — smoking pipe.

**puyuletsiyok** — smokes the pipe.

**puyût** — dried mushroom.

## — S —

### Introduction to Eskimo words beginning with the letter S

Here are some ideas expressed by words beginning with the letter S:

**SA :**
idea of surface, extension : **sâ**, the surface in front; **sagvik**, chest.
idea of obstruction taken off : **sakkerpok**, is seen unexpectedly.
idea of opposite : **sangani**, is in front of.
idea of transitory surface : **sanerk**, dust.

**SI :**
idea of contraction : **siarnartok**, is bitter.
idea of extension afar : **sila**, atmosphere; **sina**, shore.
idea of different ways of covering distances : **situyok**, slides.
idea of expansion under pression : **singortitok**, a tumour.
idea of splitting : **siikpok**, is split.
idea of noise, sound : **sirkrortok**, noise of a shot; **sirkomittok**, is broken.

**SO** and **SU** : (root word for questioning) :
**sokoersiwok** : knows why; **sukkut** ? by what ?; **sûna** ? what is it ?

## — S —

**saa** — front part.

**saapkut** — artistically done.

**saartok** — thin (as paper).

**sabgut**, saubgut — sounding stick.

**sabgutauyok** — ruler, measure.

**sablutak** — wall of protection.

**sâdlerk** — the one opposite, Southampton Island.

**sadluwalliayok** — is thinner and thinner.

**sadluyok** — is thin, skinny.

**sadvarpok** — answers.

**saggark** — short hair.

**saggarut** — month of short deer hair : July.

**sâgiarpok** — gets in front of.

**sâglu, sâgluwutit** — you lie, you are a liar.

**saglukitartok** — is a liar.

**sagluyok** — lies (does not say the truth).
**sagvaiyok** — gambling stake.
**sagvak** — rapids.
**sagvalerpok** — shoots rapids.
**sagvarpok** — occupied.
**sagvartôk** — Kazan River.
**sagverpok** — loses sight of.
**sagvik** — upper chest.
**sâgvittok**, sâvittok — takes to the high sea.
**saigut** (Padl.) — fence.
**saimarnerk** — consolation, grace.
**saimarpok** — consoles.
**saimarsarpok** — tries to console.
**saimarsaut** — that which consoles.
**saimartitsidjut** — blessing.
**sajukpok** — shakes.
**sajupidlakpok** — (earth)quakes.
**sakkamaktomik piyok** — crosswise.
**sakkayok** — conjuring, shamanism.
**sakki** — mother of one's wife.
**sakkiark** — brother-in-law.
**sakkrark** — chest.
**sakkrerpok** — is seen at once.
**sakkresarpok** — commands the dogs (harnessed).
**sakkriyaut** — monstrance.
**sakku** — point of harpoon, ammunition.
**sakkuyok** — scrapes skins.
**saksanerk** — pieces of snow blocks (left over).
**sakut** — skin scraper.
**salariyok, salaksartok** — is victorious.
**salausuitok** — cannot be beaten.
**salausuktok** — is lazy.
**saliarpok** — follows aside.
**salumaitok** — is dirty.
**salumaksaut** — rifle cleaner.
**salumayok** — is clean.
**salriyautit** — skates n.
**salrosiyok** — passes without stopping.
**samani** — here.
**sammurpok** — goes from land to sea.
**sanerk** — dust.
**sanerpok, sannerpok** — sweeps.
**sangani** — in front of.
**sangiyok** — is strong.
**sangmioreit** — two groups facing one another.
**sanguniarpok** — tries to convince s.o. to change.
**sangusaraitok** — changes often.
**sanguyok** — changes.
**saniutit** — broom.
**sannelereit** — side by side.
**sanniagut** — near by.
**sanniani** — at the side of.
**sannesiktok** — gets away from.
**sapkuyok** v. — lets go, lets fall.
**sapkut** (Okk.) — ammunition.
**sapmut**, ammut — downwards (vertically).
**sappagnak** (Okk.) — pearl, beads.
**sapperpok** — is unable, lazy.
**sappiutiwa** — prevails against someone.
**napputit** — dam (to catch fish).
**npputiyok** — protects.
**saptigorpok** — passes in front of us.

**sapviyarpok** — has something in hand.

**s[illegible]attok** — is damp.

**sarpik** — whale tail.

**sarpituyok** — walks with toes outwards.

**sarpiuyak** — fish tail.

**sarremaitok** — is sad.

**sarremasakpok** — is tired.

**sarrimanartok** — is annoying.

**sarrimaipara** — I made him sad.

**sarrimayok** — is happy.

**sârtok** — thin.

**satkomerpok** — appears.

**satkrark** — bone joining ribs.

**satkuarpok** — harpoons whale, etc.

**satornartok** (Net.) — thankful.

**satortok** — gives back to owner, etc.

**sau** — footing of iglu (outside).

**saubgut** — sounding stick.

**saudlût** — instrument to take out marrow.

**saumik** — left hand.

**saummikkut** — by the left.

**saumiôyok** — is left-handed.

**saunark** — egg shell.

**saunereik** (Okk.) — two homonyms (others : abvareik).

**saunerk** — bone, frame.

**saunittok** — choked by bone, etc.

**saupâ** — covers with snow or earth.

**saurak, sauvrak** — red phalarope (ornith.).

**sausimayok** — is covered with snow, etc.

**savatsiyok** — works at something.

**saviarpalût** (Padl.) — bell.

**saviarpaluktok** — rings the bell.

**savigauyak** — wire.

**savigayak** — tin.

**savik** — iron, steel, knife, etc.

**sâvikpok**—takes to the high sea.

**saviliorpok** — smith.

**saviliorvik** — anvil.

**savitkarpok** — has a hissing respiration.

**sayukpok** — shakes, trembles.

**sêgpâ** — rasps it.

**sêmiktok** — crushed.

**senneksak** — work to be done.

**senneksarpok** — works at. v.

**senneksorpok** — makes preparations.

**sennektaili** — sunday.

**sennektailiaruserk** — saturday.

**sennettit**, sennakrut — tools.

**sennelik** — cut tobacco.

**senneliusibvik** — tobacco pouch.

**sennetuyok** — is good at work.

**senneye** — workman, carpenter.

**senneyok** — works. v.

**sennerark** (anat.) — side.

**senneréarpok** — goes with wind on the side.

**sennengoarpok** — sculptures, paints, imitates.

**sennerarmik** — plane (tool).

**senneroark** — button, cross bar.

**senneleriyut** — they commit adultery.

**senningayok** — cross, Backs River.

**senningayolik** — crucifix.

**senningayoliorpok** — makes the sign of the Cross.

**serdlerk** — a little, skin well dried.

**serdloark** — store, reserve.
**serkirarpok** — spits.
**serleriyaut** — scraper to dry skins.
**serlerpok** — skin that is drying well.
**sermerpok** — is icing the sled runners.
**sermersît** — piece of skin for icing runners.
**sernartok**, siarnartok — is sour, bitter like vinegar.
**sertinerk** — water flows under snow.
**sertuvok** — stops one's nose not to smell.
**siak** — hair separated from skin.
**siakput** — are all in a row.
**siamangayut** — are dispersed.
**siangerpok** — loses its hair.
**siangiyaut** — clothes brush.
**siaraut, siarut** — button.
**siarkrayok** — on the move, skates. v.
**siarnak** — grey colour.
**siarusibvik** — button hole.
**siblugiwok** — is not proud of.
**sibverk** — hip bone.
**sibvêtok** — is lame.
**sibvorsiut** — wringer.
**sibvortorpok** — wrings clothes, etc.
**sidlît** — sharpening stone.
**sidlingôyok** — is not easy to digest.
**sigalak** — biscuit (hard).
**sigalarallak** — sweet biscuit.
**sigarpaluktok** — cracking of articulations.
**sigdjak** — shore.
**sigdjiark**, sidjak — fox den.
**siggiarialik** — sand piper (bird).
**siggiariktok** — accessible shore.
**siggiarluktok** — bad shore.
**sigittok** — breaks like wood, etc.
**sigguk** — beak, bill.
**siggutût** — snipe (bird).
**signerk** — shoe-lace.
**signernerk** (anat.) — ankle.
**sîgorpok**, sîkpok — is cut in strips.
**sîtsuitok** — so weak he cannot even say a word.
**sikerarpok**, sikrittok — spits.
**sikerarvik** — spittoon.
**sikiktok** — clear water, clear ice.
**sikkiwok** — chin in water to drink, etc.
**sikku** — ice.
**sikkuliark** – new ice.
**sikkuksayark** (Okk.), alelayok — paper.
**sikrinaktok** v. — the sun shines.
**sikrinerk** — sun.
**sikrinersertok** — eclipse of the sun.
**sikrinertok** — sun is hidden.
**sikrinrut** — sextant.
**sikrinruyak** (Okk.) — watch, clock, etc.
**siksik** — ground squirrel.
**siktartok** — zip.
**sikungertok** — has closed eyes.
**sila** — atmosphere, intelligence.
**silaitok** — has no intelligence.
**silakrertok** — it is fair weather.
**silaktauyok** — fair weather.
**silalereit** — neighbours.
**silaluktok** — it rains, it is bad weather.
**silami** — outdoors.

**silangerpok** — builds a new top to the iglu.

**silapak** — exterior garment.

**silaruarmiut** — the world.

**silata** — the outside.

**silatsiarpok** — it is fair weather.

**silatunerk** — intelligence, shrewdness.

**silatusarpok** — is prudent, thinks ahead.

**silatuyok** — is shrewd.

**silauyak** (Padl.) — watch.

**sili** or **hili ?** — is it not true ?

**siliktok** — is wide, broad.

**silingnerk** — wideness.

**siluk** — animal found dead (carrion).

**simmerk** — cork.

**simmersît** — corkscrew.

**simmikpok** — is obturated.

**simmiktartok** — has hiccups.

**sina** — limit of ice, shore, etc.

**sinaliarpok** — goes to the edge of ice.

**singaiyak** — embryo, fetus.

**singaiyok** — is pregnant.

**singortortok** — river that overflows.

**sinnaktômawok** — dreams v.

**sinniksaut** — edge of garment.

**sinnik** — sleep.

**sinnikpok** — sleeps. v.

**sinniktarpok** — sleeps (camps away from home).

**sinnigvik** — sleeping bag.

**siorak** — sand.

**siorauyak** — sugar.

**sipietsi** (Okk.) — cards (English corr. for spades).

**sipiksak** — keel.

**sipiyok** — is split.

**sipsangayok** — is wide open.

**sirayukpok** — reproaches.

**sirkraliwok** — puts into pieces.

**sirkreark** (anat.) — chyle.

**sirkrok** — knee.

**sirkroat** — knee cap.

**sirkromiarpok** — kneels down.

**sirkromiarvik** — prayer stool.

**sirkromikpok** — is broken.

**sirkropadlakpok** — detonates.

**sirkropserark** — egg (still in bird's body).

**sirkropterpok** — takes apart, undoes.

**sirkrortark** — chewing gum.

**sirkrorpok** — shoots.

**sirkrotidjut** — rifle, gun.

**sirkrortitok** — shot with rifle.

**sitakpok** — loses when playing.

**sitamertorpok** — does it four times.

**sitamangat** — the fourth.

**sitamat** (tisamat) — four.

**sitamerangat** — every fourth one.

**sitamerpok** — obtains four.

**siterpok** — repulses, recoils.

**sitkut** (anat.) — eyelid.

**sitsuitok**, sitisuitok — waterproof cloth.

**sittaktok** — hard wood.

**sittigak** — dog den.

**sitiksiksaiyok** — presses, hardens.

**sitiyok** — is hard.

**sitokritarpok** (anat.) — is about to vomit.

**sitorarpok** — slides.

**sitsertok** — permeated with rain water, etc.
**sittokrittok** — vomits.
**situngayok** — stretched out.
**siturarkutit** — skis.
**situyok** — slides, comes down rivers, etc.
**siudjarluktok**, siudluk — bad hearing.
**siuseriyok** — has sore ears.
**siulik** — pike (fish).
**siut** (pl. : siutit) — ear.
**siutak** — interpreter.
**siuterut** — earring.
**siuteriyok** — interprets.
**siva** (Okk.) — biscuit.
**sivanerteraut** — bell.
**sivanerterausibvik** — bell-tower.
**sivanerteriyok** — rings the bell.
**sivikiktok** — is at a short distance.
**sivituyok** — is at a long distance.
**sivu** — front part.
**sivudjet** (anat.) — front teeth.
**sivudlerk** — the first one.
**sivudlermik** — at first.
**sivudlerpok** — goes ahead.
**sivulingayok** — goes first, flirts.
**sivuranartok** — is exacting.
**sivurark** — front part of thigh.
**sivuvareit** — ancestors.
**sivuvasiktok** — clock ahead of time.
**sog ? sogli ?** — why ?
**soglikiak** — I do not know why.
**sogluartortok** — plays mouth organ.
**sokaima** (Aiv.) — it is out of question, cf. tauka (Padl.).
**sokak** — tent frame.
**sokalayaut** — kind of Eskimo dance.
**sokoersiwok** — recognizes well, understands well.
**sokoserpok** — changes.
**sokosuitok** — never changes.
**sokrark** — baleen, whale bone.
**sorangayok** — is not well disposed.
**sorarpok** — breaks, spoils.
**soriukpok** — falls in pieces, ruined.
**sorlo, -tut-*** — as.
**sorluk** (anat.) — interior part of nose.
**sororpok** — useless.
**sorosuitok** — is still useful.
**soruserk** (Okk.) — child.
**suâ ?** — what ?
**suakpok** — reprimands, corrects.
**sua-unit** (Padl.) — never mind (kuyanna).
**subluarpok** — blows.
**subluksarutit** — mouth organ.
**subluksungnark** — light wind.
**sudluarnartok** — is very interesting.
**suglunartok** — is despicable.
**sugiviuk ?** — what relation have you to him ?
**suigiyok** — despises.
**suinnak** — is no good, sinful.
**sukkittok** — wounds underfeet.
**suiksarpok** — despises others.
**sujomiyok** — is discouraged.
**sujungnerk** — legal sin.
**sukangitok** — it is not there.
**sukkaitok** — is very slow.
**sukkaliyok** — is swift.

**sukkangayok** — is stretched out tight.

**sukkaurpok** — swift dog sled.

**sukkasarpok** — urges dogs to faster pace.

**sukkaterut** — winder.

**sukkaterpok** — winds up.

**sukkatervik** — nine o'clock p.m. (lit. : time to wind the watch).

**sukkorpok** — corrects s.o.

**sukkutsia** — its side.

**sukko** — is evil.

**sukoviuk ?** — what do you want him to do ?

**suksak ?** — what is it used for ?

**suksauyok** — is useful.

**suli** — again, once more.

**suliaksak** — something to be done.

**suliarpok** — is busy with.

**suliyangit** — his actions.

**suliwok** — is busy.

**sulsriyok** — does nothing.

**suluk** — bird feather.

**suluktar** — every thing.

**sulurak** — leather part of whip.

**sumikpok** — tries to cry.

**sûmi ?** (Net.) — where ? (also nani ?).

**sumiutaôwit ?** — of which band are you ?

**suna ?** — what is it ?

**sunakasuitok** — deserted.

**sunakiak** — I do not know what it is.

**sunamerpok** — does not succeed.

**sunasorpok** — eats remains.

**sunaubva** — I had not expected this.

**sunaungitok** — it is nothing.

**sungark** (anat.) — bile, gall.

**sungauyak** — pearl.

**sungejuitok** — does not change.

**sungerutiwa** — confides in s.o.

**sungowok** — is strong.

**sungonartok** — gives bile.

**sungouyarpok** — fights until gets a black eye.

**supisiktok** — river overflows.

**suppiyok** — blows with one's mouth.

**suppogak** (Okk.) — smoking pipe.

**sutainialerpok** — about to be destroyed.

**sutaitok** — it is not there.

**sutakartok** — there is some.

**sutkorpok** — corrects s.o.

**sutô - sila ?** — what kind of weather is it ?

**sutuinnar** — any thing at all.

**suvak** — fish egg.

**suvalikiak ?** — what is the use ?

**suvertok** — permeated with rain.

**sûvinga ?** — what do you want of me ?

**suyat-una ?** — what do you want of him ?

**suyok-una ?** — what is he doing now ?

**suyoungitok** — it is nothing.

— T —

## Introduction to Eskimo words beginning with the letter T

Here are some ideas suggested by words beginning with the letter T :

**TA** : idea of the place occupied :
**takpâni**, away inland; **takanna**, that one over there; **tamna**, this one here.

**TAR** : idea of movement, change, etc. :
**tarralikitak**, butterfly; **tarraiyartut**, they have a movie show.

**TI** : idea of violence, force, etc. :
**tigliktok**, robs, steals; **tilliwok**, sends s.o.; **tiluktût**, snow beater

**TO** or **TU** : idea of foundation, base, etc. :
**tungavik**, stool, base; **tutpok**, touches the ground, has a base.

— T —

**tablikayok** — stings through clothes.

**tablu** — chin.

**tablurutit** — tatooings around chin.

**tâdgomayok** — has taken off his coat.

**tadjarpok** — gives a push.

**tadlikpok** — scratches.

**tadliksît** — skin scraper.

**tadlimangat, tadlimât** — the fifth.

**tadlimangorsaiyok** — for the fifth day in a row.

**tadlimat** — five.

**tadlimauyortok** (Okk.) — ten.

**tadluk, tadluark** — snow-shoe.

**tadlukpok, tadluktorpok** — goes on snow-shoes.

**tagga** (tagva) — therefore, here.

**taggariktok** — it is pitch dark.

**taggiarpok** — goes inland with whole family.

**tagiortorpok** — sneezes.

**tagiorksaut** — snuff (powdered tobacco).

**tagiutit** — worms in deer's nose.

**taglerpok** (Net) — usually carries on self.

**tagva** — enough, here, therefore.

**tagvadlaksinnar** — at the very same moment.

**tagvainnar** — at once.

**tagva-tagva** (Padl.) — at once.

**tagvawutit** — good bye (to those staying home.)

**taigna** — this one near by.

**taika** — here (pointing with finger).

**tailak** — indirectly.

**taima** — the end, thus.

**taimaliorpok** — does this way.

**taimanna** — so, (this way).

**taimna** — the one absent.

**taipsomani** — once upon a time, long ago.

**taiyalak** — eight (playing cards) and 8 o'clock.

**taiyauyok** — is named.

**taiyok** — names, v.

**tark** — darkness.

**takanna** — that one over there.

**takkannâluk-arnâluk** — deity of the sea (female). Myth.

**takîyok** — is long.
**takoark** — food (grub for the trip).
**takpak** (anat.) — exterior part of nose, nostril.
**takpani** — up there.
**takpiitok** — does not see well.
**takpikpok** — has a good sight, sees well.
**takrark** (anat.) — vein.
**takrayok** — is tired.
**takserk** — spot, stain, fog.
**taksertok** — it is foggy.
**taktiriyok** — that long.
**taku** (or takku !) ! — look !
**takudjutinerk** — vision, sight.
**takuganartok** — looks at pictures.
**takugit !** takulerit ! — look ! (affirmation ).
**takuksauyok** — is seen.
**takulukpok** — feeds the dogs.
**takulutiksak** — dog food.
**takuminartok** — nice to look at.
**takumortok** — is hypocrite.
**takungarpok** — is shy. (sees for 1st time).
**takuvik** (anat.) — apple of the eye.
**takuyatuartit** — that is all you see.
**takuyok** — sees, looks and sees.
**tallengonartok** — tiresome for the arms.
**talleriktok** — has strong arms.
**tallerk** (anat.) — arm.
**tallerok** — seal flipper.
**tallerpik** — right arm.
**talliarpok** — balances arms when walking.
**talliktok** — is hidden.
**tallikut** — shield.
**tallitak** — mud runner protector.
**talliuyak** — front flippers.
**talluark, tallutak** — curtain.
**tallugak** — thin snow over trap.
**tallungmiyok** — hides face in hands.
**tamadja** — these things here.
**tamaluktar** — the whole of it.
**tamamnuk** — both of us.
**tamapta** — all of us.
**tamarmik** — totally.
**tamat (krau)** — daily.
**tamatkerpok** — takes entirely all.
**tamatsiatik** — absolutely all.
**tamattomani** — once more, again.
**tammareikut** — compass.
**tammarnartok** — is deceiving, scandalizing.
**tammarnerk** — fault, error, deception.
**tammarpok** — is lost, is wrong, etc.
**tammarsaiye** — one who induces into error.
**tamuark** — a mouthful, a bite.
**tamuasukpok** — bites, eats, chews.
**tamasût** — communion.
**tamuatuar** — chewing gum.
**tamuawok** — takes a bite.
**tangertuyok** — thick juice.
**tangmarpok** — camps for the night.
**tapereik** — two with one shot.
**tapiyok** — more than one at a time.
**tapmikpok** — rebounds (cf. piglertok).

**tappaiyok** — teases on purpose.
**tappasukpok** — is teasing much.
**tapperkrut** — double seam, etc.
**tapsi** — girdle, belt, waistband.
**tapsikpok** — walks (without seeing ahead).
**tapsitarpok** — touches, feels.
**taptauyarput** — play "blind-man's buff".
**tareor** — sea, salt.
**tareormiut** — people living close to the sea.
**tareornittok** (-suniktok) — tastes salt.
**târit** — take off your coat.
**tarksiyok** — it is dark outside.
**tarnerk** — soul.
**tarrak** — shade.
**tarraiyaut** — film projector.
**tarralikitak** — butterfly.
**tarrartût**—looking glass, mirror.
**târsiut** — small hawk.
**tartitarpok** — sun hiding back of clouds, etc.
**tartikpok** — falls unconscious.
**târtok** — it is dark.
**tartuk** (anat.) — kidney.
**tasserk** — lake.
**tasserark** — small lake.
**tasserkrut** — instrum. to stretch skin.
**tassiartok** — elastic.
**tassiorpok** — guides, leads by the hand.
**tassiterpok** — stretches.
**tatabjiyok** — is suddenly frightened.
**tatamnartok** — is marvelous.
**tatapsimanartok** — is miraculous.
**tatattok** — is full.
**tatidgak** — crane (bird).
**tatiksarpok** — seeks help.
**tatisuarpok** — gets close to s.o. (confidently).
**tatilugo** — confides in s.o.
**tatiriyok** — has confidence.
**tatkramani** — inside.
**tatkrerk** — moon.
**tatkrersertok** — eclipse of the moon.
**tattokrikpok** — is too narrow, caught between two.
**tattokrut** — quince.
**tatkut** — Eskimo lamp trimmer.
**tattivok** — presses against self.
**tattuisiyok** — soles of boots (expanded by dampness).
**taunani** — down there.
**taupkoa** — those down there.
**taursiwok** — exchanges.
**tautuganark** — pictures to look at.
**tautu** (anat.) — face.
**tautukpok** — sees.
**tauturut** (anat.) — iris of the eye.
**tawa** — far away.
**tâwâwutit** — good-bye (to those going away).
**te'atna** (Padl.) — so, like that.
**tea'ha, tea'a** (Padl.) — so, like that.
**terliarpok** — acts without being noticed.
**terlikpok** (Padl.) — is doing nothing, stays home.
**teyayok** — cuts meat to be dried.
**tî** — tea (English corr.).
**tibjak** — drifted wood.
**tibjalik** — Nottingham Island.
**tibjek** — deer horn (nagdjuk).
**tiblerterut** (Padl.) — tobacco.

**tiblit** — food marks in face.
**tibviartarpok** — recalls others' bad actions.
**tibvuarpok** — spits.
**tibvurlukpok** — spits in face.
**tigartorpok** — hits with short whip.
**tigarut** — something used as a short whip.
**tiggak** — a kind of seal.
**tigittok** — is stiff dead.
**tiglertak** (anat.) — artery.
**tiglerpok** — beats like artery.
**tiglikomerpok** — steals food to eat.
**tiglikomiareik** — they commit adultery.
**tiglikpok** — steals, robs, etc.
**tigluarpok, tiglukpok** — hits with fist.
**tigluktorpok** — knocks at the door.
**tîgorpok, tîgukpok** — has a taste for tea.
**tiguark, tiguangoyok** — is adopted.
**tiguarsiye** — adopting.
**tigukat** — movable effects.
**tigumayok** — is avaricious.
**tigumiarpok** — holds in hand.
**tigumibvik** — handle, etc.
**tigumibvilik** — handbag.
**tiguyait** — wrinkles near nose, folds on heel of boots, etc.
**tiguyok** — takes in hand, takes away.
**tigutiyok** — shakes hand.
**tikerark** — newly arrived.
**tikerk** (anat.) — first finger: index.
**tikitokrat** — quite adult.
**tikitpok** — arrives from afar.
**tikkût** — arrow indicator.
**tikoarpok** — indicates with finger.
**tikorsiyok** — becomes straight.
**tikortok** — is straight.
**tikpit** — canoe ribs.
**tiktalerk** — long fish.
**tiktauyok** — carried by the wind.
**tikte** (anat.) — cerumen, earwax.
**tikuarpok** — indicates, points out.
**tîlak** — coffee (English cor.: kind of tea).
**tîliorut** — tea pot.
**tillariwok** — takes off snow from clothes.
**tilliklerpok** — sends some one.
**tilliorpok** — gives advice, sends.
**tilliwok** — sends.
**tilliya** — sent.
**tilliye** — sender.
**tilûtiksak** — deer horn (to make snow beater).
**tilûktorpok** — beats snow from clothes.
**tiluktût** — snow beater (cf. anautark).
**timâni** — on main land.
**timi** (anat.) — body, main part.
**timmurpok** — goes ashore.
**tingauyait** — small branches.
**tingmiark** — bird, goose.
**tingmikarpok** — makes a jet, squirts.
**tingmikarut** — squirt syringe.
**tingmisorpok** — goes by airplane.
**tingmisût** — airplane.
**tingmiyok** — is flying.

**tingnelrautak,** tingelrautak — sail.
**tinguk** (anat.) — liver.
**tiniktok** — the tide is low.
**tininerk** — place left dry, at low tide.
**tiningoyok**—tide is going down.
**tiniyauyok** — left dry at low tide.
**tipaitok** — has no taste, no smell.
**tipak** — tobacco (English corrup.).
**tipaksaut** — perfume.
**tipangosibvik** — tobacco pouch.
**tipiariktok** — smells good.
**tipik** — smell.
**tipiyok** — is drifted ashore.
**tipsiktok** — is funny, mocking.
**tireark** — ermine.
**tiregluit** — young seals (square flippers).
**tireksiutit** — girdle, waistband, belt.
**tireksorpok** — acts without being seen.
**tiretkroark** — corner.
**tiretokrat** — youngsters.
**tireganierk** — fox.
**tireganiutak** — fox pelt.
**tireganiersiut** — fox trap.
**tiregosukpok** — follows tabooes.
**tirinartok** — prohibited by conjurors.
**titerarpok** — writes.
**titerarte** — clerk, writer.
**titerarviksak** — writing paper.
**titerarviuyok** — receives letter.
**titerkrekreyok** — reads with eyes (silently).
**titeraut** — pen, pencil, etc.
**titerausibvik** — pencil box.
**titerpok** — makes a mark.
**titkrut** — hand of watch, clock, etc.
**toko** (anat.) — death.
**tokolikpok** — gives death blow.
**tokonartok** — poison, deadly poison.
**tokosarpok** — kills.
**tokoniluktok** — is half dead.
**tokosertok** — is as if dead.
**tokotuksak** — is going to die.
**tokoyok** — is dead.
**topkoyak,** tupkoyak — throat.
**torarpok** — aims.
**torayukpok** — aims well.
**torenartok** — falls of a sudden death.
**tork** — ice chisel.
**torkluark** (anat.) — throat, stove pipe, etc.
**torklualik** — kettle.
**torklurarpok** — calls loudly.
**torkluk** (anat.) — main artery.
**torksok** — exterior porch.
**torngark** — devil, spirit, etc.
**torngiyut** — has relations with ghosts, spirits.
**torpalakpok** — is hit by bullet.
**tôrpok** — uses ice chisel.
**tsianayuk** (Net.) ! — nice !
**tuawi !** — quick !
**tuawiorpok** — acts quickly.
**tubjagaeksauwok** — should be imitated.
**tubjarsiwok** — follows tracks.
**tubviriwa** — puts his hands on another's head.
**tudjarpok** — suffering from walking too much.
**tudlak** — opening of bullet wound.

**tuertok** — is narrow.
**tûgar** — ivory, walrus tusk.
**tûgagak** — billiard ball.
**tûgartok** — plays billiards.
**tûgarvik** — billiard table, room.
**tûgaut** — billiard cue.
**tûgautiyok** — hits with fist.
**tuglerk** (poss. : tuglia) — next.
**tuglit** — sticks worn by women for hair plait.
**tuglilereit** — one after the other.
**tuik, tuit** — extremity of shoulders.
**tukerpok** — kicks backwards.
**tukertautit** — brake made of deer horn.
**tukikangitok** — has no sense, no meaning.
**tukiliarpok** — goes straight ahead.
**tukimiarpok** — goes and shoots straight ahead.
**tukinga, tuki** — its meaning.
**tukingani** — in a line.
**tukingersît** — sight (aiming device).
**tukisiwok** — understands.
**tukkuitok** — is stingy.
**tukkuttok** — is generous.
**tuksiarkattigeit** — congregation (lit. : they who pray together).
**tuksiarnerk** — prayer.
**tuksiarpok** — prays, asks, worships.
**tuksiarvik** — church, chapel.
**tuksiarviriwa** — asked him, prayed him to.
**tuksirarpok** — begs.
**tuksiut, tuksiutit** — book of prayers.
**tuksiutiwok** — prays for s.o.
**tuktu** — deer, caribou.
**tuktukotit** — deer skin clothes.
**tuktukpok** — kills deer.
**tuktuliarpok** — goes where there are deer.
**tuktusiorpok** — is seeking deer to hunt.
**tuktuyait** — spiders (assiwak).
**tuktuyak** — sheep.
**tullakpok** — boat hits the shore.
**tullimak** (anat.) — rib.
**tullugak** — crow (bird).
**tullureark** (anat.) — eye tooth.
**tullurpok** — hits obstacle.
**tulroyok** — is heavy-haired.
**tumark** (anat.)—paralyzed limb.
**tumangayok** — is paralyzed, swollen, etc.
**tumeraut** — stepladder, etc.
**tumik** — foot track.
**tumnit** — tatooing of women.
**tunerk** — gift.
**tunerktuyok**—recoils (as a rifle).
**tunerkutiksak** — something to give.
**tunersiyok** — gives his word.
**tungani** — there between, a little lower.
**tungavik** — foundation, base.
**tungavok**—is placed on its base.
**tungunerk** — vapour over the sea (winter time).
**tungurtok** — is blue.
**tunguyurtok** — is green.
**tungumiartok** — a cloudy sky.
**tunijiviujaraekarpok** — deserves a reward.
**tunisiviuyok** — receives a gift, reward.
**tunisiyok** — gives.

**tuniorkaiyok** — distributes (cards, etc.).
**tunit** — first famous Eskimos.
**tuniyok** v. — gives.
**tunnu** (anat.) — back, fat of back.
**tunnuani** — in his back.
**tunnuksak** — white mushroom.
**tunnunermiut** — people of Pond Inlet area.
**tunnusuk** (anat.) — nape of the neck.
**tunnukpok** — turns his back.
**tunnuyak** — limestone.
**tupakpok** — is awake.
**tupaktitsiyok** — awakes s.o.
**tupangiyaiyok** — has malaria.
**tuparomitarvik**—breakfast time.
**tuparomitarpok** — eats his breakfast.
**tupilak** — harmful ghost.
**tupkrerpok** — takes tent down.
**tupkoyak** (anat.) — throat.
**tupkoyakiktok** — almost choked with emotion.
**tupperk** — tent.
**tupperkattiga** — my tent companion.
**tupperpok** — has tent up.
**tuppervivik** — place where tents were put up.
**tuppingoark** (anat.) — Adam's apple.
**tuppinartok** — makes one choke.
**tuppittok** — is choked.
**tupsiyok** — finds footprints.
**tuputak** — peg, cork.
**tuputauyak** — pin.
**tussangisartok** — is disobedient.
**tussaomayok** — it is a saying, we hear that . . .
**tussarpok** — hears.
**tussarnarut** — grammophone.
**tussarnartut** — agreable to hear, Holy Gospels.
**tussarsauyok** — is heard.
**tussiattok** (anat.) — limps.
**tussunartok** — it is desirable.
**tussusarpok** — tries to make one desire.
**tussuyuyok** — has desires.
**tussuyok** — desires.
**tutak** (anat.) — lower cheek (cf. ulluak).
**tutibvik**, tutiut — door mat, carpet.
**tutiyok** — steps on.
**tutkorpok** — puts back in its place.
**tutkuyok** — goes to sleep at neighbour's.
**tutok** — touches ground.
**tuwak** — solid ice on sea.
**tuwaertok** — breakup of sea ice.
**tuyurmiangoyok** — is visitor from afar.
**tuyurmiarpok** — goes afar to visit folks.
**tuyurpok** — sends something afar.

## — U —

### Introduction to Eskimo words beginning with the letter U

The main idea expressed by words beginning with the letter U, is the opening of the eyes and the feelings of the soul expressed by the opening of the eyes, as :

attention : **udjertortok,** is careful.
interest : **uiritsaktok,** is very interested in.
agitation : **uimaktok,** is excited.
on the watch : **ulureasuktok,** is suspicious.

There are also several derivated words with the same meaning, as :
opening, split, etc. :
**ulûtit,** saw; **ungerutit,** laces (lit. : to close an opening).

— U —

**ubjuarpok** (Padl.) — narrates other's shortcomings.

**ublangôlertok** — it is almost morning.

**ublar** — morning.

**ublakut** — at one moment in the morning.

**ublarorpok** — starts early in the morning.

**ublarpaluk** — early daybreak.

**ublarsiutit** — morning prayers.

**ublisaut** — stone trap.

**ubliyok** — spends the day waiting for good weather.

**ublukilak** — shortest day.

**ubluinnar** — all in one day.

**ubluk** — day.

**ubluluktar** — all day long.

**ublumi** — today.

**ublurât** — each day.

**ublureak** — star.

**ubluromitarvik** — noon.

**ublursaulertok** — it is daytime.

**ublursiorpok** — celebrates the day.

**ublursiutit** — calendar.

**ublurtulak** — longest day.

**ublurtuyok** — it is a long day.

**ubva !** — here it is !

**udjertorpok** — pays attention.

**udjilukpok** — exposes one's need.

**udjuk** — big seal (square flipper).

**udlayok** — runs.

**ugark** — cod fish.

**ugdjutnar** — shrew mouse.

**uglarpok** — visits close by.

**ugtuk** (anat.) — vulva.

**ui !** — how nice it is !

**uibjangôyok** (anat.) — becomes dizzy.

**uibjarpok** — walks around it.

**uigarnerk** — widow.

**uigasuk** — young maid.

**uigoriyok** — adds a new piece, extension.

**uik** — husband.

**uikait** (Okk.) — young men.

**uimakpok** — is excited.

**uimanartok** — is exciting.

**uimayarpok** — is nervous (ideas are not clear).

**uimaitok** — is calm, clear minded.
**uinganartok** (Padl.) — makes pleasure.
**uinganartok** (Aiv.) — makes one sleepy.
**uinigomasuitok** — will not marry (voluntarily).
**uiniktok** — pubescent girl.
**uiningitok** — non-pubescent girl.
**uiritsaktok** — is very playful.
**uirnerk** — front part of sled.
**uitakikpok** — eyes hardly open.
**uitayok** — with eyes wide open.
**uitpok** — opens eyes.
**uivarpok** — goes around.
**uivilraiyok** — flatters.
**uivituyok** — is avaricious.
**ukalerk** — hare.
**ukkark** (Padl.), ikkuma — fire.
**ukkartok** — ice breaking.
**ukkiak**, ukkiaksak — fall (season).
**ukkioksak** — beginning of winter.
**ukkiork** — winter, year.
**ukkiutark** — long winter.
**ukkuarannuk** — wife of one's son.
**ukkuark** — door, daughter-in-law.
**ukkuaruk** (imp.) — close the door.
**ukkueruk** (imp.)—open the door.
**ukkuerut** — key.
**ukkungayok** v. — bows, is bent forwards.
**ukpattok** — double paddle for kayak.
**ukpikarnerk** — cascade, falls.
**ukpikarpok** — falls head first.
**uksavik** — funnel.
**ukserk** — ivory joint for dog lines.
**ulamertok** — is round, circular.
**ulik, ôlik** — blanket.
**ulikattark** — shawl.
**ulikdjuark**, ulingonerdjuak — great flood, deluge.
**uliktornerk** — high tide.
**ulimakpok** — uses axe.
**ulimaut** — axe.
**ulingôyok, ôlingôyok** — tide is rising.
**ulipkartok** — overflows.
**uliusinerk** — caribou sinew.
**uliut** — sinew thread.
**ulureasukpok** — frightened, protects one's self.
**ulurnerk** — sight (rifle).
**uluark** (anat.), ulluark — cheek.
**uluarpok** — saws. v.
**uluarutit** — cheek tatooings.
**ulurksit** — chisel.
**ulut** — women's knife (half moon form).
**ulûtit** — saw.
**umerk, umit** (anat.) — beard, whiskers.
**umgiyarpok** — shaves.
**umgiyaut** — razor.
**umiark** — boat.
**umiardjuarâluk** — steam boat, ship.
**umiardjuartnar** — schooner.
**umiardjuk** — peterhead boat.
**umiarsarpok** — gets a boat.
**umiartorpok** — travels by boat.
**umiiyarpok** — has a boat wreck.
**umikjuktok** — beard full of frost.
**umiktok** — well closed in, no opening left.

**umilik** — bearded one.
**umingmak** — musk ox.
**umît** — skin tents.
**ummark** — seams of boots.
**una** — this one.
**unalerk** — indian (Cree).
**unangmiyok** — proud.
**unani** — at the East.
**unârk** — lance, harpoon.
**unatarpok** — fights.
**unatartuksak** — soldier.
**unayok** — dog plays.
**unerk** — armpit.
**ungatarpok** — is ambitious.
**ungawakjuani** — very far away.
**ungayok** — loves affectionately.
**ungêrutit**—laces at top of boots.
**ungilakpok** — it itches.
**ungnertak**—string around hood.
**ungomayok** — repulses, chases.
**unguat** — button.
**un'guk** (anat.) — wart.
**uniarpok** — pulls sled (helping the dogs).
**unikpok** — stays there.
**uningarpok** — devours.
**uniorpok** — misses shot.
**unipkarpok** — tells stories.
**unipkartuark** — fable, story, novel.
**unît** — never mind.
**uniwok** — eats any thing.
**uniyok** — dogs (jealous of each others).
**unnerpok** — tells the truth, narrates.
**unnuak** — night.
**unnuakut** — at one moment of the night.
**unnuarmi** — during the night.
**unnuk** — evening.
**unnuromitarvik** — supper time.
**unnuromitarpok** — is taking supper.
**unurtut** — many.
**unwadlerk** — the furthest.
**unwatâni** — over.
**unwatikarpok** — has a place on the bed.
**unwawarpok** — is gone very far away.
**upaluarpok** — is taken by surprise.
**upalunartok** — is ready.
**upingorpok** — surprises.
**upipok** — marvels.
**upluk** — nest (bird's).
**upseriyok** — obturates all issues.
**ussertok** — is naked.
**ussi** — I remember now.
**ussik** — lead on sled, or boat.
**ussikiktok** — has small load on sled.
**ussingayok** — is naked (in bed).
**ussiomali** — I thought . . . but.
**ussiyok** — the sled is loaded.
**ussuk** (anat.) — penis.
**ussuseriyok** — lewdness.
**utarak** (nutara) — child.
**utkosik** — cooking pot.
**utkosiksalik** — Wager Inlet.
**utnertok** — skin (losing hair).
**utartok, ôtartok** — is burnt.
**utatkriyok** — waits.
**utterpok** — returns home.
**uttimut** — on the way back.
**uttuk** (anat.) — vulva.
**uvertartok** — boat tossed about.
**uviluk,** uvilruk — oyster, clam.

**uvineriye** (Okk.) — doctor (medical), cf. idluarsaiye, aniarsiorte, etc.

**uvinerk** — flesh.

**uvingayok** — is leaning.

**uvingiarpok** — whistles.

**uvinraut** — underwear.

**uwagnartok** — N.W. wind. also **wagnark.**

**uwanga** — I, me.

**uwannamik** — it is annoying.

**uwatamanarpok** — turns on one's self.

**uwatautsiyok** — has a hole right through.

**uyakpok** — appears from beyond

**uyakterpok** — lifts oneself on tip toes.

**uyamik** — necklace, beads.

**uyamikortok** — says the beads (rosary).

**uyarak** — stone.

**uyarasukdjuk** — boulder.

**uyaratareak** — miner, prospector.

**uyaratsiark** (Okk.) — hammer.

**uyaraut** — diamond, precious stone.

**uyatsiutit** — suspenders.

**uyorok** — nephew, niece (male's sister's child).

## — W —

The words beginning with W come from **wagnark**, meaning the N.W. wind or a favorable wind to travel, work, etc.

**wadlaiwok** (Okk.) — perhaps.

**wagnilerit** (Padl.) — keep quiet.

**wakadlanga** — what a thing !

**walereit** — snow houses united by the same porch.

**walilertok** — the sun is setting.

**wagnark, uwagnark** — N.W. wind.

**warayar !** — how slow !

**warutiksak** (Padl.) — something to do.

**watsinak** (Padl.) — do not move.

**wawârtok** — it is the N.W. wind.

**wayartok, wayok** (Padl.) — is at work, in full activity.

---

End of the Dictionary

Ottawa — 1954

## APPENDIX I

# THE INFIXES

### The Infixes and Their Use

An infix is a particle inserted in the body of a word to modify its meaning. In Eskimo, the infixes are of the utmost importance. One may say that the meaning of each and every word is liable to be modified by one or several infixes. So that, even though the Eskimo vocabulary may seem somewhat restricted, it is in fact surprisingly enriched by the use of infixes to create new words or express new shades of meaning.

Infixes are governed by very definite rules. First of all, an infix is never taken as a noun or a verb, for it signifies only a quality of the being or a modification of the action. Therefore, an infix is never used alone. On the other hand, two or more infixes may be used in a single word. And here is what might be called the golden rule : **infixes always affect those parts of the word preceeding it only.**

An infix is inserted immediately after the radical of the word and followed by the termination expressing case, person of conjugation. In inserting an infix into a word care must be taken to observe the rules of euphony. For instance a **k** or a **t** meeting certain consonants will be changed into an **l** or a **g**. (See grammar.)

The general use of infixes explains why the Eskimo language is without articles, prepositions, pronouns, possessive and demonstrative adjectives, etc. All these particles are rendered by infixes or by flexions of the noun and the verb.

Here is an example of the use of infixes :
"Nuna-tsia-ungi-tok" meaning : It is not a nice country. Note how a good translation must begin by the end of the word.

4 3 2 1 1 2 3 4
Nuna- tsia- ungi-tok : It is - not - a nice - country.

# A LIST

## OF THE MOST COMMONLY USED INFIXES

---

**aikutit** — protection, prevention, etc.; mattar**aikutit,** a kind of a belt to prevent dogs from unharnessing.

**alayok** — ease, quickness, repetition; pissu**alayok,** he is a good walker.

**âluk** — big, tall, large; umiardjuar**âluk,** (lit. : a great big boat) 'a steamer.

**anik** — end, finishing, stop; nerre**anik**tok, he has finished eating.

**âpik** — greatest, highest, strongest; iksiradjuar**âpik,** the pope. (Sometimes apik is used to express the exact opposite of greatest : nutara**âpik,** a tiny little child.)

**ar** — movement towards; tuktuli**ar**pok, (lit. : he goes where there are some deer) he goes to hunt the deer.

**ardjuk** — small, little; nutara**ardjuk,** a little child.

**atnar** (Padl.) — soon; tiki**katnar**lerpogut, we shall soon arrive.

**dgu** — strongly, persistently, with force; tô**dgu**yok, he is strong with the ice chisel.

**djar** — possibility (with negation, impossibility); tiki**djangi**tok, he cannot arrive.

**djuteri** — cause, motive; ninga**djuteri**lugo, (lit. : it is the cause of his being angry) that makes him angry.

**dlarpok** — with force, passion, intensity; pi**dlar**para, I treated him harshly.

**dlerk** — preference, localisation, rather than; ûna**dlerk,** this one, rather than any other.

**erpok** — finished, exhausted, no more; tuktukaru**erpok,** he has no more deer.

**ertarpok** — multiplication, a definite number of times: pingasu**ertar**luni, he did it three times.

**ertorpok** — about the same meaning as ertarpok, only insisting rather on the number of times.

**erutiwok** — completely exhausted, absolutely no more; nerkriksa**erutiwok,** he has no more food.

**gajuk** or **gayuk** — usually, habitually, tendency, repetition; ninga**gayuk**tok, he often gets angry.

**gak** — in the state of . . . constituted; nâle**gak,** constituted chief, master, lord.

**galluar** — however; takujoma**galluar**pagit, however, I want to see you.

**gar** — privation, lost, is without; ui**garne**ôyok, (lit.: she is without husband) a widow.

**gayar** — would . . . if, almost; audla**gayar**pok, would leave if . . .

**gêk** — relationship, affinity, parenthood; nullia**gêk**, wife and husband.

**gi** — motive, object (a kind of possessive case); nuka**gi**wara, (lit.: I have him as my brother) he is my brother.

**giar** — beginning, being about to; nerre**giar**pok, he is beginning to eat.

**gik** — goodness, perfection, beauty, fairness; kringme**gik**tok, he has good dogs.

**gior** — begins to, does it for the first time; okra**gio**lisarpok, he speaks for the first time.

**goark** — imitation, similitude, play; inun**goark**, (lit.: imitation of a man) statue, etc.

**gor** — says he or she (quoting words); sagluwunga**gor**, he says I am a liar.

**gorti** — makes it his, possession; annoran**gorti**pa, (lit.: he uses it as his garment.)

**gosuk** — physical feeling, need, want, impulse, tendency; merea**gosuk**ama, I feel like vomiting.

**guark** — imitation, similitude, play; sennen**guar**tok, he is sculpturing (carving ivory, etc.).

**guk** — has taste, is wanting; tî**guk**pok, he has a thirst for tea.

**î or ii** — privation, none of it, negation; inuîtok, (lit.: no human being there) no one there.

**i** — is incidentally so; takpâni-**i**tok, he is up there.

**îjar** — completely lost; umî**jar**tok, he has lost his boat.

**îliwok** — temporarily loses the use of . . .; adgaî**liwok**, right now, has a useless hand.

**innar** — does only that, does not do much more than that; pissu**innar**pok, (lit.: he just walks) he goes for a walk.

**jartor** — goes to do something, moves towards; nerre**jartor**itsi, go and eat!

**je or ye** — profession, occupation, duty; sâvileri**je**, (lit.: professional iron worker) a smith.

**ji** — present participle, having influence on . . .; nerre**ji**yok, he makes s.o. eat.

**jui** — absolute privation, negation, absence; tussa**jui**tok, (lit.: deprived of the sense of hearing) is deaf.

**jungnar** — possibility; tigu**jungnar**piuk ? can you reach it ?

**kalluar** — however; tiki**kalluar**pok, however, he has arrived.

**kammer** — recently (with negation : a long time ago); takusuer**kammingi**tagit, it is a long time since I have seen you.

**kanner** — once again, once more, repetition; **attilukannerk,** do it once more.

**karani** — without (in a verb); nerre**karani,** without eating, he . . .

**kartok** — he has some, there is some; tuktu**kartok,** there are some deer, or he has some deer.

**kasak** — almost; toko**kasak**tok, he is almost dead.

**kasaur** — idea of competition, race; piala**kasaur**tut, they race.

**katnar** (Padl.) — the proximate future; tuksia**katna**niarpogut, we shall soon pray.

**katti, katta** — together, companion, with; nerre**katta**uwunga, I eat with them.

**ki** — once more; ningar**ki**wok, he, once more, gets angry.

**kiark** — doubt, ignorance; kina**kiark,** I do not know who it is.

**kik** — little, small; iye**kik**tok, he has small eyes.

**kisaur** — competition, race; piala**kisaurtut,** they are having a race.

**ko** — order, command; per**ko**yiyok, he gives orders.

**koluk** — small, little, despicable; nutara**koluk,** a small child.

**kortuyok** — big, large, long; kringa**kortuyok,** he has a long nose.

**kosar** — same size, equal; akti**kosar**tut, are of the same size, they are equal.

**krar** — once it is done, after doing it; tuktu**krar**luni, once he killed the deer, then . . .

**kraur** — each for himself; atâta**kraur**mannik, they both have their own father.

**kraut** — container; imme**kraut,** a container for liquids.

**krauyok** — recently, just now; audla**krauyok,** he left a moment ago.

**krut** — instrumental; issi**krut,** a skin scraper.

**ksak** — something to be; attigi**ksak,** something to make a shirt.

**kunuk** — depreciative; okra**kunuk**tutit, you speak badly.

**kut** — family, tribe; Josepi**kut,** Joseph's family.

**lai** — impossibility; tiki**lai**tok, he cannot arrive.

**lak** — superlative form; angi**lak,** the biggest.

**langayok** — is about to do it; pissika**langayok,** he is about to begin singing.

**lar** — a future that will be realized; tiki**lar**pok, he shall arrive.

**lâr** — he pronounces that word; atâta**lâr**pok, he says the word "father."

**lasiwok** — on the point of, about to; tiki**lasiwok,** he is about to arrive.

**laur** — form of the past tense; pissu**laur**tok, he has walked.

**laur** — a polite form; taku**laur**langa, please let me see.

**layok** (Padl.) — ease, facility; ninga**layut**nar, he easily gets angry.

**ler** — about to be done; tiki**ler**pogut, we are almost arriving.

**lerangat** — each time; sennektaili**lerangat,** each Sunday.

**lerai** — if it should happen; aju**lerai**guma, if it should happen that be in need.

**lerêk** — mutuality; tuki**lerêk,** two following one another.

**leri** — busy with; titirkre**leri**wunga, I am busy writing.

**li** — but; igvil**li,** but what about you ?

**liar** — going where there are some; tuktu**liar**pok, he goes deer hunting, where there are some.

**lijar** — carries with one's self; anauta**lijar**pok, he carries his snow-beater with himself.

**lik** — there is some; iglu**lik,** a place where there are some houses.

**limar** (Okk.) — all, completely; inu**limar**âluit, all the people.

**lior** — works at, makes; iglu**lior**tok, he is building a snow house.

**lisar** — recently; tiki**lisar**put, they have recently arrived.

**litak** — protection; mamauta**litak,** an apron.

**lônit . . . lônit** — either . . . or; kablunail**lônit,** inuil**lônit,** either the white men or the Eskimos.

**lônit** — even; atâtaga**lônit,** even my father.

**lorik** — much, fluently; okrad**lorik**tok, he speaks much.

**lorluk** — not much, sadly; okrard**lorluk**tok, he is sad, he does not speak much.

**lu** — and; kablunail**lu** inuil**lu,** the white men and the Eskimos.

**luar** — too much; okrard**luar**tok, he speaks too much.

**luavik** — real, genuine; inu**luavik,** a real man, an Eskimo.

**luba . . . luba** — either this or that; ûna**luba** tamna**luba,** either this one or that one.

**luktar** — all of it, completely.

**lutaôwok** — the cause, the motive; idlui**lutaôwok,** he is the cause of the trouble.

**mar** — simply, only that; nerre**mar**pok, he is simply eating.

**marik** — true, real; î**marik,** yes truly.

**mi** — once again; tiking**mi**yok, he arrives once again.

**miar** — simply; pingoar**miar**pok, he is simply playing.

**mik** — asking, requesting; tî**mik,** let me have some tea.

**miok** (pl. miut) — people of that place; Arviar**miut,** the people living at Eskimo Point.

**najar** or **nayar** — would . . . if; pissu**najar**pok, would walk . . . if.

**nalrear** (Padl.) — maybe, perhaps; aniarto**nalrear,** maybe he is ill.

**nar** — small, little; umiardjuart**nar,** (lit. : a small ship) a schooner.

**nartok** — is cause, makes one do something; pâdla**nartok,** it makes one stumble.

**nasar** — late, slow, behind schedule; krai**nasar**pok, he comes late.

**nasuk** — tries, makes an effort; pitsiar**nasuk**tok, he tries to be good.

**nasuri** — is thought so; tigli**nasuri**yauyok, they think he is a robber.

**neluktok** or **nerluktok** — is well, more or less; nerre**neluktok,** he eats well, more or less.

**niar** — future tense; audlar**niar**pogut, we shall leave, go away.

**ngi** — negative form; nagli**ngi**tok, he does not love.

**ngor** — transformation, changed into; inu**ngor**tok, he is becoming a man.

**nuar** (Net.) — cute, agreeable, nice; nutara**nuar,** a cute little child.

**ô** — is substantially so; nerdjuta**ô**wok, it is an animal.

**oma** — is willing, wants; nerrey**oma**yok, he wants to eat.

**ômangat** — wonders if it is so; anguta**ômangat,** he wonders if it is a male.

**omar** — a future, more or less proximate; tikits**omar**pok, he will arrive sometime.

**onar** — probably; tokoy**onar**tok, he is probably dead.

**orkraiyok** — idea of distribution; tuni**orkraiyok,** he is distributing.

**pak** — usually, habitually; pissuk**pak**pok, he usually walks.

**pallia** — more and more; pissuk**pallia**wok, he walks more and more.

**paluk** — sounds as if . . .; okrar**paluk**tok, it sounds as if s.o. was talking.

**panar** — depreciative; tuktu**panar**pok, surprisingly, he got a deer.

**pangni** — prohibition; pissu**pangi**lutit, you are forbidden to walk.

**pkar** or **kkar** — almost not; maki**pkar**punga, I almost failed to get up.

**psiluk** — communicates its colour; aupalu**psiluk**tok, it communicates reddish colour.

**raikutit** — protection, prevents; matta**raikutit,** something that prevents unharnessing.

**rallak** — more or less big; aive**rallak,** a more or less big walrus.

**rar** — obtains a determined quantity; pingasu**rar**punga, I obtained three of them.

**rasuar** — makes an effort, tries, would like; taku**rasuar**pok, he tries to see.

**rear** — goes to do something; pa**rear**torpok, he goes to meet.

**rêk** — mutuality; erne**rêk**, son and parent together.

**ri** — repetition, motive; atâta**ri**lugo, he acts as if it was his father.

**rik** — beautiful, good, nice; kînatsia**rik**tok, he has a beautiful face.

**ruar** — big, great, large; iglu**ruar**, a big house.

**ruer** — no more of it; pitaka**ruer**mat, because there is no more of it.

**ruluk** — depreciative, evil, bad; ûna**ruluk** ! this evil one !

**sai** — goes to see if . . .; taku**sai**yok, he goes to see if . . .

**sali** — will soon; tiki**sali**niarmat, he will soon arrive.

**sar** — recently; tiki**sar**tok, he arrived recently.

**sâr** — goes and fetches; umiar**sâr**pok, he goes and fetches a boat.

**sarai** — facility repetition, often; ningar**sarai**tok, he often gets angry.

**ser** — action going on; panner**ser**tok, it is drying.

**seri** — busy, occupied; su**seri**wit ? what are you doing ?

**sertor** — simulates; pitsiart**sertor**pok, (lit. : he acts as if he was good) he is a hypocrite.

**si** — finds, acquires, etc.; tumi**si**yok, he finds foot-marks.

**sior** — seeking, searching, looking for; nanuk**sior**tok, he is looking for polar bears.

**sît** — instrumental; sermerk**sît**, skin for icing sled runners.

**siut** — instrumental; tuk**siut**, prayer; tuk**siut**it, prayer-book.

**sor** (Padl.) — possibility; nerre**sor**tok. he is able to eat.

**suar** — wants, tries, makes an effort; audla**suar**tok, he wants to go away.

**sui** — privation, impossibility; mami**sui**tok, it cannot heal.

**sunnik** — smells, tastes; tareor**sunnik**tok, it tastes salt.

**tâ** or **tânga** — possessive case of a past action; tuktuk**tâ**, the deer that he has killed.

**ti** — physical influence; nerre**ti**tsiyok, he makes s.o. eat (physically).

**taili** — is prohibited, forbidden; nerre**taili**bvik, time of fasting.

**tainnar** — at last; tikili**tainnar**tok, at last he has arrived.

**talik** — there are some; amarok**talik**, there are some wolves.

**târ** — makes an acquisition; kamik**târ**punga, I acquired boots.

**tau** — passive form of verbs; toko**tau**yok, has been killed.

**tauk** — also; igvit**tauk**, you also (sing.); illipsi**tauk**, you also (plur.).

**te** — profession, occupation; nâlek**te**, a professional radio-man.

**tillu** — while, during; nerre**tillu**nga, while I was eating.

**tô** — only one; inotôwunga, I am the only one here.
**tôk** — how desirable ! inotsiarlangatôk ! How I wish I would live well !
**tokrark** — possessed since a long time; kringmetokraga, my old dog.
**tor** — direction, swallowing, etc.; tîtorpok, he swallows tea.
**tsiar** — beautiful, nice, good; pitsiar ! how nice !
**tsomar** — a future definitely sure to be realized; tikitsomarpok, he shall surely arrive.
**tuar** — unique, only one; ernetuar, the only son.
**tuinnar** — does nothing else but that; nerretuinnarpok, does only eat.
**tuksak** — should be; tikituksak, he should arrive.
**tulli** — is making; piungitulliyok, he is committing (lit. : making) sins.
**tungar** — at last, finally; tikitungarpok, at last he arrived.
**tut** — as; inuktut, as an Eskimo.
**tuyok** — easily, often, much; nerretuyok, he eats much.
**ungnaer** — impossibility, unable any more; tikiyungnaermat, because he can no longer arrive.
**ut** — any instrument or tool; kokiut, rifle; ulut, woman's knife.
**uti** — motive, for; tuksiutiwa, he prays for him.
**uyar** — similitude; innuuyar, a doll.
**vik** — place, time; Aklavik, the place where the brown bear is found.
**vinerk** — formerly of; attigivininga, (lit. : a shirt formerly belonging to him) his used shirt.
**viri** — place, motive; tikibviriwa, he arrived at it.
**wak** — usually, habitually; nerrewaktok, he usually eats.
**walliar** — more and more; piosiwallialerpok, he is improving more and more.
**yau** — passive form of verbs; nerreyauyok is eaten
**yorkraiyok** — distribution one by one; tuniyorkraiyok, he distributes (vg. the cards).
**yortau** — superlative form; krauyimayortauyok, he knows the most.
**yuksak** — should be; nerreyuksauwok, he should eat.
**yuyok** — frequently; nerreyuyok, he eats frequently.

APPENDIX II

# THE DECLENSION OF NOUNS

In Eskimo, nouns and substantives are declined as in Latin. However, there is but one declension comprising eight cases, and each case has a special form for the singular, the dual and the plural. There is no special termination to denote the gender. If need be, it is expressed by adding the word **male** or **female.**

As for the Infixes, the rules of euphony will sometimes cause the last consonant of the radical to be changed before the first letter of the termination.

## HOW TO USE THE CASES

### The Absolute Case

A noun or substantive is used in the absolute case:

a) when it is subject of an intransitive verb (In Eskimo, that verb is called intransitive which does not contain in itself its direct object, when this is a personal pronoun.)

Ex. :**Tuktu pangalikpok,** the deer gallops.

**Inuk tautukpok,** the Eskimo looks and sees.

b) when it is the direct object of a transitive verb (The transitive verb is that which contains in itself its direct object when this is a personal pronoun.)

Ex. : **Tuktu takuwara,** I see the deer (Lit. : the deer it is my seen; i.e. I see it).

### The Transitive Case

The termination for the transitive case is **b** for the singular, and **t** for the plural.

a) The transitive case is used to express **the subject of a possession.** It is similar to the possessive case in English. Ex. : **The deer's horn, tuktub nagjuâ.** However, in Eskimo, the "possessed" also takes the possessive form. Ex. : **Tuktub kigutinga** or **Kigutâ,** the deer's tooth (Lit. : of the deer its tooth);

b) The transitive case is also used when the noun is subject of a verb in the transitive form. Ex. : **Tuktub kappiaringmanga,** The deer fears me; **Kringmerk tuktub takuwa,** The deer sees the dog.

### The "Modalis" Case

The termination for this case is **mik** for the singular, and **nik** for the plural.

The "modalis" (mode) case is used :

a) when the noun is direct object of an intransitive verb. Ex. : **Tuktumik takuvunga,** I see a deer; **îmmermik piyomavunga,** I want water;

b) when the noun denotes a mode or way of doing, which is expressed with the aid of the particles : of, with, by, etc. Ex. : **Savingmik sennesimayok,** It is made of iron;

c) When a noun or an adjective is used as an adverb. Ex. : **Angiyomik tuktukpunga,** I killed a big deer; **Unvasiktomik ingelravunga,** I travel far;

d) when a noun is used alone in the sense of "please give me . . .". Ex. : **Timik,** Please give me some tea; **Immermik,** Please give me some water.

### The "Localis" Case

The termination for this case is **mi** for the singular, and **ni** for the plural.

The "localis" (locative) case is used to denote place or time. Ex. : **tareomi,** At sea; **tuktumi,** on the deer; **ublumi,** today; **tayalarmi,** at eight o'clock; **ukkiumi,** in the winter.

### The Ablative Case

The termination for the ablative case is **mit** for the singular, and **nit** for the plural.

This case expresses :

a) extraction; ex. : **Tuktumit tiguwara,** I took it from the the deer; **Nunamit unvasiktomit,** From far inland;

b) beginning of time, as : From that time . . .; ex. : **Ublarmit unnuarmut,** From morning till night;

c) the second part of a comparison; ex. : **Tuktumit mikinersauyok,** It is smaller than the deer.

### The "Vialis" Case

The termination of the "vialis" (way, via) case is **kut** for the singular, and **tigut** for the plural.

It is used to express the way or means taken, and is rendered in English by the particles : through, by, across, etc. Ex. : **Tuktukut karjuk piyok,** The bullet passes through the deer; **Nunakurutikut tikitunga,** I arrive by train.

The plural form of this case when used alone means : "We the . . .". Ex. : **Innuktigut,** We the Eskimos; **Kablunatigut,** We the white men.

### The "Terminalis" Case

The termination for this case is **mut** for the singular, and **nut** for the plural.

The "terminalis" (terminal) case expresses :

a) progression towards a term; This is rendered in English by the particles : towards, to, at, etc. Ex. : **Tuktumut torartunga,** I aim at the caribou; **Iglumut tikitunga,** I arrive at the igloo;

b) the purpose or motive of an action; Ex. : **Naglingnermut okrarpok,** He speaks through love;

c) the instrument with which something is done; Ex. : **Kayareamut ikârpok,** He crosses by canoe.

### The "Aequalis" Case

The termination for this case is **tut** for the singular, and **titut** for the plural.

The "aequalis" (equal) case is used to express likeness, similarity, equality, etc; Ex. : **Tuktutut,** As the deer; **Inuktut,** as the Eskimo.

This case is also used for the terms of a comparison; Ex. : **Tuktutut mamartiriwok,** as good as the deer; **Taimannatut,** just like that.

# TUKTU, the deer

## SINGULAR (only one)

| | |
|---|---|
| **absolute** — tuktu | the deer |
| **transitive** — tutu-b | of the deer |
| **modalis** — tuktu-mik | the deer (direct object) |
| **localis** — tuktu-mi | on the deer |
| **ablative** — tuktu-mit | from the deer |
| **vialis** — tuktu-kut | through the deer |
| **terminalis** — tuktu-mut | towards the deer |
| **aequalis** — tuktu-tut | as the deer |

## DUAL (only two)

| | |
|---|---|
| **absolute** — tuktu-k | the two deer |
| **transitive** — tuktu-k | of the two deer |
| **modalis** — tuktu-nik | the two deer (direct object) |
| **localis** — tuktu-ni | on the two deer |
| **ablative** — tuktu-nit | from the two deer |
| **vialis** — tuktu-tiguk | through the two deer |
| **terminalis** — tuktu-nut | to the two deer |
| **aequalis** — tuktu-titut | as the two deer |

## PLURAL (more than two)

| | |
|---|---|
| **absolute** — tuktu-t | the deer |
| **transitive** — tuktu-t | of the deer |
| **modalis** — tuktu-nik | the deer (direct object) |
| **localis** — tuktu-ni | on the deer |
| **ablative** — tuktu-nit | from the deer |
| **vialis** — tuktu-tigut | through the deer |
| **terminalis** — tuktu-nut | to, towards the deer |
| **aequalis** — tuktu-titut | as the deer |

## DECLENSION OF THE POSSESSIVE FORM

### FIRST PERSON (one possessor only)

| SINGULAR (of "possessed") | PLURAL (of "possessed") |
|---|---|
| **absolute** — tuktu-**ga** (my one deer) | tukta-**kka** (my many deer) |
| **transitive** — tuktu-**ma** | tuktu-**kka** |
| **modalis** — tuktu-**mnik** | tuktu-**mnik** |
| **localis** — tuktu-**mni** | tuktu-**mni** |
| **ablative** — tuktu-**mnit** | tuktu-**mnit** |
| **vialis** — tuktu-**pkut** | tuktu-**pkut** |
| **terminalis** — tuktu-**mnut** | tuktu-**mnut** |
| **aequalis** — tuktu-**ptut** | tuktu-**ptut** |

### FIRST PERSON (more than one possessor)

| SINGULAR (of "possessed") | PLURAL (of "possessed") |
|---|---|
| **absolute** — tuktu-**wut** (our one deer) | tuktu-**wut** (our many deer) |
| **transitive** — tuktu-**pta** | tuktu-**pta** |
| **modalis** — tuktu-**ptingnik** | tuktu-**ptingnik** |
| **localis** — tuktu-**ptingni** | tuktu-**ptingni** |
| **ablative** — tuktu-**ptingnit** | tuktu-**ptingnit** |
| **vialis** — tuktu-**ptigut** | tuktu-**ptigut** |
| **terminalis** — tuktu-**ptingut** | tuktu-**ptingnut** |
| **aequalis** — tuktu-**ptitut** | tuktu-**ptitut** |

### SECOND PERSON (one possessor only)

| SINGULAR (of "possessed") | PLURAL (of "possessed") |
|---|---|
| **absolute** — tuktu-**it** (your one deer) | tuktu-**tit** (your many deer) |
| **transitive** — tuktu-**wit** | tuktu-**tit** |
| **modalis** — tuktu-**ngnik** | tuktu-**ngnik** |
| **localis** — tuktu-**ngni** | tuktu-**ngni** |
| **ablative** — tuktu-**ngnit** | tuktu-**ngnit** |
| **vialis** — tuktu-**kkut** | tuktu-**kkut** |
| **terminalis** — tuktu-**ngnut** | tuktu-**ngnut** |
| **aequalis** — tuktu-**ktut** | tuktu-**ktut** |

### SECOND PERSON (more than one possessor)

| SINGULAR (of "possessed") | PLURAL (of "possessed") |
|---|---|
| **absolute** — tuktu-**si** | tuktu-**si** |
| **transitive** — tuktu-**psi** | tuktu-**psi** |
| **modalis** — tuktu-**psingnik** | tuktu-**psingnik** |
| **localis** — tuktu-**psingni** | tuktu-**psingni** |
| **ablative** — tuktu-**psingnit** | tuktu-**psingnit** |
| **vialis** — tuktu-**kkut** | tuktu-**kkut** |
| **terminalis** — tuktu-**ngnut** | tuktu-**ngnut** |
| **aequalis** — tuktu-**ktut** | tuktu-**ktut** |

### THIRD PERSON (one possessor only)

| SINGULAR (of "possessed") | PLURAL (of "possessed") |
|---|---|
| **absolute** — tuktu-**nga** (his one deer) | tuktu-**ngit** (his many deer) |
| **transitive** — tuktu-**ngata** | tuktu-**ngita** |
| **modalis** — tuktu-**nganik** | tuktu-**nginik** |
| **localis** — tuktu-**ngani** | tuktu-**ngini** |
| **ablative** — tuktu-**nganit** | tuktu-**nginit** |
| **vialis** — tuktu-**ngagut** | tuktu-**ngitigut** |
| **terminalis** — tuktu-**nganut** | tuktu-**nginut** |
| **aequalis** — tuktu-**ngatut** | tuktu-**ngitigut** |

### THIRD PERSON (more than one possessor)

| SINGULAR (of "possessed") | PLURAL (of "possessed") |
|---|---|
| **absolute** — tuktu-**ngat** (their one deer) | tuktu-**ngit** (their many deer) |
| **transitive** — tuktu-**ngata** | tuktu-**ngita** |
| **modalis** — tuktu-**nganik** | tuktu-**nginik** |
| **localis** — tuktu-**ngani** | tuktu-**ngini** |
| **ablative** — tuktu-**nganit** | tuktu-**nginit** |
| **vialis** — tuktu-**ngatigut** | tuktu-**ngitigut** |
| **terminalis** — tuktu-**nganut** | tuktu-**nginut** |
| **aequalis** — tuktu-**ngatitut** | tuktu-**ngititut** |

**N.B.** — A special form of declension is used when the possessor is subject of the verb. We refer to the Grammar for this particular case.

## DECLENSION OF THE PERSONAL PRONOUNS

### THE FIRST PERSON : UWANGA : I, me, we, us

| SINGULAR (I) | DUAL (we both) | PLURAL (we, more than two) |
|---|---|---|
| **absolute** — uwanga | uwaguk | uwagut |
| **transitive** — uwanga | uwaguk | uwagut |
| **modalis** — uwamnik | uwaptingnik | uwaptingnik |
| **localis** — uwamni | uwaptingni | uwaptingni |
| **ablative** — uwamnit | uwaptingnit | uwaptingnit |
| **vialis** — uwapkut | uwaptiguk | uwaptigut |
| **terminalis** — uwamnut | uwaptingnut | uwaptingnut |
| **aequalis** — uwaptut | uwaptitut | uwaptitut |

### THE SECOND PERSON : IGVIT : thou, you

| SINGULAR (you) | DUAL (you both) | PLURAL (you, more than two) |
|---|---|---|
| **absolute** — igvit | illiptik | illipsi |
| **transitive** — igvit | illiptik | illipsi |
| **modalis** — illingnik | illiptingnik | illipsingnik |
| **localis** — illingni | illiptingni | illipsingni |
| **ablative** — illingnit | illiptingnit | illipsingnit |
| **vialis** — illipkut | illiptigut | illipsigut |
| **terminalis** — illingnut | illiptingnut | illipsingnut |
| **aequalis** — illiktut | illiptitut | illipsitut |

### THE THIRD PERSON : UNA : he, they

| SINGULAR (he or she) | DUAL (they both) | PLURAL (they, more than two) |
|---|---|---|
| **absolute** — una | ukkuak | ukkua |
| **transitive** — oma | ukkuak | ukkua |
| **modalis** — ominga | ukkoninga | ukkoninga |
| **localis** — omani | ukkonani | ukkonani |
| **ablative** — omangat | ukkonangat | ukkonangat |
| **vialis** — omûna | ukkutigûna | ukkutigûna |
| **terminalis** — omunga | ukkonunga | ukkonunga |
| **aequalis** — otunak | ukkotitunak | ukkotitunak |

# NUMERALS

1 — atauserk

2 — malrok

3 — pingasut

4 — sitamat

5 — tadlimat

6 — arvinilli

7 — malronik arvinilli

8 — pingasunik arvinilli

9 — kolingiluartok, kolikangituinnartok

10 — kolit

11 — kolillu atauserglu.

12 — kolillu malroglu

13 — kolillu pingasullu

14 — kolillu sitamallu

15 — kolillu tadlimallu

16 — kolillu arvinillilu

17 — kolillu malroniglu arvinilli

18 — kolillu pingasuniglu arvinilli

19 — kolillu kolingiluartorlu

20 — awatit; or : malrok aggait; or : inuk atauserk nâvlugo

21 — awatillu atauserglu

40 — awatit malrok; or : sitamat aggait

100 — awatit tadlimat; or : kolit aggait

1000 — awatit tadlimat koliertarlugit; or : kolit aggait koliertarlugit

4000 — tadlimat aggait (or adgait) koliertarlugit sitamaertarmilugit

**first** — sivudlerk

**second** — alrak or tuglia

**third** — pingasuat

**fourth** — sitamangat

**fifth** — tadlimangat

# I – Conjugation of intransitive form of verbs

(giving only the termination)

**INDICATIVE Mode**

| | | |
|---|---|---|
| 1 | sing. | — -unga |
| 2 | " | — -utit |
| 3 | " | — -ok |
| 1 | dual | — -oguk |
| 2 | " | — -utik |
| 3 | " | — -uk |
| 1 | plur. | — -ogut |
| 2 | " | — -usi |
| 3 | " | — -ut |

**CAUSATIVE Mode**

| | | |
|---|---|---|
| 1 | sing. | — -ama |
| 2 | " | — -awit |
| 3 | " | — -mat |
| 1 | dual | — -amnuk |
| 2 | " | — -aptik |
| 3 | " | — -mannik |
| 1 | plur. | — -apta |
| 2 | " | — -apsi |
| 3 | " | — -matta |

**INTERROGATIVE Mode**

| | |
|---|---|
| sing. | — -ik ? |
| " | — -it ? |
| " | — -a ? |
| dual | — -inuk ? |
| " | — -itik ? |
| " | — -ak ? |
| plur. | — -ita ? |
| " | — -isi ? |
| " | — -at ? |

**CONDITIONAL Mode**

| | |
|---|---|
| sing. | — -uma |
| " | — -uwit |
| " | — -pat |
| dual | — -umnuk |
| " | — -uptik |
| " | — -pannik |
| plur. | — -upta |
| " | — -upsi |
| " | — -patta |

**IMPERATIVE Mode**

| | | |
|---|---|---|
| 1 | sing. | — -langa |
| 2 | " | — -rit |
| 3 | " | — -li |
| 1 | dual | — -luk |
| 2 | " | — -itik |
| 3 | " | — -lik |
| 1 | plur. | — -ta |
| 2 | " | — -ritsi |
| 3 | " | — -lit |

**GERUNDIAL Mode**

| Simple Form | | Reflexive Form | |
|---|---|---|---|
| sing. | — -lunga | sing. | — -larma |
| " | — -lutit | " | — -larpit |
| " | — -luni | " | — -larmi |
| dual | — -lunuk | dual | — -lamnuk |
| " | — -lutik | " | — -laptik |
| " | — -lutik | " | — -larmik |
| plur. | — -luta | plur. | — -lapta |
| " | — -lusi | " | — -lapsi |
| " | — -lutik | " | — -larmik |

**Note :** The future is expressed by the infix **-niar-** or **-omar-**.
The past is expressed by the infix **-laur-** or **-sima-**.

# II — Conjugation of transitive form of verbs

## INDICATIVE MODE

| | 1st person being object | | 2nd person being object | | 3rd person being object | |
|---|---|---|---|---|---|---|
| Subj. | sing. | plur. | sing. | plur. | sing. | plur. |
| 1 s. | — — | — — | -agit | -apsi | -ara | -akka |
| 2 | — -arma | -aptigut | — — | — — | -at | -atit |
| 3 | — -anga | -atigut | -atit | -asi | -a | -ait |
| 1 pl. | — — | — — | -aptigut | -apsi | -awut | awut |
| 2 | — -apsinga | -aptigut | — — | — — | -asi | -asi |
| 3 | — -anga | -atigut | -atit | -asi | -at | -ait |

(Ex. : takuw-arma, you see me; takuw-ara, I see it; takuyawut, we see them.)

## INTERROGATIVE MODE

| | 1st person being object | | 2nd person being object | | 3rd person being object | |
|---|---|---|---|---|---|---|
| Subj. | sing. | plur. | sing. | plur. | sing. | plur. |
| 1 | — — | — — | -agit ? | -apsi ? | -igo ? | -akka ? |
| 2 | — -inga ? | -itigut ? | — — | — — | -iuk ? | -igit ? |
| 3 | — -anga ? | -atigut ? | -atit ? | -asi ? | -auk ? | -agit ? |
| 1 | — — | — — | -itigut ? | -apsi ? | -itigo ? | -itigik ? |
| 2 | — -isinga ? | -itigut ? | — | — — | -isiuk ? | -isigik ? |
| 3 | — -anga ? | -atigut ? | -atit ? | -asi | -atsuk ? | -agit ? |

(Ex. : takuwinga, do you see me ? takuwatit, does he see you ? takuwiuk, do you see him ?)

## GERUNDIAL MODE

| | 1st person being object | | 2nd person being object | | 3rd person being object | |
|---|---|---|---|---|---|---|
| Subj. | sing. | plur. | sing. | plur. | sing. | plur. |
| 1 | — — | — — | -lutit | -lusi | -lugo | -lugit |
| 2 | — -lunga | -luta | — — | — — | -lugo | -lugit |
| 3 | — -lunga | -luta | -lutit | -lusi | -lugo | -lugit |
| 1 | — — | — — | -lutit | -lusi | -lugo | -lugit |
| 2 | — -lunga | -luta | — — | — — | -lugo | -lugit |
| 3 | — -lunga | -luta | -lutit | -lusi | -lugo | -lugit |

(Ex: takulunga, seeing me; takulutit, seeing you; takulugo, seeing it.)

## IMPERATIVE MODE

| | 1st person being object | | 2nd person being object | | 3rd person being object | |
|---|---|---|---|---|---|---|
| Subj. | sing. | plur. | sing. | plur. | sing. | plur. |
| 1 | —— | —— | -lagit | -lapsi | -lago | -lakka |
| 2 | —-nga | -tigut | —— | —— | -leruk | -kit |
| 3 | —-linga | -litigut | -litit | -lisi | -liuk | -ligit |
| 1 | —— | —— | -laptigit | -lapsi | -lawut | -lawut |
| 2 | —-singa | -litigut | —— | —— | -siuk | -sigik |
| 3 | —-linga | -litigut | -litit | -lisi | -litsul | -ligit |

(Ex: takunga, see me; takulagit, let me see you; tukulago, let me see it.)

## CAUSATIVE MODE

| | 1st person being object | | 2nd person being object | | 3rd person being object | |
|---|---|---|---|---|---|---|
| Subj. | sing. | plur. | sing. | plur. | sing. | plur. |
| 1 | —— | —— | -apkit | -apsi | -apko | -apkit |
| 2 | —-amga | -aptigut | —— | —— | -angni | -angni |
| 3 | —-manga | -matigut | -matit | -masi | -mago | -magit |
| 1 | —— | —— | -aptigit | -apsi | -aptigo | -aptigit |
| 2 | —-apsinga | -aptigut | —— | —— | -apsiuk | -apsiuk |
| 3 | —-manga | -matigut | -matit | -masi | -matsuk | -magit |

(Ex: takungmanaa, he saw me; takungmatit, he saw you; takugapko, I saw it.)

## CONDITIONAL MODE

| | 1st person being object | | 2nd person being object | | 3rd person being object | |
|---|---|---|---|---|---|---|
| Subj. | sing. | plur. | sing. | plur. | sing. | plur. |
| 1 | —— | —— | -upkit | -upsi | -upko | -upkit |
| 2 | —-umga | -uptigut | —— | —— | -ungni | -ungni |
| 3 | —-panga | -patigut | -patit | -pasi | -pago | -pagit |
| 1 | —— | —— | -uptigit | -upsi | -uptigo | -uptigit |
| 2 | —-upsinga | -uptigut | —— | —— | -upsiuk | -upsigit |
| 3 | —-panga | -patigut | -patit | -pasi | -patsuk | -pagit |

(Ex.: takukpanga, if he sees me; takukpatit, if he sees you; takurupko, if I see him.)

## N.B.

1 — In order to be complete, the conjugation with the dual as subject and as object should have been added. There is also a reflexive form which is used when two verbs have the same subject. As this special form is not used very often, we refer to the Grammar for want of space.

2 — There is no special form of conjugation when the same person is subject and object of a verb. Two dashes in the table of conjugation mean that there is no special form. To translate "I see myself" the pronoun object should be expressed: **takuwunga uwamnik.** On the contrary, when there is a special form, the personal pronoun object is not expressed, since it is included in the verb. For example, I see you, **takuwagit.**

3 — When the subject is a personal pronoun, it is never expressed but included in the verb. Example : **pissukpunga,** I walk; **naglikpunga,** I love; **takuwagit,** I see you. However, for reason of emphasis the personal pronoun subject is sometimes expressed, as : **uwangali pissukpunga,** but it is **I** who walk.

4 — Verbs ending in **-pok** keep the **p** right through the conjugation, the **p** preceding all the terminations given here. Verbs ending in **-wok** keep the **w** in the same way.

5 — The past and the future tenses are expressed by the use of infixes : **-laur-** for the past, and **-niar-** or **-omar** for the future. These infixes are inserted between the radical and the termination of the conjugation.

6 — The terminations of verbs never change and are used with every single verb. However, care must be taken to observe the rules of Eskimo euphony in adding the termination to the radical.

A careful study of the conjugations along with an attentive ear to native pronounciation will soon enable one to speak correctly and understand well.

# GEOGRAPHICAL NAMES OF PLACES IN THE ARCTIC

**Aivilik** — Repulse Bay (also Nauyak).
**Akkilasardjuk** — Prince River (near Baker Lake).
**Akkilinerk** — Beaverly Lake.
**Akpatorardjuk** — Walrus Island (near Southampton).
**Akpatordjuark** — Coats Island.
**Akrearornerk** — Duke of York Bay (Southampton).
**Alanaryuk** — Garry Bay.
**Arviark** — Eskimo Point.
**Arviligdjuark** — Pelly Bay.
**Igluligardjuk** — Chesterfield Inlet.
**Iglulik** — Igloolik.
**Ikkerasar** — Bellot Strait.
**Ikpik** — Thom Bay.
**Inugdjuark** — Harrison.
**Irkaluit** — Frobisher Bay.
**Irkalutsiark** — Cambridge Bay.
**Kalâdlit** — Greenlanders.
**Kangerdlinerk** — Rankin Inlet.
**Kangerdluâlugdjuark** — George River.
**Kangerdlukadlak** — Wolstenholme.
**Kangerdluk** — Payne Bay.
**Kangerdludjuark** — Wakeham Bay.
**Kangeruatsiak** — Minto Inlet.
**Kattiktalik** — Fullerton.
**Kekertardjuk** — Read Island.
**Kekertauyak** — Cape Smith.
**Kidlinerk** — Burwell & Mackenzie district.
**Kimmerut** — Lake Harbour.
**Kingait** — Cape Dorset.
**Kingark** — Burnside (also Kringau).
**Kingarualik** — Padlei.
**Kôrgluktok** — Coppermine.
**Kôrviuyardjuk** — Mistake Bay, Tavanee.
**Kramaniktuar** – Baker Lake.
**Kuraryuk** — Pelly Bay, cf. also Arviligdjuark.
**Kurdjuark, Kôrgjuark** — Churchill, Chimo, Perry River (all big rivers).
**Kurk, Kôrk** — Thelon River.
**Maluksitak** — Lyons Inlet.
**Mittimatalik** — Pond Inlet (also Tunnunerk).
**Nagdjurtôk**—Richardson Island.
**Nauyak, Naujak** — Repulse Bay (also Aivilik).
**Naukorvik** — Rabbit Island.
**Omanerdjuark** — Black Lead Island, Baffin Land.
**Oksoreak** — Marble Island.
**Oksortôk** — King William Island.
**Padliardjuk** — Spence Bay.
**Pikiulerk** — Depot Island.
**Pitsiulartok** — Fairway Island.
**Povernittok** — Povangitok.
**Putjurnark** — Mansel Island.
**Sadlerk** — Southampton Island (Coral Harbour).
**Sagvartôk** — Kazan River.
**Senningayok** — Back River South.
**Tasseuyak** — Wager Inlet and Leaf Bay.
**Tikerardjuark** — Tern Point (all long points).
**Tinnitsortok** — Mistake Bay, cf. Korviuyardjuk.
**Tudjakjuark** — Nottingham & Resolution Islands.
**Tunnuneruserk** — Arctic Bay.
**Tuwâluk** — Diana Bay.
**Unguniarvik** — Whale River.
**Utkosiksalik** — Wager Inlet & Back River North.

# HOW TO EXPRESS RELATIONSHIP AND PARENTHOOD

Eskimo words expressing relationship and parenthood are more specific and therefore more numerous than English words. Indeed, relationship among the Eskimos is based on four different sources : blood, adoption, marriage, name. As a rule, the name an Eskimo has, gives him certain relationship to the person who first bore this name. Thus a boy having the name of his grandfather, will not be called "my son" by his father, but "my father," even if the boy should be only two or three years old.

There is also a traditional law among the Eskimos forbidding one to pronounce the name of certain persons, as the mother-in-law, for instance. Should this name be requested by religious or civil authorities, then they will arrange for a third person to pronounce the name. They themselves will not pronounce the personal name, but only that of their relationship.

## USUAL NAMES OF RELATIONSHIP

### I — FATHER and MOTHER

The husband is called **UI** and the wife **NULLIA.** **Nulliarêk** or **uigêk** designates the couple, one being named in relation to the other.

**Anânakukka** or **atâtakukka** means my father and mother, one being named in relation to the other.

Different words express different sources of relationship :

1 — by blood : **Atâtak**, father; **anânak**, mother.
**Atâtatsiak**, grandfather; **anânatsiak**, grandmother.

2 — by adoption : **Atâtaktar, Atâtaksak, Angutiksak, Tiguarsiye**, adopted father.
**Anânaktar, Anânaksak, Arnaksak, Tiguarsiye**, adopted mother.

3 — by marriage : **Sakki**, father-in-law or mother-in-law, for both husband and wife.

4 — by name : It will be the same name of relationship that the person had who first bore this name.

## II — SON and DAUGHTER

1 — by blood : **Ernerk**, son; **Panik**, daughter; **Erngutak**, grandson, granddaughter.

2 — by adoption : **Tiguak**, adopted child; **Ernerktar**, adopted son; **Paniktar**, adopted daughter.

3 — by marriage : **Ningauk**, son-in-law (the husband of one's daughter).
**Ukkuark**, daughter-in-law (the wife of one's son).

4 — by name : Varies according to the person who had this name before.

## III — BROTHER and SISTER

1 — by blood : **Nukak** for an elder brother speaking to a younger brother.
**Nukak** for an elder sister speaking to a younger sister.
**Angayok** for a younger brother speaking to an elder brother.
**Angayok** for a younger sister speaking to an elder sister.
**Ani** means the brother of a female.
**Naya** means the sister of a male.

2 — by adoption : This is expressed by adding **-tar** to **Nukak, Angayok, Ani** or **Naya.**

3 — by marriage : **Brother-in-law** and **Sister-in-law :**

A — If it is a man speaking, he will call his **brother-in-law :**
**Sakkiark,** the brother of his wife.
**Ningauk,** his sister's husband.
**Nukaunrok,** the husband of the younger sister of his wife.
**Angayunrok,** the husband of the elder sister of his wife.

If it is a man who speaks, he will call his **sister-in-law :**
**Ai,** the sister of his wife.
**Ai,** the wife of his brother.

B — If it is a woman speaking, she will call her **brother-in-law :**
**Ai,** the brother of her husband.
**Ai,** the husband of her sister.

If it is a woman who speaks, she will call her **sister-in-law :**
**Ukkuark,** the wife of her brother.
**Sakkiark,** the sister of her husband.
**Nukaunrok,** the wife of her husband's younger brother.
**Angayunrok,** the wife of her husband's elder brother.

4 — by name : It will be the same name of relationship that the person had who first bore this name.

IV — **UNCLE and AUNT**

1 — The father's brother : **Atkak,** uncle.
The mother's brother : **Angak,** uncle.

2 — The father's sister : **Attak** or **Atsak,** aunt.
The mother's sister : **Arnabvik, Arnarvik, Ayakoluk,** aunt.

V — **NEPHEW and NIECE**

1 — Child of one of two brothers or first cousins :
**Kangiak,** nephew or niece.

2 — Child of one of two sisters or first cousins :
**Noak,** nephew or niece.

3 — Child of a man's sister :
**Oyorok** or **Uyorok,** nephew or niece.

4 — Child of a woman's brother :
**Arngak,** nephew or niece.

VI — **SUMMARY of RELATIONSHIP by MARRIAGE**

1 — **Ai,** brother-in-law (for a female) :
the brother of her husband;
the husband of her sister.
**Ai,** sister-in-law (for a male) :
the wife of his brother;
the sister of his wife.

2 — **Ningauk,** son-in-law, the husband of a daughter.
**Ningauk,** brother-in-law, the husband of one's sister.

3 — **Sakki,** father-in-law or mother-in-law (either for the husband or the wife).

4 — **Sakkiark,** brother-in-law (for a male), the brother of his wife.
**Sakkiark,** sister-in-law (for a female), the sister of her husband.

5 — **Ukkuark,** daughter-in-law, the son's wife.
**Ukkuark,** sister-in-law (for a female), the sister of her husband.

6 — **Nukaunrok,** brother-in-law (for a male), the husband of the younger sister of the wife.
**Nukaunrok,** sister-in-law (for a female), the wife of the younger brother of the husband.

7 — **Angayunrok,** brother-in-law (for a male), the husband of the elder sister of the wife.
**Angayunrok,** sister-in-law (for a female), the wife of the elder brother of the husband.

## Words relative to the human body

**Adgak** — hand.
**adgaut** — wrist.
**aglerok** — jaw.
**ailak** — perspiration.
**ajuwak** — abscess.
**akkuliark** — between the eyes.
**akrark** — second birth.
**akrearok** — stomach.
**aksakrok** — outer part of arm.
**allornerk** — sole of the foot.
**amerk** — skin.
**amilreak** — second tibia.
**anark** — excrement.
**ânernangertok** — breathes his last.
**ânernartok** — it hurts.
**ânerteriyok** — breathes v.
**âniartok** — is ill.
**angmalerk** — vulva.
**aok** — blood.
**areak** — upper spinal column.
**arvak** — part of palm of hand.
**aumidjaktok** — sweats v.
**aunartok** — bleeds.
**avuyok** — has miscarriage.
**awârtok** — is unconscious.
**awatit** — extreme limbs.
**ayuwak** — cf. ajuwak, abscess.
**eriek** — shoulder blade.
**erkravit** — intestines.
**erkrok** — buttocks.
**erksak** — temple.
**ernikpok** — gives birth to.
**idgiark** — throat.
**idjuk** — testicle.
**idjuyak** — ovary.
**idjortok** — coagulated blood.
**idluarsaut** — remedy.
**idluarsaiye** — medical doctor.
**idluarsaiyekoluk** — graduated nurse.
**igalauyak** — ear drum.
**iggiark** — gullet, throat.
**ikit** — wound.
**ikkuserk** — elbow.
**ikritkrok** — little finger.
**ilravit** — intestines.
**immerkrotak** — groin.
**innaluak** — intestine.
**inungayok** — is ill.
**iplaut** — embryo, also iblaut.
**itterok** — urine.
**ittigak** — foot.
**ittimak** — palm of the hand.
**iviangek** — breast of woman.
**iye** — eye.
**kakerdluk** — under-chin.
**kakki** — nasal mucus.
**kakluk** — inferior lip.
**kalaserk** — navel.
**kamorayak** — wisdom tooth.
**kanak** — tibia.
**kanerk** — mouth or kranerk.
**kaniwaut** — peritonium.
**kapilrok** — thorax (front part).
**karetak** — brain, also karesak.
**katsoak** — biceps.
**kattigait** — thorax.
**kaveroak** — ear drum.

**kemmerdluk** — vertebral spine.
**kiasik** — omoplate.
**kîgut** — tooth.
**kilerok** — healed wound.
**kimmik** — heel.
**kimmikrok** — hamstring.
**kînak** — face.
**kobluk** — thumb.
**koertortok** — coughs v.
**koiyok** — urinates v.
**komilaktok** — it is itching.
**kongasinerk** — neck.
**kôtok** — collar bone.
**kotserk** — basin.
**koversak** — white of the eye.
**krarsortok** — is blistered.
**krau** — forehead.
**krek** — white hair.
**kreluliyok** — has cramps.
**kremereak** — eye lash.
**krepinrut** — appendix.
**krersortok** — is epileptic.
**kresaroak** — envelop of stomach.
**krilak** — palate.
**krinerksit** — tonsils.
**kringak** — nose.
**kriterdlerk** — middle finger.
**kudvit** — tears (from the eyes).
**kuinaktok** — it tickles.
**kuttik** — pelvis bone.
**makreyok** — suppurates v.
**mami** — thin new skin.
**mapsak** — spleen.
**merearpok** — vomits v.
**mikilerark** — ring-finger.
**mikliark** — umbilical cord.
**miluk** — extremity of breast.
**naak** — belly, abdomen.
**nabgoak** — joint.
**nabluk** — joint of the knee.
**nakasuk** — bladder.
**nakasungnartok** — calf of the leg.
**natakrok** — cartilage.
**nerreliktak** — uvula.
**nerrokak** — interior of second stomach.
**niuk** — leg.
**nutaraksalik** — is pregnant.
**nuvak** — saliva.
**nuvaktok** — has a cold.
**nuyak** — hair.
**okpat** — buttock.
**okrajuitok** — dumb.
**okrark** — tongue.
**ônartok** — is hot, warm.
**ônerk** — armpit, unerk.
**pameodluk** — coccyx.
**paterk** — marrow.
**pikuk** — hump of the back.
**pubvak** — lung, puvak.
**pudjuk** — end of fingers.
**punerk** — pus.
**puvittok** — is swollen.
**sagvik** — upper chest.
**saumik** — left hand.
**saunerk** — bone.
**sayukpok** — shakes v.
**sennerark** — side.
**sibviark** — upper thigh.
**singnernerk** — ankle.
**sikungertok** — has closed eyes.
**sinikpok** — sleeps v.
**sirkreak** — chyle.
**sirkrok** — knee.
**sirkroat** — knee cap.
**siut** — ear.

**sivudjet** — canine teeth.
**sivurak** — front part of thigh.
**sorlok** — int. part of nose.
**sungak** — bile, gall.
**tagiortorpok** — sneezes.
**takpak** — exterior of the nose.
**takrak** — vein.
**takuvik** — apple of the eye.
**tallerpik** — right arm.
**tartuk** — kidney.
**tautu** — face.
**tauturut** — iris of the eye.
**tiglertak** — artery.
**tiglerpok** — has pulsations.
**tikerk** — index, first finger.
**tikte** — cerumen, ear wax.
**timi** — body.
**tinguk** — liver.
**toko** — death.
**tupkoyak** — throat.
**tullimak** — rib.
**tullureak** — eye tooth.
**tunnu** — back.
**tupingoark** — adam's apple.
**tutak** — lower cheek.
**ulluak** — cheek.
**umik** — beard, whiskers.
**ungilaktok** — itches.
**unguk** — wart.
**ussuk** — penis.
**uttuk** — vulva.
**uvinerk** — flesh.

# ARCTIC GAME

## 1 — LAND ANIMALS

**aklak** — brown bear.
**amarok** — wolf.
**awingak** — lemming.
**kapvik** — wolverine.
**kiggiak** — beaver.
**kulawak** — doe without fawn.
**nanuk** — polar bear.
**nanertak** — bear cub.
**norrak** — fawn.
**norralik** — doe with fawn.
**okalerk** — hare.
**omingmak** — musk ox.
**pangnerk** — male, buck.
**pertoserark** — lynx.
**siksik** — ground squirrel.
**tireak** — ermine.
**tireganierk** — fox.
**tuktu** — deer.
**tuktuwak** — moose.
**ugdjutnar** — shrew-mouse.

## 2 — SEA ANIMALS and FISHES

**aiverk** — walrus.
**arverk** — black whale.
**arluk** — killer whale.
**irkaluk** — fish.
**idlôrak** — fresh water fish.
**ivitaruk** — red trout.
**kaerolik** — kind of seal.
**kanayok** — small speared fish.
**kakiviartût** — white fish.
**kenalogak** — beluga (white whale) kelaloqak.
**kinguk** — small crabs.
**netserk** — seal (netjerk).
**orvilruk** — clam (uviluk).
**tiggak** — seal (has a smell).
**udjuk** — big seal (square flipper).
**uviluk** — clam, oyster.

## 3 — BIRDS

**a'agnerk** — squaw duck.
**aggiardjuk** — squaw duck.
**akpak** — kind of penguin.
**akridgek** — ptarmagan, partridge.
**amauligak** — snow bunty (bird).
**amaulikdjuark** — American eider.
**atkonarsiut** — small black bird of the sea.
**immitkrotailak** — arctic tern.
**ikkiariardjuk** — sabine gull.
**issungnak** — jaeger.
**kaglulik** — loon (large size).
**kakoluk** — kittiwake.
**kaksaut** — loon (common).
**kanguk** — white goose.
**kaslutût** — pintail duck.
**kaubvik** — blue goose.
**kayok** — yellow hawk.
**kiggavik** — small hawk.
**kodlikodliak** — killdeed plover.
**kopanoar** — snow bird (common).

**kopanoardjuk** — snow bird of darkish colour.

**kuakuak** — crow (cf. tullugak).

**kringalik** — king eider.

**kugdjuk** — swan.

**massilik** — hawk.

**mîterk** — duck.

**nauyak** — gull.

**nektoralik** — eagle.

**nerlerk** — goose (Canadian)

**okpigdjuark**—white owl, okpik.

**pitsiulak** — sea pigeón.

**sauvrak** — red phalarope.

**siggiariardjuk** — plover, long spur.

**târsiut** — night hawk.

**tattidgak** — crane.

**tonravik** — black sea bird.

**tingmiak** — bird.

**tudlik** — small black bird.

**tudligdjuark** — loon.

**tullugak** — raven, crow.

**ulluadlik** — seems to have cheeks.

## 4 — INSECTS

**assiwak** — spider.

**auviark** — hairy caterpillar.

**iguppak** — bee;
others : iguptak.

**kraurutnar** — black fly on water.

**kiktoreak** — mosquito.

**komak** — louse.

**komarok** — kind of louse.

**kopilrok** — worm, maggot, etc.

**kromak** — nits inside deer skin

**milugiak** — black fly.

**mingniut** — kind of fly.

**missiktartut** — fleas.

**nanuyak** — spider.

**niviugak** — common fly.

**pôlik** — water worm (in weeds).

**sakraitok** — loach.

**tarralikitak** — butterfly.

## Words relative to the Eskimo clothing

**aek** — sleeve.
**agvak** — mattress.
**akkiserk** — pillow.
**akko** — tail of garment.
**alak** — sole of boot.
**alertik** — socks.
**amaut** — pouch in women garment to carry baby,
**amerk** — deer skin.
**angmak** — opening in children trousers.
**annorak** — clothes in general.
**arnagodjutit** — women's dress.
**atailitak** — dress.
**atayolik** — union suit.
**âttartar** — long pants.
**attigi** — shirt.
**attirak** — waterproot deer skin boots.
**attiyok** — puts clothes on.
**atungaksak** — skin for soles.
**auyaksiutit** — summer clothes.
**awapsilarekut** — edge of garment reenforced.
**ikinroak** — short socks.
**illudlit** — underwear.
**illupak** — underwear.
**ingnorek** — skin or canvas to put under the load.
**iperausit** — waterproof seal skin boots.
**ipialik** — boots with side braids.
**iptadjangitok** — waterproof.
**itkrorutit** — white spots on women's trousers.
**ittigamâk** — short slippers.
**ittigarutit** — seal skin low shoes.
**ittik** — top of low shoes.
**kablunartak** — clothes from stores.
**kaksungautit** — kind of button used to carry baby.
**kamâluk** — white men's shoe.
**kamidlarpok** — takes off shoes.
**kamikpak** — outer socks.
**kamiktorpok** — puts on boots.
**karlik** — breeches.
**kidlalik** — has a tear.
**kilu** — the sewing.
**kiluklukpok** — sews badly.
**kiluartok** — in unsewn.
**kinerk** — front part of garment.
**koliktar** — coat, overcoat.
**krepik** — quilt.
**kresik** — sea animal skin.
**kresiuyak** — leather.
**kringor** — skin of deer's forehead used for soles.
**kritikisautit** — belt.
**kukukpak** — point of hood.
**mangiptark** — table cloth.
**manu** — under chin.
**manuilitak** — drip flat.
**maptersimayok** — patched.
**mattarpok** — takes off shirt.
**merksorpok** — sews.
**mitkrut** — needle.
**nangmaut** — line or bag to help carrying on shoulder.
**nanurak** — bear skin.
**nassak** — head gear.
**nassarmiutak** — decoration of head gear.

**nassauyak** — point of hood.
**netsikotit** — seal skin clothes.
**nigdjelik** — shawl.
**nigdjet** — fringes.
**noversak** — white men's clothes.
**nuilak** — fur around hood.
**nuiyakattar** — sweater, pullover.
**okkorutit** — clothes.
**peruvait** — amulets sewn on garment.
**piluiyaut** — clothes brush.
**pitukotit** — amulets sewn.
**poaluk** — glove, mitten.
**puyak** — dried oil on clothes.
**siangiyaut** — clothes brush.
**siaruservik** — button hole.
**siarut** — button.
**signernerk** — shoe lace.
**sîktartok** — zip.
**silapak** — outer garment, mostly trousers.
**sinigvik** — sleeping bag.
**siniksaut** — edge of garment braid etc . . .
**sitisuitok** — waterproof.
**sungauyait** — pearls for decoration.
**tapsik** — belt.
**tarit** — take off your coat.
**tireksiutit** — belt.
**tuik** — shoulder of garment.
**tukłukotit** — deer sk. clothes.
**ungerutit** — boot laces.
**usserpok** — takes off all clothes.
**uvinersiutit** — underwear.

## Common Verbs

accepts - angerpok, pibviriyauyok
accuses - passiyok, passitiksakartok.
acquires - pissiariwok, pitârpok, -târ-*.
adheres - nippittok, nippingayok.
admires - ôpipok, ôpigosukpok.
advances - sivumuarpok.
affirms - angerpok.
agrees - issumakattauyok, angertok.
allows - perkoyiyok.
appears - takuksauyok, satkomertok.
applauds - patiktarpok.
arises - makkitpok, makkilerpok.
arranges - ikpariksarpok, atkrikpok, senneyok.
arrives - tikitpok.
asks (begs for) - tuksiarpok, tukserarpok.
attempts - pinasukpok.
avoids - uivarpok, nigorpok.

barks (dog b.) - krelukpok.
begins - pilisarpok, pigiorpok, pigiarpok.
believes - okperpok.
bites - kiisiwok, mikkikpok.
blames - sukkorpok.
blushes - kangusukpok, aupadlakpok.
bounces - piglertarpok.
brakes - tukertarpok.
breaks - sirkropterpok, sirkromikpok.
brings - adiarpok, nerksarpok.
builds ( a house) - igluliorpok.
bursts - krarpok.

calls - krainkoyiyok.
carries - adgiarpok, nerksarpok,
catches - tigusiwok.

ceases - areowok, pianikpok.
changes - sanguwok, sokosiwok.
cheats - sagluwok, tiglikpok.
chooses - anneriwok.
climbs - majorarpok.
collects - kattersiwok.
commands - perkoyiyok.
complies - nâleksinnarpok.
complins - ipkolukpok, ômilarpok.
congratulates - nakoriwok.
connects - kattitsiwok.
consents - angerpok.
conserves - papatsiwok.
consoles - saimarpok.
contributes - pikattauyok, illauyok.
converts - sanguniarpok.
copies - adjiliorpok.
corrects, scolds - inerterpok.
coughs - koertorpok, kadlaktorpok.
counts - kissitsiwok.
creates - pingortitsiwok.
cries, yells - ereadlakpok, erealârpok.
crushes - sêmikpok.
cultivates (farming) - perorsaiyok,
cuts - kipiwok.

dances (White men's dance) - mominguarpok,
dances (Eskimo dance) - momerpok.
deceuves - tammarsaiyok.
demonstrates - sukkorpok.
departs (leaves) - audlarpok.
desires - tussuyok, pissuartok, ikligosuktok.
destroys - asserorpok.
develops - agliwallialerpok.
dies - tokowok.
digs - adgasarpok.

dines - ubluromitarpok.
disagrees - issumakattigengitok.
dislikes - mamiasukpok, mamiatsakpok.
dissolves (vg sugar in tea) - ingularpok.
distributes - tuniorkraiyok, ningerpok.
divides, separates - awikpok.
divorces - awikpok.
drags (by force) - nutsukpok.
dreams - sinnektomawok.
dries - pannerserpok.
drinks - immerpok.
drops, falls - katakpok.

eats - nerreyok, nerrewok.
embraces - erkrikpok.
enters - iterpok, illuanuarpok.
equalizes - maniksarpok.
escapes - annakpok.
exceeds - piluartok.
expands - issiviktok.
expects - nerriukpok.
expires - tokowok, anernangerpok.
explodes - sirkrortok.

fails ( misses one's shot) - uniorpok.
faints - awârpok, âwok.
falls - katakpok.
fasts (is not eating) - nerretailiwok.
feeds - nerretitsiwok.
feels - ikpiriwok.
fights - unatarpok.
files - agiarpok.
fills - illudlerpok, tatatpok.
finds (after searching) - nennisiwok.
finishes - pianikpok, nâwok, -anik-*, innerpok.
floats - poktalarpok.

flows - kûrktok.
follows - mallikpok.
forbids - pitailiwok, perkoyingitok.
forgets - puigorpok.
forgives - issumariyungnaerpok.
freezes - kekrewok, koangowok.

gives - tunisiyok, kraintsiyok.
goes - inuerutiyok.
gossips - okrarayukpok.
grows - agliwok.
guesses - nellautpok.

happens - nedliutikpok.
hears, listen - tussarpok, tussawok.
helps - ikayorpok.
honors - nertorpok.
hopes - nerriukpok
hunts - angunasukpok.

ignores - naluyok, krauyimangitok.
improves - piosiwallialerpok.
increases - akkiitolik.
indicates (with finger) - tikoarpok.
inquires - apersorpok, aperiwok.
inspects - takusaiyok.
instructs - ajokertuiyok.
interprets - siuteriwok.
invites - kraiyiyok.

joins, meets - aporpok.
jokes - pingoarsinnarpok.
jumps - missikpok.

kicks - ittimgiarpok.
kisses - kunikpok.

knits - noversarpok.
knows - krauyiwok, krauyimawok.

laughs - iglarpok.
leads - sivutiksauyok.
leaks - ernrartok.
learns - illiarpok, illisaiwok, krauyisaiwok.
leaves, goes way - audlarpok.
lies (tels falsehood) - sagluyok.
lives - ômayok, inôyok.
loves - naglikpok, ungayok, pinnariyok.

marries (female ) - uitârpok.
marries - (male) - nulliatârpok.
meets - kattiwok, pârpok, aporpok.
mixes - akkuttsiyok, akkutsiwok.
moves - aulayok
murders - inuarpok, tokotsiwok, inungmik.

narrates - ubberpok.
needs, is used - atortok.

obeys - tussartok, nâlaktok.
obliges - perkoyiyok, pititsiyok.
obtains (vg. five) - (tadlima), -rartok-*
occurs - nedliutikpok.
opens - erkpakpok.
overcomes - salaksarpok.
overflows - ulipkartok, singortok.

paints - mingoarpok.
participates - illauwok.
patches - illârpok, mabliarpok.
pauses - nutkarpok.
pays (he pays it) - akkiliwa.
perspires - aumidjaktok, kiagortok.

places - illiwok, illiorkraiwok.
practices - illisaiyok.
praises - nertorpok.
prays - tuksiarpok.
preaches - ajokertuiwok.
predicts - nellautpok.
prefers (in love) - pinnariwok.
proceeds - pituinnarpok.
progresses - pitsiarpallialertok.
promises - satuiyok.
protects - napputiwok.
protests - naggarpok.
proves - nalunailiwok.
punishes - pidlarpok.
purchases - pitârpok, nioverpok.
pursues - mallikpok.
pushes - pingowook, ajaurpok.

quarrels - aivayok.
questions - aperiwok, apersorpok.

rains - makuktok, nipaluktok.
raises - napaiwok, makitayok.
reads (with eyes only) - titirkrekrewok.
receives - pibviriyauyok, tunisibvioyok.
recognizes - illitarsiwok, sokoersiwok.
refers (in love) - pinnariwok.
reflects, thinks - issumaksasiorpok.
refuses - krepilukpok, krepariwok.
refuses - orkserterpok.
regrets - ogguarpok.
remembers - aulayiyok, puigungitok.
repairs - atkrikpok, illârpok.
repeats - akkiorpok, immiatsiyok (echo)
replies, answers - akpikpok, kiowok.
reports - unnerpok.

resumes - pikannerpok, kayusiwok.
reveals - krauyititsiwok.
reverses - pussittok.
rewards - akkiliwok.
rides - ikkimayok.
rises - kungmuarpok.
robs - tiglikpok, arktayok.
rocks (chair) - nivertarpok, aulakattarpok.
rolls, vg. snow balls - aksaliksiwok.
rubs, vg with ointment - niogarpok.
rubs feet on mat - alorluiyarpok.
rug or mat - tutikviksak, alorluiyaut.
runs - akpattok, udlaktok.
rushes - parlaiyok.

saves - piuliwok.
seeks - kenerpok, ivârpok, -sior-*.
sees - tautukpok, takuwok.
sells - nioverpok.
sends s.o. - tilliwok, tillidlerpok.
shakes - sajukpok.
sharpens - ipiksarpok, kîneksarpok.
shouts - erealârpok.
shovels - poagresarpok.
shows - takutitsiyok, sakkrertipok.
sings Eskimo songs - ayayarpok.
sits down - iksiwayok.
skates - salriyarpok.
sleeps - sinnikpok.
slides - situyok.
smiles - kunwaktok, kungutortok.
smokes (it) - issertok, pujortok.
sneezes - tagiortorpok.
snores - kamguyok, kripsiyok.
spares - illipayok.
speaks - okrarpok.

speeds - nakkersartok.
spits - ôriarpok, sikerarpok, kretserarpok.
splits - koblurpok.
spoils - sorarpok.
starts - audlarpom.
steals - tiglikpok.
stops - nutkarpok.
strikes - anaurpok.
submits - manigutiwok.
succeeds (accomplishes his purpose) - pitorarpok, kayusiwok.
suffocates - ibjangoyok, ipiyok, tupittok.
suggests - issumaliutiwok.
suspects - passagosukpok.
sweats - aumidjakpok, kiagorpok.
sweeps - sannerpok.
swells - puviyok.
swims - iperatuarpok, nalugalarpok, immarpok.

takes away - perpok, tiguwok.
talks - okrarpok.
tastes, tries - ôksiwok, ôksitarpok.
tastes (has taste for) - -guk-*.
teaches - ajokertuiyok, illiniartitsiyok.
tears - aliktorpok.
tells s.o. - okrautiwa.
thanks - kujariwok.
thaws - auksertok, aulertok.
thinks - issumawok.
thinks, remembers - erkrarpok, erkraiyok,
thinks, tries to remember - erkrasarpok.
threatens - kappiasarpok.
throws - êgitpok, iksikpok.
tickles - kuinakpok.
ties - kellakpok, pitukpok, krepikpok, nimerpok.
touches - aktorpok, kalitpok.
touches - aktorpok, kalitpok.

tows - kallitpok.
trades - nioverpok.
translates - tukiliorpok.
travels - ingelrawok.
tries - pinasuktok, -nasuk-*.
troubles (makes t.) - idluiksartok.

understands well - sokoerpok.
understands - tukisiwok.
undertakes - pigiarpok.
undoes - sirkropterpok.
undresses (completely) - usserpok.
unfolds - issivikpok.
unhooks - naktingilertok.
unites (joins) - illautiwok.
unloads - nioraiyok.
urinates - koiyok, kuiyok.
uses, habits etc. - illitkroserk, illitkrosit.

vagabonds - awamurtok.
vibrates - sajukpok.
vomits - merearpok.
votes - anneriwok.

waits - utatkriwok.
wakes s.o. - ittersarpok tupatitsiyok.
walks - pissukpok.
walks (for walking) - pissuinnarpok.
walks (on sidewalk) - pissubviksami piyok.
walks (in water) - iperarpok.
walks (ahead of the dogs) - kangelrarpok.
wants - -suar-*, -oma-*, piyomawok.
washes - ermikpok.
watches - mianersiwok.
weeps loud - kreawok.
wets - kinikpok.

whips - iperartorpok, tiggartorpok.
whispers - issibjukpok.
whistles - uvingiartok.
winds (clock etc.) - sukkaterpok.
winks - kablursorpok.
wipes (face, hands etc.) - ivikpok, adlaterpok.
wishes - tussuwok, ikligosukpok.
wishes (makes one wish) - tussunartok.
works - senneyok, senneksakartok, senneksorpok.
worries - niviorpok.
worships - tuksiarkattauwok.
wrestles - pâyok.
wrings - sibvortorpok.
writes - titerarpok, aglarpok (Okk.).

yawns - aitaurpok.
yells (human) - erealarpok.
yells (dog) - mâlarpok.

**colours**

black - krernertok.
blue - tungortok.
green - tungoyortok.
pink - aupayartok.
red - aupaluktok.
violet - krenerkasaktok.
white - kakortok.
yellow - koksortok, kayok.

---

**directions**

east - unani.
east - unani.
north - kannernark.
north - kannernark.
west - wagnark, uwagnark.

---

**Numbers**

1 one - atauserk.
2 two - malrok.
3 three - pingasut.
4 four - sitamat; (Okk: tisamat).
5 five - tadlimat.
6 six - arvinilli.
7 seven - malronik-arvinilli.
8 eight - pingasunik-arvinilli.
9 nine - kolingiluartok, kolikangituinnartok.
10 ten - kolit.
20 twenty - awatit, malrok-adgait.
40 forty - awatit-malrok, sitamat-adgait
100 hundred - tadlimat-awatit, kolit-aggait.

**Time, Day and Date Related**

day (to-day) - ublumi.
day (every day) - krau-tamat, ublurât.
day after tomorrow - akragoago.
day (shortest day) - ublukilak.
day (all day long) -ubluluktar.
day - ublur.
day (longest day) - ublukortulak.
day after tomorrow - ungwatago.
day (in only one day) - ubluinnar.
day (to-day) - ublumi.
day - ublur.
daylight - kraumayok.
evening - unnuk.
forenoon - ubluromitarvik, pingitillugo sulli.
hour (one) - krauyisautib ikarninga atauserk.
long time - akkuniâluk.
midnight - unnuar kretirarlugo.
month (moon) - tatkret.
morning - ublar.
night - unnuar.
nine o'clock - sukkatervik (vg. time to wind up)
six (o'clock) - kaivattok.
summer (season) - auyark, auyak.
sun sets - sikrinerk nipingmat.
sun shines - sikrinaktok.
sunday - sennektaili.surprises - opingarpok.
sunrises - sikrinaksarpok.
to-day - ublumi.
to-morrow - akrago.
watch, clock - krauyisaut, silauyak (Padl.).
week (one) - sennektaili-akkuningani.
winds (clock etc.) - sukkaterpok.
winter - ukkior.
year (next y.) - alrago.
year (winter) ukkior.
year (last y.) - alrani.
years (has so many years) - ukkiulik..-nik.
yesterday (day before y.) - ikpaksani.
yesterday - ikpaksak.

**Metals and Minerals**

gold - kanosak.
iron, metal - sâvik.
lead (metal) - akrilrok,
lime-stone - tunnuyak.
mica - kiblereark, kriblereark.
salt - tareor.
steel - iyariyartok.
tin (sheet of tin) - savigayak, amertak.

---

**Musicical Instruments**

fiddle - agiarialik.
grammophone - tussarnarut.
harmonica - erkrerpallût.
harmonium, organ - nakrittaut.
mandolin - nokrarsarpallût.
organ (mouth organ) - subluksarutit.
organ, harmonium - nakrittaut.
trumpet - kokoarut.
violin - agiarialik.

---

**Nature**

daisy - kanguyak.
flower - nunangoark, perusiatsiark.
forest - napârtolik.
grass - ivik.
seed (garden s.) - kangaksaut.
shrubs - okpigait, okpit, awalakret.
straw - ivik.
timber - kreyuksak, igluksak.
tree - napârtok.
trees (forest) - napârtolik.
weed (sea weed) - kerkoak.
wood - krejuk.
wood (lumber) - iglusak,krejuksak.

**Tools, Equipment and Miscellenous Items**

arrow (for bow) - kardjuk.
axe - uimaut.
bait (for fish) - manak.
bait (for traps etc.) - nareakpok.
battery (electric) - aumagertaut.
bow (for arrows) - pitiksik.
bullets (small) - kardjurauyait.
camera - adjiliorut.
cartridge (ammunition) - kardjuk,
chain - ipiutak.
chisel for ice - tôrk.
chisel (wood c.) - pokuliut.
compass (marine c.) - tammareikut.
crane (mechanic) - amuakattaut, amulrut.
engine - ikkuma, ikkumalik.
flashlight, lamp - ikkittartok.
flint - kukiksaut, kukiksak.
funnel - kubvivik, kuvitît, ikkiyarsît, uksavik.
furnace - ikkualausibvik.
gasolene - ikkisareitok, orkso.
gear - maniilait.
gun - sirkotidjut, kokiut.
gun (shot gun) - miterniut.
hammer - kautauyark.
harpoon for fish - kakkiwak.
harpoon, lance - nauligak, unark, kapût.
hook (for fishing) - kardjuksak.
kerosene - ikkiyark, orksork.
knife (snow k.) - pannar.
knife (pocket k.) - okkutartok.
knife - pilaut, aktût.
ladder - majorautit, tumerautit.
lamp (electric) - ikkittartok.
lamp with a wick - iperalik.
lamp, lantern - kodlerk, naneraut.
lantern - naneraut.
leather - kresiuyok.
lever - ibjutak.
lighter (insrum.) - ignaut.

microscope - agliut
mirror - tarratût.
nail (iron) - kikierk.
needle (sewing n. etc.) - mitkrut.
nets Fish) - mattitautit, nulluat, nulludjet
oil - orksok.
oil (coal oil) - orksok, ikkiyark (Padl.).

paint - mingoarut.
paint-brush - mingaut.
paper - alelayok, sikuksayak (Okk.)
paper (sand paper) - okroiyaut.
paper - alelayok, sikuksayak (Okk.)
paper (tiolet paper) - erkroiyaut.
paper (wrapping paper) - immutiksak.
paper (tiolet paper) - erkroiyaut.
pen, pencil - titeraut, iksiraut, aglaut (Okk.).
plane (tool) - sennerarmik, saviarut.
powder for rifle, gun etc.. - ariek.
primus-lamp - iktutût, kôdlerk.
projector (for films) - tarraiyaut.
pulley - aksaludjak.
pump (air pump) - publurtaut.
pump (for liquid) - immaiyaut.
radio receiver - nâlaut.
razor - umgiyaut.
reservoir for oil - orksôsibvik, orksût.
rests - takrerserpok, mingoerserpok.
revolver - iglupinnarsût.
rifle - sirkotidjut, kokiut.
rivet - ôriungnerk.
root - mângut, amâk.
rope - aklunak.
rule, measure - ôktoraut.
scale, balance - ôktût.
scissors - kipyautit, aglerouyait.
screw-driver - kaibjarsit, pitiksiliut.
sharpening stone - kînaut, ipiksaut, sidlît.
shell (ammunition) - kardjuk.

square (carpenter's s.) - kippariksaut.
stove (cooking s.) - îgak.
stove (furnace) - aumaliorsibvik.
switch (electrical) - audlalik.
tank - immausibvik.
tar - kûtsok.
telephone - okralût.
telescope - krinrut.
television - nâlaulit-tarraiyautit.
tent - tûperk.
thermos bottle - niglisuitok.
tools - sennetit.
tube, pipe - sublulik.
typewriter - titeraut-nâkritaut.
vacuum bottle (thermos) - niglisuitok.
wheel - aksaluak.
winch - amulrut.
wiper - ibgut, adlarutiksak.
wire - savigauyak.
X-ray (instrum.) - adjiliorut

---

**Transportation**

automobile - nunakorutiâlak.
helicopter - kolimigulik.
plane, airplane - tingmisût.
submarine - atkasût.
train (railroad) - nunakorutialuit.
wagon - aksalualik.

## Games and Sport Related

ball (foot-b.) - aksark.
ball (base-b.) - anauligak, aitaliyak.
billiard ball - tûagagak.
billiard table - tûgarpok.
billiard cue - tûgaut.
billiard ball - tûagagak.
dart - kardjuk.
diamond (at cards) - kaksungaut.
juggling balls - iglukitartok.
kite (plaything) - tingmiuyak.
puzzle (chinese p.) - ikperititak, atkrisugak.
rope (for jumping) - kiggertartaut.

## jewellary

necklace - uyamik, kangiksak (Padl.)
pearls, bead - sungauyait, sappagnait (Okk.).
wrist-bracelet - adgaumik.

## Snow and Snow Related

snow (spread out) - aput.
snow beating (is beating snow) - tiluktortok.
snow block (for building) - auverk.
snow drifting (it is drifting) - perksertok.
snow (is soft) - mauyak, mauyaôlertok.
snow (first snow fall) - apingaut.
snow knife - panar.
snow (for melting into water) - aniuk, anio.
snow (like salt) - pokaktok.
snow is hard - sitidlorak.
snow (mixed with water) - massak.
snow (newly drifted) - akerrorak.

snow (on clothes, boots etc.) - aṿak.
snow-beater - anautak, tiluktût.
snow-house - iglu.
snows (it) - kannertok.

---

**food and food related**

almond - sauniub inua.
appetizer - kâlersaut.
apple - paunrak.
beans - nilernait.
berries - paunrait.
berry (yellow b.) - akpik.
berry (black b.) - kablak, (plur: kablait).
biscuit - sigalak, nerdleogak.
bread - akrelkoyak, adgiksak, niakrouyak.
butter - immuyak.
candy - nungusserak, okkomiakattar.
cheese - immuyartok.
chewing gum - tamuatuar.
chicken - akrigeuyak.
chocolate - koko (Engl. corr.)
cod fish - ôgark.
coffee - kâpik, tîrdlak.
dried meat - mipko.
dries fish - pipsi
dry meat - mipko.
dry fish - pipsi or pepsi.
egg yoke - itserk.
egg white - kauk.
egg - mannik.
egg (fish e.) - suwak, plur. suwait.
fish eggs - sûwait.
fish (red trout) - ivitaruk.
fish - irkaluk.
fish (cod fish) - ôgark.
fish (white fish) - anâdlerk, kakiviartok.

flour - akrekoyaksak, adgiksak.
food - nerkriksak.
fork (table f.) - kakiak.
frozen meat - koak.
fruits - paunrait.
gravy - immerark, kayok.
grease, lard - punernerk.
hen - akrigerdjuark, arnaviak.
honey - mamaksaut, iguptait nerkringa.
jam (edible) mamaksaut.
juice, soup - immerak, kayok.
kettle - torklualik.
knife (table k.) - papkuyak.
meat - nerkri.
milk - immuk.
molasses - malasi (engl. corr.).
mug (cup) - ermosek, ermoseuyak.
mushroom - tunnuksak.
oats - alugaksak, katseogak (Padl.), alugak.
orange (fruit) - paunrak-koksortok.
pie - akkulroalik.
rabbit - ôkalerk, ukalerk.
raw meat - mikkigak.
rice - kopilrouyak, komauyar.
root (edible) - airark.
salt - tareor.
sauce (gravy) - immerark.
soup, juice - immerark.
spoon - alût, orviuyak (Padl.)
sugar - siorauyak, auksereartok.
sweets (candies) - okkomiakattar, nunguserark.
syrup (edible) - mamaksaut.
syrup (cough s.) - novaksiut.
tea - tî(Engl. cor.).
trout - irkaluk.
trout (black) - idlorak.
trout (red) - îvitaruk.

NOTES

NOTES

**NOTES**

NOTES

NOTES

NOTES

**NOTES**

**NOTES**

NOTES